Consuming passions

D0109778

Consuming passions

Food in the age of anxiety

edited by
Sian Griffiths and **Jennifer Wallace**

MANDOLIN

Copyright © Times Higher Education Supplement 1998

While copyright in the volume as a whole is vested in the Times Higher Education Supplement, copyright in individual chapters belongs to their respective authors, and no chapter may be reproduced wholly or in part without the express permission in writing of both author and the Times Higher Education Supplement.

The right of Sian Griffiths and Jennifer Wallace to be identified as the editors of this work has been asserted by them in accordance with the Copyright, Designs and Patents Act 1988.

Published by Mandolin
an imprint of Manchester University Press
Oxford Road, Manchester M13 9NR, UK
and Room 400, 175 Fifth Avenue, New York, NY, 10010, USA

Distributed exclusively in the USA by
St. Martin's Press, Inc., 175 Fifth Avenue, New York,
NY 10010, USA

Distributed exclusively in Canada by
UBC Press, University of British Columbia, 6344 Memorial Road,
Vancouver, BC, Canada V6T 1Z2

British Library Cataloguing-in-Publication Data
A catalogue record for this book is available from the British Library

Library of Congress Cataloging-in-Publication Data applied for

ISBN   1 901341 06 2   *paperback*

First published 1998

05   04   03   02   01   00   99   98   10   9   8   7   6   5   4   3   2   1

Typeset in Hong Kong
by Graphicraft Typesetters Limited, Hong Kong

Printed in Great Britain
by Bell & Bain Ltd, Glasgow

Contents

Notes on contributors

William Arens is professor of anthropology, State University of New York at Stony Brook. His 1979 book *The Man-Eating Myth: Anthropology and Anthropophagy* (Oxford University Press) provoked controversy because of its argument that cannibalism was much less prevalent than is commonly thought.

David Bederman is professor of law at Emory University in Atlanta, Georgia.

David Booth holds a personal chair in psychology at the University of Birmingham, is an accredited nutritionist and helps lead the Society for Chemical Industry (SCI) Working Party on Education and Training in Consumer Science.

Derek Burke is former vice-chancellor of the University of East Anglia. A scientist, he recently retired as chairman of the Advisory Committee on Novel Foods and Processes, which advises the Department of Health and the Ministry of Agriculture, Fisheries and Food on the acceptability of genetically manipulated foods.

Ian Christie is professor of film studies at the University of Kent. He is also *The Times* visiting lecturer in film and a fellow of Magdalen College, Oxford, and a regular broadcaster on cinema. His books include *Arrows of Desire: The Films of Michael Powell and Emeric Pressburger* (2nd edn, Faber and Faber, 1994) and *The Last Machine: Early Cinema and the Birth of the Modern World* (BFI Publications, 1994).

Roger Dickinson is a lecturer at the Centre for Mass Communication Research, University of Leicester, and director of the university's social sciences graduate school. He is co-editor (with R. Harindranath and O. Linne) of *Approaches to Audiences*, published by Edward Arnold, 1998.

Mary Douglas is retired professor of social anthropology at University College London. The pioneer of the study of food within the social sciences in Britain, she is author of several books, including *Purity and Danger* (Routledge, 1991) and *Risk and Blame* (Routledge, 1992).

Tim Dyson is professor of population studies at the London School of Economics. He is the author of *Population and Food: Global Trends and Future Prospects* (Routledge, 1997).

Terry Eagleton is Thomas Warton professor of English literature at the University of Oxford and author of *Heathcliff and the Great Hunger: Studies in Irish Culture* (Blackwell Verso, 1995). His collection of essays on Irish culture, *Crazy John and the Bishop*, is published by Cork University Press, 1998.

Emily Gowers is honorary research fellow in the Department of Greek and Latin, University College London. Her book *The Loaded Table: Representations of Food in Roman Literature* (Oxford University Press, 1993) was awarded the *Premio Langhe Ceretto per la cultura del cibo*.

Sian Griffiths is features editor of *The Times Higher Education Supplement* and editor of *Beyond the Glass Ceiling* (Manchester University Press, 1996).

Brian Harrison is professor of modern history at the University of Oxford and fellow of Corpus Christi College. Among his books are *Drink and the Victorians* (Oxford University Press, 1971) and *The Transformation of British Politics, 1860–1995* (Oxford University Press, 1996).

Geoffrey Ainsworth Harrison is emeritus professor of biological anthropology at the University of Oxford. He has researched various aspects of human adaptation in a number of traditional societies around the world. Key books include *Human Biology* (with J. M. Tanner, D. R. Pilbeam and P. T. Baker) (Oxford University Press, 1988).

Philip James is director of the Rowett Research Institute, Aberdeen, and author of the report *Food Standards Agency: An Interim Proposal* (London, 1997).

Richard Lacey is a medical doctor. He is currently a visiting professor at the University of Leeds and health service consultant in infectious diseases at Leeds General Infirmary. He is working on *Food for the Future*, to be published by Thames and Hudson in 1998.

Tim Lang is the only professor of food policy in a British university. His chair is at Thames Valley University. He is co-author of *The Unmanageable Consumer* (Sage, 1993), *The New Protectionism* (Earthscan, 1993) and *Food Standards and the State* (Thames Valley University, 1997).

Simon Leader is research associate and part-time distance-learning tutor at the Centre for Mass Communication Research, University of Leicester.

Prue Leith is deputy chairperson of the Royal Society of Arts and chairperson of The British Food Heritage Trust. Her publications include *Leith's Vegetarian Cookery* (Bloomsbury, 1993), *The Cook's Handbook* (Papermac, 1984) and *Leith's Cookery Bible* (Bloomsbury, 1991).

Lydia Martens is a lecturer in sociology at the University of Stirling. She is joint author, with Alan Warde, of *Eating Out: A Sociological Analysis*, to be published by Cambridge University Press in 1999.

Anne Murcott is director of *The Nation's Diet: The Social Science of Food Choice*, a research programme funded by the Economic and Social Research Council. She is professor of the sociology of health at South Bank University, London and is co-author of *The Sociology of Food: Eating, Diet and Culture* (Sage, 1992). The programme's findings will be published in *The Nation's Diet: The Social Science of Food Choice*, edited by Anne Murcott and published by Longman, 1998.

Susie Orbach is a psychotherapist and writer. She pioneered approaches to eating problems in her books *Fat is a Feminist Issue* (Paddington Press, 1978) and *Hunger Strike* (Faber and Faber, 1986).

Shannan Peckham is a research fellow at St Catharine's College, Cambridge and an affiliated lecturer in the Faculty of Modern and Medieval Languages. He is completing a book entitled *Frontier Fictions: Literature and Nationalism in Greece*.

Hugh Pennington is professor of bacteriology at Aberdeen University. He chaired the expert group set up by the Scottish Office to inquire into the fatal outbreak of *E.coli* in Scotland which produced the *Report on the Circumstances leading to the 1996 outbreak of infection with E.coli 0157 in Central Scotland, the implications for food safety and the lessons to be learned* (Edinburgh, 1997).

Ann Ralph is a nutritionist and scientific assistant to Philip James, director of the Rowett Research Institute, Aberdeen.

Peter Singer is professor of philosophy, Monash University, Melbourne, Australia. He is best known as the author of *Animal Liberation: A New Ethics for Our Treatment of Animals* (Pimlico, 1995). His other books include *Practical Ethics* (Cambridge University Press, 1979), *How Are We To Live?* (Oxford University Press, 1997) and *Rethinking Life and Death* (Oxford University Press, 1994).

Jennifer Wallace is lecturer in English at Peterhouse, University of Cambridge. Her academic publications include *Shelley and Greece: Rethinking Romantic Hellenism* (Macmillan, 1997).

Graham Ward is Dean of Peterhouse, Cambridge. He teaches philosophical theology and critical theory at the University. He is senior editor of the journal *Literature and Theology* (Oxford University

Press), and his most recent books are *Theology and Contemporary Critical Theory* (Macmillan, 1996) and *The Postmodern God* (Blackwell, 1997).

Alan Warde is professor of sociology at Lancaster University. The research featured in his and Lydia Martens's essay was part of the programme *The Nation's Diet: The Social Science of Food Choice*, funded by the Economic and Social Research Council. Their book *Eating Out: A Sociological Analysis* is to be published by Cambridge University Press in 1999.

Preface

The *Times Higher Education Supplement*, as the trade paper of the academic profession, has a taste for topics which combine many disciplines. Food is such a subject, drawing together experts from medicine, the sciences, social sciences and humanities.

Interest in food and food policy has been sharpened in recent years by outbreaks of *E.coli* poisoning and fear of an epidemic of Creutzfeldt–Jakob Disease resulting from BSE infection in cattle. Uncertainty among scientists and bungling by politicians have made the public sceptical. 'What should we do?' has become as important a question as 'What do we know?'. Debate has moved from 'Is it safe?' to how we assess risks and who should be appointed to protect our interests in the face of huge retail and agricultural businesses. The new Food Standards Agency is now getting going, thanks partly to the efforts of a handful of experts at the forefront of a new academic subject – that of food policy. But the study of food is driven by more than scares. As world populations rise and the climate warms, producing enough food preoccupies plant scientists. As populations in advanced countries age and demand on health services threatens to overwhelm them, people have become more concerned with how to eat to stay well. Modern technologies – and a less stuffy approach to what can be regarded as historical documents – are telling us more about what our ancestors ate and how they lived. Food is moving into the heart of archaeology, history, anthropology. Nor is food just an academic matter. Prue Leith is campaigning to get children cooking at school. Marco Pierre White and others are icons for a generation of wannabe chefs. Terence Conran is storming Paris. Tourism is a person-hungry industry. In response, cooking and catering are looming larger among the courses offered in colleges and universities.

In the last couple of years the *THES* has been tracking this growing interest in a series of articles. These are brought together in this book. The series owes its origin to the insight and imagination of the paper's features editor, Sian Griffiths. It owes its success to the academics who have contributed – in particular to Jennifer Wallace, for her introduction to and inspired co-editing of the book. Thanks also to Roy Porter, who was enthusiastic at the critical moment, Andrew Lever and Shannan Peckham for their advice.

I would also like to thank the *THES*'s head of design, Adrian Norris, for his work on the illustrations and the cover; Mike Daley for letting us re-use his incomparable illustrations; Val Pearce for indispensable clerical help; and, at MUP, Vanessa Graham, Carolyn Hand, Claire Blick and Gemma Marren who shepherded the book to press.

Auriol Stevens
Editor *THES*

Introduction

Jennifer Wallace

We are living in uncertain times. Though the end of the millennium may only in fact have fictional value, yet the mythical resonances invoked by 'the end of two thousand years of history' can stir up panic and disorientation. How far have we departed from our roots? In what direction do we set out to meet the not-so-fresh new dawn of the third millennium? Other centuries have experienced *fin de siècle* weariness or disturbance. The end of the nineteenth century worried about syphilis, the evolutionary degeneration of humankind and the amorality of decadent artists and writers, but now we are witnessing a *fin de millénaire* panic of apocalyptic proportions. What has been called a 'dark-ages-type millennial fever' is sweeping the Western world in which isolated cases of disease, famine, crime and genocide are feverishly taken up as indications of the world's degeneration. Terrible murders and statistics on drug addiction provoke scares about human moral decline; global warming and deforestation point to upheavals in nature. This, in short, is the age of anxiety.

Like the end of the tenth century, as Sarah Dunant and Roy Porter point out in their book *The Age of Anxiety* (Virago, London, 1996), the end of the twentieth is characterised by a popular feeling of powerlessness. While a thousand years ago humans worried about God's wrath in the form of fire and plague, now we worry about innercity decay, youth brutality, complicated machinery. 'Our sense of powerlessness is not limited to the environment or acts of random violence', Dunant writes. 'For many people in the western world the unprecedented expansion of everything from technology through communication to shopping has brought with it not only increased demands of choice (in itself something of an anxiety) but also an expanding potential for feeling out of control' (p. xi).

The modern feeling of powerlessness stems not from awesome natural or divine forces, but paradoxically from humans themselves. Like Frankenstein's monster, who returns to terrify his creator, the machinery which replaces human employment or the huge multi-national companies and global money markets which can overpower local interests or even national governments are our own creation. Humankind, it seems, has assisted in its own demise, using its ingenuity to deny itself the power to alter the course of history or to impose the certainty of moral principles. We are thus implicated in the millennial panic, not just the innocent victims. We are terrified by the consequences of our own power.

The American commentator Gore Vidal noted recently that now 'everything is politics'. Powerful interest groups dominate every sphere of activity, from sport and the arts to the environment and agriculture. Every decision is more complicated than it seems, because it is determined by unseen factors, by large political lobbies or by financial considerations. The Kafkaesque mystique of global politics and business, of which the public is granted glimpses every so often, gives rise to the popular sense of modern-day complication and inaccessibility. The powerlessness of anxiety, in other words, is chiefly located in a feeling of ignorance, in the recognition of our lack of privileged knowledge. We seem to be moving further and further away from the natural and simple, from a time when, ostensibly, there was the comforting permanence of the world beyond humankind's control, the consolation of nature.

It is because of this feeling of divorce from the natural world that environmentalists become so passionate about the few wild or green places which are left. In Britain, the efforts of Swampy and his friends to halt the continual incursions into the green belt have highlighted how far along the road of 'development' we have travelled, while the world loses forests half the size of Wales each day with the chopping down of the Amazon rainforest. Yet even passionate environmentalists concede that it is difficult any longer to determine what can be considered pure and natural. The countryside is owned and farmed intensively, with the liberal use of pesticides and fertilisers encouraging the 'natural' crops. Animals are bred to an ever greater degree of efficiency, offering more value for money, supposedly for our benefit. Even the great wildernesses of the Arctic and the Antarctic have been found to be affected by the growing hole in the ozone layer. There is apparently no such thing as pure nature left, and it is as the public comes to realise this that its certainty and confidence are irrevocably undermined. If an uncomplicated nature no longer exists, is there anything sacred left?

It seems to some that the answer to this question is food. Everyone has to eat and food is the irreducible factor of daily life which seems to remain impervious to the sources of anxiety, to politics and ideology, to mental or spiritual hopelessness. When all is said and done, the argument goes, you are what you eat and no more, regardless of beliefs and background, class and culture. Food constitutes the last link with our nostalgic notion of natural man who was simple, certain of his world – and fed each day. Commerce and the media have recognised the apparent natural comfort of food in the last decade. Advertisers stress the close connection between their food product and a well-loved and purely imagined nature, by depicting, for example, creamy milk pouring into a bar of chocolate or ears of wheat falling into a cereal bowl. Cookery programmes market what they do as a leisure activity, a way of relieving stress. Chop a few porcini mushrooms, mix your pesto into your pasta and you can forget about the anxiety of modern living in the age-old traditional process of cooking.

Yet the notion of food as natural and therefore restorative is problematic. For a start, questions have been raised in the last decades of the twentieth century as to whether the most apparently natural form of food is the most healthy. Not long ago, medical evidence was published proving that traditional butter caused heart disease. Consumers were encouraged to buy margarine, particularly the polyunsaturated variety. The artificially manufactured food, with listed ingredients which were incomprehensible to most people, seemed paradoxically to be better than the natural one that had been eaten for centuries. But later, speculation was aired about the link between margarine and cancer. Some people reverted to butter; others remained confused, their notions about food, nature and health disturbed and no longer of any guidance.

Similarly, as Derek Burke describes in his essay in this book, crops are now cultivated or even genetically engineered in order to offer the public products which are supposed to seem fresher or riper than the so-called natural ones. Tomatoes, for example, can be created which stay fresh for longer and therefore can be picked from the plant later when they are already ripe. The ordinary tomatoes, in contrast, must be picked when they are only half ripe so that they can ripen on the journey to the shop and not become squashy. Which tomato, in this case, is the more natural and which is the healthier?

With trade and the increased importation of food, with continual advances in nutritional and scientific knowledge, food is becoming less and less 'natural', whatever that might mean, and less and less of a benchmark of the simple and traditional. To fear some foods because they are somehow 'less natural' is therefore misguided, for the cultivation of food calls into question our very notions of nature and purity. Indeed, as Tim Lang points out in his essay, food production is now very far from the popular conception of a simple chain of transmission from farm to shop to dining-table. It involves influential lobbies, the farmers and the retailers, who manipulate supply and demand and control what we eat even when the consumer appears to be spoilt for choice. As with the other sources of anxiety, food production highlights the powerlessness of consumers and their ignorance in the face of the big political hitters, the government, the scientists and the unseen might of business.

The high-profile health scares in Britain of the last few years have particularly intensified consumer fears. Salmonella, listeria, BSE or mad cow disease, *E.coli* – each of these food scares has struck at staple ingredients of the basic British diet and so caused maximum nutritional and emotional damage. Crucially, with each food crisis the traditional trust between the government and the public has weakened. In fact, the events have been marked by political cover-up and revelation. First, a Conservative health minister, Edwina Currie, shocked her parliamentary colleagues to the point of resignation when she broke government ranks and admitted that 'sadly most of British egg production is infected with salmonella'. A few years later John Selwyn Gummer fed hamburgers to his brave daughter in an effort to quell growing public concern about BSE, but it was not long before another government minister, Stephen Dorrell, refused to confirm that he himself loyally ate beef, so accelerating the BSE crisis with all its wide-ranging and still continuing repercussions. And just last year the *E.coli* outbreak in Scotland demonstrated that previous lessons about abattoir hygiene and the licensing of butchers had not been learned. Indeed, as Hugh Pennington describes in his hard-hitting essay in this book, the suspicion remains that inquiries into food safety are often set up by the executive 'to avoid doing things that it has decided not to do'.

In each of these cases, the public has found that the truth about the health risk is muddied by conflicting scientific evidence, by rumour and counter-rumour. The scientific investigation of many of the diseases, and particularly BSE, as Richard Lacey explains in his essay, is actually extremely difficult to conduct and remains controversial in its findings. But in the dearth of hard facts, the government has been frequently all too happy to deny a problem. Indeed, Hugh Pennington suggests that there has been a rather sinister collusion between scientists and the politicians who have wished to repress the problem and have drawn support from scientific uncertainty and weakness. For politicians do not have only the consumers to please, and it has been the fact that the Ministry of Agriculture, Fisheries and Food represents the interests of the constituency of farmers as well as those of the general public, rendering it both gamekeeper and poacher, so to speak, that has lost it so much public confidence and trust.

To re-establish public trust, the new Labour government elected in 1997 is in the process of establishing the much-discussed Food

Standards Agency, a body which will aim to lift food policy out of politics. Philip James has drafted the proposals for the agency and explains in his essay here the complicated political factors that shaped or hindered his ideas. The powerful lobbies of business, retailing and farming, which basically run the management of food production, have stymied changes for years, even when the last government might have wanted to implement them. Indeed, the BSE crisis helped to reveal just how ineffectual the British government could be when faced by the big supermarkets and the European Union. In developing a Food Standards Agency, James has had to confront the question of who should form the agency: elected politicians or so-called experts? Neither group is entirely satisfactory. Politicians are always open to the charge of denying truth for short-term gain; experts are unaccountable to the people and might turn out to serve some particular interest group. Who is most qualified to speak on a subject which affects everyone: the democratically elected or the most qualified? Who will run the food chain most effectively?

The problems surrounding the establishment of the Food Standards Agency raise a question addressed by several essays in this book. Although the abundance of food now on supermarket shelves has created the expectation of a limitless freedom to shop, and although modern consumer culture has come to mean the freewheeling, unaccountable right to any product, nevertheless there is a growing call among influential thinkers for greater public responsibility and control over our eating habits. Philip James is proposing to allocate more power to experts to monitor the nation's diet and less to freely elected politicians. Similarly, in arguing the case for vegetarianism, Peter Singer calls for an end to the belief that the individual bears no responsibility to the wider world. If individuals continue to believe that their private eating of meat will not make any significant difference to the global environmental problems of intensive cattle farming, he argues, the consequences to our natural world could be catastrophic. Addressing the same question of individual rights, David Bederman offers an American perspective. The McLibel trial and a recent dispute with Texas cattlemen over the alleged health risks of beef have put to the test libel laws concerning food safety in the United Kingdom and the United States. We have reached a point when a careful balance must be struck between the crucial freedom to investigate and report food safety and the public duty not to stir unwarranted rumours with disastrous effect upon consumer demand and prices. Food has traditionally been seen as one of the most democratic and freely available aspects of our daily lives, demanded in surplus as a right by the consumer of the developed world. These writers, however, seem to be striking a new note in their description of the call for some degree of responsible restraint on our cherished free-market liberalism.

The public credibility gap between producer and consumer is being bridged by regulation and by the establishment of an independent management and monitoring body. After years of *laissez-faire* politics, in which consumers have had to run the health gauntlet of relying on profiteering farmers, ineffective scientists and unscrupulous politicians, all in the name of the free market, an effort is being made to confront the causes of consumer anxiety and to replace confusion with clarity, chaos with control. But besides cleaning up the whole food production process, politicians are beginning to recognise that it is important for consumers to be heard. The ignorance about food goes both ways. The public has so often been left in the dark about the way in which our meat, for instance, is farmed and slaughtered, and only realises its ignorance at the height of some health scare. But scientists, nutritionists and food policy-makers are themselves ignorant about consumers, about their daily diets and about – what has become the buzz phrase in the field – their 'food choices'.

Traditionally, scientists and nutritionists have always assumed that, as they are clearly the experts, they can advise and educate the public about diet and that those recommendations will be obediently followed. Derek Burke, in his essay, follows the accepted line amongst scientists in arguing that decisions about food safety – in his case in the field of genetic engineering – should be left to scientists. In his former role as chief adviser to the government on genetically engineered food, he investigated the various experiments in food cultivation being conducted, and prescribed which were acceptable and which were not. Similarly, Ann Ralph and Prue Leith, nutritionist and restaurateur respectively, argue here that it is public ignorance which is the main cause of poor health and food poisoning and that people must be taught what to eat and how to cook it. Both are unequivocal in their call for better public education in food and nutrition. But the problem is that people will not necessarily do what they are told. Recalcitrant baked-beans-and-chips, sugary-tea-and-sticky-bun consumers continue in their well-worn habits, despite a decade or more of advice about healthy eating. As David Booth argues in his essay, nutritionists must plug the hole in *their* knowledge of the public's eating habits before they can presume to educate others.

It is for this reason that nutritionists are beginning to turn to sociologists and anthropologists. For many years, Mary Douglas was really the lone British voice on the social significance of food. Inspired by the examples of two Frenchmen, Claude Lévi-Strauss and

Roland Barthes, who first recognised the potential of food to convey the wider beliefs of any culture, Douglas set about, as she put it, deciphering a meal. For her, the ordering of a meal, its arrangement into different courses, is as complicated and aesthetic as the creation of a painting or a poem and just as open to interpretation. While Lévi-Strauss had concentrated in his book *The Raw and the Cooked* (Cape, 1970) on the cooking and eating habits of the Bororo Indians of Brazil, Mary Douglas turned her attention closer to home. Nothing was deemed too trivial or mundane, and she describes in her contribution here the resistance she encountered when setting up a study of the working-man's diet. Now her pioneering example has been taken up by others who are eager to study the meal customs of a whole range of different social groups and to whom terms like 'food event' for meal or 'food choice' for shopping do not seem unusual or otiose. Indeed, the growth in the sociology of food has climaxed in a large, publicly funded sociological research project led by Anne Murcott, under the title 'The nation's diet'; we have included a short account of some of the work in this programme (see the essays by Anne Murcott and Alan Warde and Lydia Martens).

Sociology hopes to fill the gap in the nation's knowledge about its own eating habits. If ignorance is a source of anxiety, then the greater self-awareness afforded us by social science should eventually bring some comfort. It is for comfort too that many academics working within the arts are turning to a re-evaluation of food and its significance. For too long, the emphasis within academia has been upon the intellectual and spiritual maxim 'I think therefore I am', not to mention the seductive other-worldliness of Romanticism in which, as in Shelley's poem *Alastor*, poets could be depicted starving to death in their all-engrossing quest of the imagination. Now, as Graham Ward describes with relish, literary critics, theologians, historians and philosophers are beginning to rediscover their bodies, *the* body. The worrying abstraction of the mind has, in the last few years of the twentieth century, been replaced – or at least quelled – by the solid materialism of the flesh.

The academic recourse to the body and food has not been all milk and honey, however. Debates inevitably still rage about the precise significance of the semantics of food. Some celebrate the irreducible materialism of food, the fact that it cannot be interpreted or analysed for hidden meanings, but it is just there, as solidly real and unambiguous as the apple on the table or the cabbage in the pot. Susie Orbach, for example, is angered by those who seek to make eating a metaphorical activity and eating disorders a symptom of purely mental – rather than also physical – distress. By putting the physical weight of food and body image back into psychoanalysis, rather than transforming everything into narrative, she argues that psychoanalytic psychotherapy can actually help women with eating disorders in a practical way rather than just speculate about their difficulties. Orbach aims to rescue anorexia and bulimia from what she sees as the recent hijacking of it by cultural studies. But for many critics, food is never unambiguously material and its metaphorical possibilities are endless. As Emily Gowers argued in her book *The Loaded Table: Representations of Food in Roman Literature* (OUP, 1993), the apple on the table which classical philosophers used as an example of reality could also signify the fall of Eden or the judgement of Paris. At the opposite extreme from Orbach's plea for the non-metaphorical study of food is Terry Eagleton's elegant contribution, a masterpiece of writing in which the boundaries between food and language, or indeed eating and imagining, are very blurred indeed.

Another major influence upon the study of food in the arts, besides the growth of interest in the body, has been what is known as the *Annales* school of history. Popularised by the Frenchman Emmanuel Le Roy Ladurie, who wrote the seminal history *Montaillou* in 1975, the school was dedicated to studying the whole picture of a particular time or people rather than, as it was thought, restricting the account to the political and supposedly more important events. Depicting all the details of a society, Le Roy Ladurie intended to convey the *mentalité* of the times. Of course any claim to offer a 'whole picture' is bound to be beset with the problems of selection and priority. Historians since, from Simon Schama to Piero Camporesi, have put more weight on material culture than on abstract beliefs and replaced Ladurie's *mentalité* with what could be described as a *substantialité*. But the basic aim, to draw upon ostensibly trivial detail in order to achieve a broader understanding of any culture, is the same. In the spirit of this type of history, Brian Harrison investigates in his essay the vast changes in the cooking and eating habits of the last fifty years in order to gain a broader sense of the post-war years. In the years of comparative peace and stability in Britain, he argues, it is the changes in technology and lifestyle which constitute the only historically interesting revolution.

The interest in material culture has been taken further by those working in the field of cultural studies. Influenced by the Marxist view that art and culture are shaped by objects and their means of production, followers of thinkers such as Jean Baudrillard and Pierre Bourdieu have investigated what has been described as 'the complex interdependence of cultures and goods', and looked at the way in which the production and consumption of commodities tells us much about a society. Food, of course, is no exception, and often, indeed, acts as a symbol or symptom of other types of consumption in a society. It is in line with this thinking that Ian Christie explores the links between cinema and food, taking into account the context of the popcorn-eating cinema audience, which consumes foodie films. Shannan Peckham wonders what happens when food is potentially globalised and mass-produced. The strong force of national identity, he argues, creates an imagined community of consumers, held together by what is perceived to be the national dish or ethnic cooking.

Food, as many of the contributors acknowledge, can be studied across a wide variety of academic subjects. Because it involves the physical act of eating as well as the symbolic significance of mealtimes, the risks and regulations of health as well as the pleasure of gastronomy, it can genuinely be described as an interdisciplinary subject. One of the aims of this book is to reflect the extent to which the study of food is now stretching from the sciences and sociology to the humanities and beyond. As a result, we have endeavoured to include contributions from most academic disciplines and areas of intellectual food study and welcome the consequential range of approach and interpretation. The interest in food in these last years of the millennium also spans the academic/popular divide, with the rise in cookery programmes and the sale of recipe books mirroring the growing increase in academic food studies. Many of the academics included in this book are working in public life, making crucial decisions about food policy which will affect millions of lives. Others, though highly intellectual, are studying popular culture or popular eating habits to deduce more about food today. In order to convey the hands-on, practical messiness of food (and of course to be useful), as many of our contributors as could be persuaded have provided relevant recipes or diet tips with their articles. All the essays, we hope, will be accessible to the lay reader and slip easily like tasty morsels into the public consciousness.

The mood of the essays is by and large optimistic. Although nearly all the contributors are aware of the anxiety of the age, and not a few are directly engaged with the consumer's anxiety about food, the prevailing tone is one of cautious expectation of improvement and comfort. Some contributors, such as Tim Dyson and William Arens, take great pleasure in scotching our worst, most primitive and basic fears – famine and cannibalism respectively. Others, such as Tim Lang and Philip James, acknowledge the potential chaos in late twentieth-century food provision, but believe that, with the active intervention which is now promised, things should get better. All are convinced that the cause of the anxiety is widespread ignorance and uncertainty and that the secret solution to the anxiety is greater public *and* expert knowledge about food, greater recognition of its importance. With food still a marginalised subject within universities, they call for a more serious acceptance of it as an academic discipline and for more scholars to follow their pioneering example. Once the study of food is established and recognised within academia, the public consciousness of the vital contribution of cooking to popular health and culture should follow suit. Then perhaps, like these contributors, we too can turn our unthinking daily consumption into a consuming passion.

Consumer anxiety

Towards a food democracy

Tim Lang

Twenty-five years ago I decided I was more interested in the intellectual pursuit of food than in that of social psychology, in which I was
then completing a doctorate. I thought that psychology was caught
in a theoretical cul-de-sac of reductionist individualism and that the
understanding of human behaviour and thought could be better
pursued through the novels of William Faulkner than through the
psychology journals.

Over the last quarter century, my love affair with food as an intellectual pursuit has grown. Whereas being a psychologist felt a bit
academically constricting – the subject, like any that is well established, comes with clear intellectual baggage – studying and working
in the world of food policy has been a feast of opportunities.

What I still love about working in food policy is its plasticity, the
way it draws upon many disciplines. This multi-disciplinary potential
has appeared to be its weakness to many people, but I revel in the
fact that to understand food we need to grapple with the relationship between people and food, politics as well as science. Since this
relationship is both constantly changing and definable, the field of
study, the methods and the framework are themselves up for grabs.

We require anthropology as much as agricultural science, cultural studies as well as chemistry.

My mother, a classicist who also studied psychology at university, was fairly horrified at my change of direction; throwing up that good career – for what? Food was a subject for women, a practical issue. (She gave a series of talks on the BBC radio programme *Woman's Hour* in the 1960s on time-saving hints and taught me the virtues of pressure-cooking; aged nearly 85, the other day she again advised that it could save me time since I was so busy. Ah, the mother–child relationship through food!) And when I went farming, literally to get my hands dirty in one end of the subject, this was, in my mother's view, akin to a rejection of the intellect itself.

In the mid-1970s I began to meet others through the now defunct British Society for Social Responsibility in Science, who, like me, were fascinated by the policies and politics of food. We set up two specialist groups to explore food, one focusing on health, the other on production, intrigued by the growing evidence in the rich world of food's impact on health both among consumers of food and among those who produced it. It seemed to us that the interesting things to study in what was then always called 'the food chain' were the connections. The farmworkers' health and safety problems with pesticides, for example, were connected to consumers' consumption of minute amounts of residue. At least farmworkers had some chance of finding out what the toxic stuff they were using was; usually consumers weren't even informed of the residues' presence. Even when they were, 'neutral' scientists and ministries were on hand to reassure consumers about the residues' negligible effect.

Studying modern food systems, I was struck by their complexity. The old distinction between production and consumption was becoming obsolete. Far from being a chain, the modern food economy is like a well-mangled plate of spaghetti that has to be delicately unravelled to bring pleasure. Since the 1970s, I have been intrigued by the thought that, far from food being a sector of modern life that late capitalism has resolved in a remorseless march of progress, one set of food problems has merely been replaced by another. Western food culture has moved from an era of scarcity to one of surfeit. The dynamics of today's food system can be better understood as an attempt to control the tendency to over-produce than to under-produce. As researchers have shown, hunger is almost always the result of human decisions, a triumph of systematic greed and power politics, laid over the chance of birth and the world order. The food world's capacity to turn common sense on its head has fascinated and incensed me in equal proportion.

Food history teaches us that the biological need for nourishment and pleasure may be an opportunity for creativity – witness the diversity of cuisines – but it also offers the chance to control. The privilege of studying food policy is that it offers an opportunity to ask the subversive questions: who is controlling, or trying to control, what and why? What usually emerges is a complex picture of different interest groups vying for influence and power. Most grotesquely, this happens on a mass scale in hunger, but it also happens mundanely within families; parents and children controlling, fighting and loving through food.

Food policy is inevitably, therefore, a study of conflict relations. The UK crises over food safety since the mid-1980s, wherein diverse explanations can be offered for agreed facts, are ample illustration of this rule. Recorded and proven incidence of food poisoning, for example, has risen inexorably since the early 1980s; no one denies that. Where differences emerge is over how many cases go unrecorded and why this rise should have taken place. Is it incompetence by consumers in handling foods at home and their failure to cook meats properly, as elements of the food industry would have us believe? Or is it, as consumer-advocates argue, that contaminated feedstuffs are fed to animals reared in battery conditions whose slaughter on speeded-up abattoir lines and poor handling by butchers result in consumers being sold contaminated food? Trying to walk through such a minefield of analysis makes food policy a lively and sensitive field. Someone's interests are bound to be hurt or compromised.

Although the term 'food policy' has begun to be used in public discourse, it is young as an academic discipline and the term still lacks the resonance of, say, economic or foreign policy. Perhaps we should not be surprised that people are somewhat perplexed by the possibility that policies might actually affect their food. Everyone likes to think that they control what they eat. Consequently, when it can be shown that someone has been adulterating or altering or short-changing food, emotions can get heated, particularly where children are concerned. Many of the recent food scandals in Britain have underlined this sensitivity, as government, business, farmers and, worst of all, meddling foreigners – a.k.a. the European Union (EU) – have been tried in the media dock. But the academic task of studying food policy is more than mere scandal-watching. The scandals are like the tip of an iceberg, not necessarily an indicator of the shape below the surface. So, what is food policy?

One of the only attempts to set out a workable definition of what is meant by food policy comes from the Organisation for Economic Co-operation and Development (OECD), better known as the West's free-market think-tank and regular auditor of its members' economies. A little quoted report from its Agricultural Policies Working Party in 1981 defined food policy as those policies affecting food – its supply and impact – which reflect 'the dominant priorities and objectives of governments'. This definition is brilliantly circular; food policy is whatever the government of the day does and thinks about food. As others before the OECD have noted, food policies do change with the whim of political economy, but academically (and sometimes personally) our task shouldn't be just to go along with this but to study and explore why this happens.

William Beveridge, father of the welfare state, highlighted this political charge in choosing the title *Food Control* for his magisterial historical review of food policy in the United Kingdom in World War One. In that book, he showed how war allowed government to intervene where hitherto ideology forbade action – at least since the repeal of the Corn Laws in 1846. For the OECD, food policy has been a sphere of governmental action which has grown dramatically since World War Two. As the food economy became more complex, policies inevitably had to cover this widened remit. Even if food policy is strictly defined as those policies that affect the food economy or food system, the field's complexity has grown immensely in the late twentieth century. It now covers not just agriculture, but processing, catering, retailing and culture as well. Whole new sectors such as logistics – moving the food about – have emerged. For the OECD, food policy is 'dynamic', a process of policy-making 'in which there is continual interaction and re-action'. I agree entirely.

Since the 1980s, we have seen how previously immutable forces could suddenly bend to new contingencies and pressures. I remember how companies began to play with consumer reactions against unnecessary food additives. First, companies insisted that the additives were necessary; then, when shown that over 90 per cent of additives were purely cosmetic, they began to drop some, continued to use others, but only after labelling them with their full name, rather than with an E number. The OECD in 1981, incidentally, saw that food additives were likely to become a sensitive issue. This was well before the EU had woken consumers up to these new food ingredients by insisting on a scheme for labelling them – designed to show that such additives were approved. Such examples illustrate how food policy can become a game of cat and mouse, a far cry from the lofty world of government policy that commentators from William Beveridge in the 1920s to the OECD in the 1980s have described.

Reviewing the formal works on food policy, my main reservation is that they are too government-focused. In the example of additives, for instance, many more players than government were involved.

Corporations are today more often of greater significance in setting food policies than either governments or consumers. The political myth is that farmers are the most powerful lobby in food; the reality is that retailers are.

In the crisis over the epidemic of BSE, or 'mad cow disease', in British cattle, observers knew that the Conservative government's approach was failing when the retailers, with one exception, said they wouldn't go along with the 'calm it all down' approach, but instead themselves decided to set up systems to trace the origin of the meat they were buying. Protecting consumer brand loyalty was more important than supporting a government many of their chairs or chief executives had publicly supported in the 1992 election. On their own and in consortia, the big food retailers and some brand manufacturers have been dominating how food is grown, harvested, stored and transported for years. The 1996 BSE crisis meant that this ratchet of control was tightened further as the supermarkets rationalised how they order food from suppliers and farmers in order to trace where every batch came from. (By implication they didn't know this before; their trust in suppliers was shaken too.) This insistence on traceability was partly driven by the 1990 Food Safety Act, which extended the European notion of 'due diligence' to food. A company now has to show that it has exerted maximum effort to ensure that food is safe in order to be free from legal liability. The policy of traceability is also driven by public relations considerations and management control; simply wanting to know everything about what is being sold. The buzz phrase now in retailing circles is Efficient Consumer Response (ECR).

ECR is code for further integration across the supply chain. Logistics is in the driving seat – how to get goods across the food chain at maximum efficiency. ECR might seem an esoteric and managerialist subject for study were it not a symbol of something much more significant. Quietly, the retail giants are setting up their own systems of standards and regulation, parallel to, and potentially in conflict with, publicly accountable standards. A conflict in food policy is in the making.

Britain's giant supermarket chains will now argue strongly, but as yet in private, that standards and consumer relations might be better left to them rather than government. We shall see whether this strategy works, or, indeed, if it survives once the new UK Food Agency is set up. The point stands, however, that in the 1980s and 1990s, the driving force of food policy is no longer government, either alone or possibly at all, but the unleashing of private capital's control over food. Through loyalty cards and the like retailers know more about us than even the banks. (They are becoming banks, too, note.) To the authors of the 1981 OECD report, this trend away from governmental control over food policy must be rich in ironies. Rightly, they pointed to the dangers of having fragmented food policies, with different wings of government going off in contrary directions. The purpose of conceiving of food policy as a separate focus of study, the OECD argued, was to avoid 'the competing views and claims imposed on policy-makers'. What has happened within less than two decades of that report is that private capital looks to be usurping government's right to set policy and govern. This tendency suggests we have entered a new phase in the long-term struggle for what we might call food democracy, the inverse of food control. Viewing food policy as a command and control perspective is self-evident to any reader of food history. Barons, governments, corporations have all sought to control food systems. But democracy, its counter? I think so. We can only make sense of modern food policy history as an epic tension between these two visions of public policy.

Anyone who has read of food riots or the demand for bread or for better wages to enable a decent standard of living is aware of a democratic thread of food demands in the wider political process. I use the phrase 'food democracy' to highlight the great struggle over the centuries, in all cultures, to achieve the right of all citizens to have access to a decent, affordable, health-enhancing diet, grown in conditions in which they can have confidence. Since the mid-nineteenth century, this has been a remarkable social tradition – from the Luddites to the creation of the Co-operative movement to demands for school meals and an end to food poverty.

In recent years the struggle for food democracy has itself been torn between a neo-liberalism which promises that better food emerges from unfettered markets ('leave it to the supermarkets') and an older, welfarist and socialist perspective which has argued that markets suit the affluent not the poor. It is not accidental that some of the greatest voices in twentieth-century food policy – Beveridge, R. H. Titmuss, F. Le Gros Clark – came from a social policy, welfarist tradition. Until the food scandals of the 1980s and 1990s, scientific and technological solutions seemed quietly to have replaced their more social vision within food policy. All this is changing once more. Productionism and commerce have been on trial. Food poverty and inequalities in food-related health have political priority again.

It is shameful that here in Britain, as rich a country as human history has produced, there are millions experiencing food poverty. But we cannot understand why this is, let alone argue for policies which may prevent it, if we only focus on the poor or on nutrition. The lesson of studying food policy is that we need a socio-political context too. So does this leave food policy as a subject blown hither and thither, at the whim of political and economic exigencies? I think not. The point about highlighting food democracy as a tendency within food policy is that we need to see the whole historical picture, not just the fragments. Food policy is made by actors in the field, not just handed down by governments like tablets of stone.

For me, the study of food policy is the study of those decisions that affect who eats, what, when, where and how. I study and advise on the shape of the food system, how food appears and disappears from tables, how it gets (or does not get) from primary producer to end consumer, how competing forces vie to affect the form of the system. In studying this dynamic weave of interests and decisions, one inevitably has to be cross-disciplinary and panoramic. At one point in its treatise the OECD defines food policy as 'a strategy that views the food economy and policies relating to it in an integrated way and in a broad economic and political context'. The subject and the practice of food policy link policy inputs from environment to social justice, from farm to fart (a small but measurable factor in global warming, particularly in the form of cows' methane!).

Food policy, like any policy area, is affected by and infused with ideology. In the great era of post-war prosperity, common sense suggested that food problems were in the past, a historical episode in the long march of progress. Today, this interpretation of history looks jaded. There is ample evidence that the poor are heavily burdened by food problems and, although the wealthy can buy their way out, to argue that rich cultures and the rich within food cultures therefore have no problems would be misleading. The environmental and public health impact of food affects us all, but unequally at the same time. Coronary heart disease, for example, is a great divider but a great leveller, too. Parents, rich and poor, worry equally about their children's food. It is just that some can throw more money at their worries than others.

People have an intensely personal relationship with their food. Whatever the diet – be it the 'shovel it in, never mind the quality' parody of a British diet or the chic-est Mediterranean cuisine – it comes wrapped with meanings and messages. And it is amusing to unravel from where our food actually originates, both as raw commodity and as food. Which Italian likes to admit that tomatoes come from Central America; which Brit that potatoes are from the Andes? And now that the pizza is the most popular food for British children and curries the national dish, geographical and cultural boundaries get somewhat blurred. It was always thus. Food is one of the oldest traded commodities, yet once you eat it, it becomes yours.

Even today, the sensitivities remain. Social scientists have taught us how food is an object of style and desire. Yet despite the plethora of TV programmes on food, and despite the remarkable improvement in good food one can buy in Britain, ours is a food culture in distress. One-tenth of the population cannot afford to eat a healthy diet. Shops groan with food, yet there are food deserts in our towns. Issues like these keep food a politically charged subject and campaigns in the 1980s and 1990s on issues as diverse as pesticide residues and sweets sales at checkouts targeting bored children have caused endless headaches to politicians and food bosses.

Politicians consistently think of food policy as a peripheral issue, to be handled under the agricultural brief, itself a political backwater, when food ought to be at the forefront of thinking about the modern economy. Food was globalising when manufacturing and services were entirely local. Now that they are globalising, a counter-trend is emerging, formed by environmental pressure for food to be relocalised. I am one who believes that, among other indicators, the health of the food economy should be judged by the distance that foods travel, which is why we should study and reduce what I have called the 'food miles' phenomenon, the growth of long-distance food on supermarket shelves. This is driven less by consumer demand, as the retailers claim, than by their own search for cheaper and more malleable sources. The result is long-distance beans in mid-winter for elite dining-tables, and a cultural collusion with late capitalism's suspension of any connection with the seasons – what has been called, in a memorable phrase, the 'refashioning of nature'.

The depth of food culture's distress should not be underestimated, which is why I am bemused that food policy is a Cinderella subject, attracting big attention only when in crisis, usually wartime. That's what is particularly interesting about the current period. We are in 'peace' yet food policy is in crisis for the first time since the mid-nineteenth century, when the battles, first over free trade and protectionism, and then over food adulteration, marked the role of government in protecting the public interest and the economy.

Passionate though I am about my focus of work, I remind myself frequently that food policy is only one among many microcosms of modern politics. Official food policy today is infused with the common fear of government intervention, refusal to confront the rise of the super-rich transnational corporation, the love affair with post-modernism and globalisation, and so on. From my own work on food retail concentration, observing the rise of this modern food baronial class, it has become clear to me that food contributes an early warning for the twenty-first century. The very definition of a market is being rewritten. When four or five companies account for a half to two-thirds of all food sold in Britain, the language of the 'market' is perhaps obsolete. We inhabit a hypermarket economy, not a market economy. Similar warnings are posted in areas as diverse as the cultural industries (media, music), chemicals and cars.

Is the policy challenge to create a new framework to let markets work, or do we sit back and allow retail concentration to continue? Exploring this question may necessitate the questioning of economic conventions. 'Efficient' food distribution, for instance, externalises environmental costs. The price of the so-called cheap food policy is not only that some cannot afford it, but that everyone experiences clogged roads and a contribution to worsened air quality, as the food belts up and down motorways and we travel further to shops in cars rather than on foot. Another question concerns the pathetic state of competition policy, which has allowed a growth of corporate giantism. This is not just a failure of public policy but an illustration of how mainstream economics – J. K. Galbraith and a few honourable others excepted – has let us down by legitimising the erosion of public controls in pursuit of lean government and a low burden on business. The retreat from food governance has been an ideological exercise. Is public policy best subsumed by commercialism?

Looking ahead, I am excited by the possibilities for food policy, both for its students and practitioners. Expansion of the EU means that the pressure on the Common Agricultural Policy (CAP) to change is immense. CAP reform is currently driven more by the political desire to lower its fiscal drag than by any notion of consumer justice or the prevention of public ill-health. Only Britain and Sweden talk of fundamental CAP reform. No government really worries about CAP's appalling impact on public health – subsidising dairy fat and tobacco, constraining affordable fruit and vegetable production – but this might be changing. In February 1997, EU President Jacques Santer gave an extraordinarily powerful speech in response to a damning report on the handling of the BSE crisis from the European Parliament. He called for CAP to become a Common Food Policy, for a shift away from intensive agriculture and for more notice to be taken of consumers, the environment and public health. As a wish list, I cannot fault it, but four months later, the EU's Agenda 2000 document outlining the actual CAP reform programme showed little of this imagination. We are back to the old policy of piecemeal reform.

Despite this sober reality, I am hopeful. The growth of a strong public-interest food movement across Europe is paralleled in most countries and regions of the world. On the back of globalised media, the capacity for ordinary people to see what eludes the specialists offers great promise. The need is to integrate environmental, health, consumer and economic imperatives where, in the past, productionism has triumphed. Everywhere I see continuing tension between the local and the global within food policy. On the one hand, global companies want global standards, but ones which they can 'play' best. On the other hand, with biodiversity under great threat, the monocultures of food production are themselves in the spotlight. With concerns growing about the impact of genetic engineering on food, I see no diminution of such tensions. In the United Kingdom, food governance, far from being the means for implementing food policies, has itself become a problem. Fifteen years of scandals will undoubtedly yield change in Whitehall. The Food Standards Agency is to be welcomed, but I am as interested in the role of the rump Ministry of Agriculture left behind. What will it do? Will it survive? Will it have cloned itself into the new agency, as some fear? Heaven preserve us!

I also discern growing tension over food education, not just in schools but the wider instillation of food-consciousness. The 1990s school curriculum removed most traces of practical food education. This so incensed the Department of Health and the Ministry of Agriculture, Fisheries and Food that they backed a project to re-inject cooking classes into schools. To be fair, a health component was inserted into the curriculum, but its effectiveness needs to be monitored. I doubt that it will compensate for the £600 million a year that the food industries spend on food advertising. For a glimpse, observe the effectiveness of the advertisements on children's TV. The current government is aware of the complexity of food issues in schools. A working group on school food and physical activity has already reported to the Minister of Public Health and the Secretary of State for Education and Employment has promised new standards for school meals. The challenge to education is considerable.

Unless there is a concerted effort to empower future consumers by giving them the skills not just to cook if they want to, but to shop and to look after their bodies through food, we will see an acceleration of the US obesity phenomenon. Does it matter? In the case of obesity, yes. In hard cash the cost to the NHS is immense, and lives are lost prematurely. In wider cultural terms, a dependency culture could be in the making. Food is becoming more complex and pre-processed. It comes from factories, not our own transformation at home. The challenge was to get men to cook, not to remove the skills from women as well.

After a decade in which food policy has returned to the public policy agenda, led by concerns about food safety, I am hopeful, but only if a literate, multi-disciplinary, educational process is maintained. In truth, no one discipline has all the answers. Here lie opportunities for universities in the next century. It is really ridiculous that, to my university's knowledge and to mine, my chair in food policy is the only one in this country. There are professors of food marketing and agribusiness – some sponsored by corporations – but too few independent voices on food policy. Subjects which traditionally kept a food-consciousness academically alive have been changing rapidly. Home Economics has been transmogrified into Consumer Studies and the food element has too often been submerged by commercialism. Nutrition has become ever more sophisticated, but has often lost the social vision which gave birth to it. Economics and management try to increase efficiency without asking for what goals. New insights are pouring out of environmental and human sciences which beg to be integrated. With food policy so popular an issue, now is a good time for a flowering of multi-disciplinary work. Certainly, food policy's challenges won't be met by specialisms on their own, but by teamwork for the public good.

Further reading

Beveridge, W., *Food Control*, Oxford University Press, London, 1928.
Leather, S., *The Making of Modern Malnutrition*, Caroline Walker Trust, London, 1966.
Organisation for Economic Co-operation and Development, *Food Policy*, OECD, Paris, 1981.
Tansey, G. and Worsley, T., *The Food System*, Earthscan, London, 1995.
Thrupp, L. A., *Bittersweet Harvests for Global Supermarkets*, World Resources Institute, Washington DC, 1995.

A recipe

Porridge

Oats
Water
Heat

The best porridge, to my mind, is made from pinhead oatmeal, really coarse oatmeal. This, my mother thinks, can be best made in a pressure-cooker, but actually it's very simple without, but requires a moment's planning the evening before. Put one scoop of oatmeal with three scoops of water into a pan. Bring it to the boil, stirring occasionally. Turn it off and go to bed. The next day, it'll just need bringing slowly to the boil. Eat and enjoy.

If you cannot cope with this, buy jumbo whole oats and add water and bring to the boil in the morning. Porridge has a special place in our household. My partner's granddaughter's first complete sentence was 'Granny, eat your porridge', at which our jaws dropped. Scots traditionally take porridge with a pinch of salt, but this is not needed and is undesirable for your heart. Canadians add fruit. I have a drop of skimmed milk. My mother, of course, loves it with honey or treacle and she'll outlive us all.

Dining with death

Hugh Pennington

Long experience has led many of us to believe in a hidden hand which starts public health catastrophes on a Friday and propels them to develop their full horror over the weekend. At just after noon on Friday 22 November 1996, 3 confirmed cases of *E.coli* 0157 were reported to the Lanarkshire Department of Public Health in central Scotland. By the evening the number of likely cases had risen to 15. The outbreak grew rapidly and went on to become one of the world's largest outbreaks of food poisoning, with 20 deaths, almost 500 cases and 151 patients admitted to hospital.

Even the most cursory study of this outbreak shows that food safety – or the lack of it – is a subject which is multi-disciplinary in the widest sense. This particular outbreak (which resulted from eating contaminated meat) threw up issues relating to interactions between subjects as varied as medicine, science, sociology, politics, philosophy and the law. It provoked the Scottish Office to establish an Expert Group of specialists in food safety, microbiology and public health to inquire into the catastrophe and seek lessons from it. During the course of its deliberations, the group, which I chaired, tackled basic questions about science and politics, such as 'is there any truth in the view that the appointment of an advisory committee is the last refugee of administrative incompetence?', 'how often are such groups appointed as an easy way for the executive to avoid doing things that it has decided not to do by studying a problem until the issue has quietened down and then advising not to do it?' and 'are the members of advisory groups, including those drawn from the civil service, always sufficiently objective?'

Scotland has a well developed set of legislative, administrative, medical, scientific and enforcement structures for the protection of the public health. They are as well developed as those of any other nation – indeed better than most – yet Scotland has a notoriously poor record not only in food poisoning but also in cancer and heart

disease. Why is this? Who or what is to blame? Is it a matter of the basic principles being right but errors being made in their implementation, or are Scotland's fundamental approaches to the prevention of disease seriously flawed?

A less public by-product of the *E.coli* outbreak was the establishment of a Cabinet Committee to handle issues arising from the catastrophe. Why did the government do this? The Cabinet Office document *Question of Procedure for Ministers* states:

> [C]abinet and ministerial committee business consists of (i) questions which significantly engage the collective responsibility of the Government because they raise major issues of policy or because they are of critical importance to the public, (ii) questions on which there is an unresolved argument between Departments.

Researchers in politics will probably have to wait the customary thirty years until government papers are made public to find out which of these caused the Cabinet to act. Nevertheless, those of us close to the affair might deem it hubristic for food specialists to imagine that an outbreak of food poisoning was significant enough to fall into the first category. Were there unresolved arguments about the handling of the affair between, on the one hand, the Scottish Office in Edinburgh and, on the other, the two London-based government

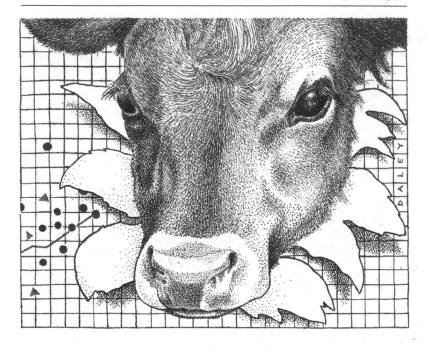

departments with responsibility for regulating food safety and public health: the Ministry of Agriculture, Fisheries and Food and the
Department of Health?

All these issues and problems are important. Even more significant
is the fact that, at the end of the day, many of them are addressing
really big debates, not just in public policy, but in biology, such as
evolution; in political science, such as the constitution; and in the
philosophy of science, such as how do we know when scientific knowledge becomes reliable.

Because I am a microbiologist I firmly believe that science has
shown that microbes cause disease. I have no time for the wilder
excesses of any constructivist sociologist of science who thinks otherwise – even if I accept that social factors may be pre-eminent in
determining the incidence, spread and victims of infectious diseases.
So before discussing the role that the impact of *E.coli* can play as a
starting point for the study of big questions, it is worth considering
the organism and its science. The central Scotland outbreak was
caused by a particular strain of *E.coli* 0157, characterised by the production of a toxin and a particular kind of chromosomal DNA structure
identical to that possessed by a strain that in 1994 caused the world's
largest milk-borne outbreak. This also happened in central Scotland

– in West Lothian – hence its laboratory designation, the West Lothian sub-clone.

Because *E.coli* reproduces by binary fission without the need for sex, all daughter cells are identical twins, and its populations, by definition, are clonal. But because individual bacteria can occasionally exchange pieces of DNA by a sort of *coitus interruptus*, and because they suffer from random mutations, the original *E.coli* clone has long since split into many different sub-clones, one of which is the disease-producing 0157 – which itself is now beginning to divide into further sub-clones. Most *E.coli* strains can coexist happily with us in our bowels. They have the greatest difficulty in killing people. Not so *E.coli* 0157. It regularly causes fatal infections in the very young and the very old, because its toxin attacks small blood vessels. Even more frequently it causes serious disease in individuals in these age groups by damaging their kidneys, often permanently. This complication is called the haemolytic uraemic syndrome (HUS).

There is nothing remarkable about these events. Many other bacteria cause disease through the activity of toxins of one sort or another, although only a few are as nasty. What makes *E.coli* 0157 particularly interesting scientifically is its novelty – there can be little doubt that it is a brand new organism – and its almost complete failure to cause disease in its natural home, the intestines of cattle and sheep. These observations raise as yet unanswered questions about microbial evolution.

It is generally accepted that the organism appeared for the first time in the 1970s – with the first cases of disease documented in the United States in 1982. Did it evolve there? What selective advantage do its virulence genes, like the one coding for its toxin, confer? Why does it keep them if it doesn't use them in its natural host? That these genes confer an advantage seems self-evident because, since its first appearance, the organism has spread to all continents. This has occurred very unevenly, raising another set of fundamental questions, this time about bacterial ecology and natural history. Why are *E.coli* 0157 human infections particularly common in Scotland, but not in Ireland, and in Canada but not in Scandinavia? Why is HUS a major health problem in Argentina but not in South Africa? Are answers to these questions to be found in national differences in carriage rates in cattle, or in the geographical distribution of particular sub-clones, or in varying predilections for beef or differences in farming practice, or because of what happens in slaughterhouses and butchers' shops, or are the differences due to chance? One cannot say. So the mantra 'more research must be done' has been uttered. It is happening. Results will come. Nevertheless, public and political pressure requires that action be taken *now*.

How did the Expert Group cope with all this? Although our remit prevented and absolved us from apportioning blame at the personal level, it did not require a profound analysis to conclude that the occurrence of a massive outbreak, the frequent recording of other smaller ones, and the continued existence of bacterial food poisoning as a major public health problem indicate that the food safety system is failing, either because of faults in its design or because of faults in its operation. The only comfort was that in spite of many unanswered questions about the biology of *E.coli* 0157, existing knowledge about its virulence (as measured by deaths, which are better recorded and easier to count than illnesses) and transmissibility (eating fewer than ten bacteria can have lethal consequences) was sufficient to show that it constitutes about the severest test of the food safety system one could imagine. Even so, it is clear that a century and a half of sanitary reform, a hundred years of bacteriology, and half a century of antibiotics have not closed the highways that bacteria use to transport themselves from the intestines and faeces of animals to the mouths of people. Indeed, they are still wide open, and from time to time very busy.

It was against this background, of the failure of an extensive regulatory system, an impressive degree of scientific uncertainty, political pressure for rapid results and intense media scrutiny, that the Expert Group conducted its inquiry. Coping required a pragmatic approach: we did not have the luxury of time to conduct an in-depth review of general principles. Nevertheless, such principles were there – tacitly – in our thinking. They often derived from areas remote from food safety, such as the principles guiding policy-making based on inadequate scientific information and those governing the reduction of risk by means of regulation. These are controversial and topical subjects. Contemporary British examples include arguments between doctors, scientists and politicians about the nature of the Gulf War syndrome, and the debate about the impact of a deregulatory philosophy on safety in the off-shore oil industry.

It is not difficult to show that most scientific theories are under-determined by evidence. With the cataloguing of the world's species of birds, and human anatomy at the macroscopic – surgical – level as the only exceptions that spring to mind, it is hard to think of any biological subject even remotely approaching scientific closure. It follows that policy-making in just about any medical or related area is going to have a scientific basis characterised by incompleteness and error. While it has to be admitted that such a basis has not inhibited doctors from implementing drastic and dangerous treatment regimes in the past, and that the continued popularity of 'alternative' medicine shows how acceptable the lack of a scientific underpinning is to members of the public, most professionals aim to base their practice on sound and rational principles. Experience from other fields gives them clues about how to avoid major errors when basing decision-making on incomplete scientific evidence. One obvious and successful way to compensate for uncertainty is to incorporate substantial degrees of redundancy and overdesign into one's plans. These have long been a feature of the design of buildings, boilers and bridges, no doubt because of the fatal consequences of failure not only for the life of the user, but for the reputation of the designer.

Overdesign and redundancy are an engineer's response to uncertainty, technical fixes that are not always available or appropriate in policy-making. Philosophers and lawyers can point to the precautionary principle as another way of protecting human life in the face of hazards marked by scientific uncertainty. It is neatly summarised in Principle 15 of the Rio Declaration made at the 1992 United Nations Conference on Environment and Development:

> In order to protect the environment, the precautionary approach shall be widely applied by States according to their capabilities. Where there are threats of serious or irreversible damage, lack of full scientific certainty shall not be used as a reason for postponing cost-effective measures to prevent environmental damage.

The ringing tones of the Declaration and its underpinning by international agreement should not, however, be taken as evidence that it is operational. It is not. One reason is that it presents a major challenge to current legal principles – such as the presumption that no harm has occurred until a party can demonstrate harm and causation. This is an issue of immense practical importance in food safety. Sooner or later every environmental health officer has to face the situation of finding a hazard but being unable to take formal action because the evidence falls short of the high level of certainty required by the courts. Officers in Scotland have been particularly influenced by the outcome of an application in 1995 for a Condemnation Order on forty-four batches of a blue cheese. This expensive process (evidence from twenty-six witnesses was heard over nineteen days and 253 documents were lodged as evidence) culminated in the refusal of the Order by the Sheriff and the incurring of heavy costs by the local council. Argument centred on the scientific evidence relating to the ability of certain strains of *Listeria* to cause disease in humans; many expert witnesses were heard, and a high degree of scientific certainty was demanded. The precautionary principle was clearly not in operation.

Another powerful force that prevents the routine application of overdesign, redundancy and the precautionary principle as responses to scientific uncertainty is that they are seen as luxuries because of their cost. In considering food safety, a major issue that we faced was the trade-off between safety costs and commercial considerations. Industry often finds the scientific community helpful here because scientists are more interested in avoiding false positive than false negative errors in situations of uncertainty, placing a greater burden of proof on the person who postulates some, rather than no, effect. At least one body we consulted – the government Advisory Committee on the Microbiological Safety of Food – took this attitude. Its scientific and industrialist members made representations to us that because we could not produce a minute-by-minute detailed account of the spread of *E.coli* 0157 from the gut of a cow to the residents of Wishaw – the epicentre of the 1996 outbreak – our recommendations somehow lacked scientific weight. In fact, this outbreak will almost certainly turn out to have a degree of abundance of epidemiological and microbiological data that will make it one of the best documented ever for *E.coli* 0157.

Nevertheless, it has to be admitted that policy-making in the microbiological safety of food often has to be conducted without the strength of scientific evidence that one would like – partly because of the difficulties in obtaining evidence. More often than not, for example, when investigators arrive, the food that contained the offending microbe cannot be studied because it has all been eaten.

Fundamental problems also attend the methods that are used to investigate food poisoning. Heavy reliance is put on epidemiology, which tries to establish associations between factors – such as the consumption of a particular food item – and the occurrence of disease. This approach must be one of the last bastions of induction, or the drawing of a general principle from particular facts, and is essentially Baconian in logic. Lord Macaulay exposed the banality of its intellectual underpinning in the *Edinburgh Review* in 1837:

[W]e are not inclined to ascribe much practical value to that analysis of the inductive method which Bacon has given in the second book of the *Novum Organum*. It is indeed an elaborate and correct analysis. But it is an analysis of that which we are all doing from morning to night, and which we continue to do even in our dreams. A plain man finds his stomach out of order. He never heard Lord Bacon's name. But he proceeds in the strictest conformity with the rules laid down in the second book of the *Novum Organum*, and satisfies himself that minced pies have done the mischief. 'I ate minced pies on Monday and Wednesday, and I was kept awake by indigestion all night.' This is the *comparentia ad intellectum instantiarum convenientium*. 'I did not eat any on Tuesday and Friday, and I was quite well.' This is the *comparentia instantiarum in proximo quae natura data privantur*. 'I ate very sparingly of them on Sunday, and was very slightly indisposed in the evening. But on Christmas-day I almost dined on them, and was so ill that I was in great danger.' This is the *comparentia instantiarum secundum magis et minus*. 'It cannot have been the brandy which I took with them. For I have drunk brandy daily for years without being the worse for it.' This is the *rejectio naturarum*. Our invalid then proceeds to what is termed by Bacon the *Vindemiatio*, and pronounces that minced pies do not agree with him. (T. B. Macaulay, *Critical and Historical Essays Contributed to the Edinburgh Review*, vol. 2, 2nd edn, Longman, Brown, Green and Longman, pp. 280–429)

Very often it is not even possible to get as far as Macaulay's plain man. Thus a food source was not identified in three quarters of the 1,744 cases of *E.coli* 0157 reported in Scotland between 1990 and 1996. This was because most of these cases occurred in isolation, not as part of an outbreak, which makes them difficult and expensive to investigate by epidemiological methods.

It is plain that epidemiological data will nearly always fall significantly short of providing the sort of evidence that scientists look for when they set out to 'confirm' a hypothesis – even if what they mean is not 'confirmation' in the strict logical sense, but the provision of strong support for its probability. The Victorian polymath William Whewell, Master of Trinity, showed how a scientist's 'confirmation' could be massively strengthened. His 'consilience of inductions' is now a forgotten term, but the technique is still used all the time. In essence, it involves the demonstration of supporting evidence for a hypothesis by two completely different and unrelated methods. In the case of a food poisoning outbreak this is commonly done by showing that cases of infection related epidemiologically – say, by having eaten the same suspect food – have also been infected with an identical microbe. The development of techniques to type bacteria using DNA fingerprinting methods is a very active field for this reason. Lawyers have been among the keenest exploiters of this information because of the courts' requirements for evidence that satisfies well beyond reasonable doubt and because they know the power of DNA fingerprinting as a marker of human individual identity. But some bacteriologists have been reluctant to use the new methods. Resolution of this problem will come from the operation of Planck's principle: 'a scientific truth does not triumph by convincing its opponents and making them see the light, but rather because its opponents eventually die and a new generation grows up that is familiar with it.'

Food safety legislation – even if defective – requires enforcement. The current regulatory system is imperfect, not only because its scientific basis is incomplete and error-ridden, but because it fails more often than it should. In addition, enforcers have to cope with a legal milieu that sometimes places too heavy a burden of proof on them. They also have to face hostility from those they regulate. The anecdotes related to the Expert Group about abattoir inspectors, whose car tyres were deflated after they had ordered the slaughter line to be slowed, were probably apocryphal, but illustrate the point.

The regulation of hazardous substances is a subject with a large literature and a very long history. Attempts to control infectious diseases go back to the late Middle Ages – a typical example is the edict of the Aberdeen town council of 21 April 1497 concerned with the control of sexually transmitted infection – the French disease:

> [I]t was statut and ordanit be the Alderman and Counsale for the eschevin [overcoming] of the infirmity cum out of Franche and strang partis, that all licht woman be chargit and ordanit to decist fra thar vices and syne of venerie, and all thair buthis and houssis skalit [demolished].

Such regulations and their successors have played a key role in directing the evolution of municipal government in the succeeding 500 years. In his book *Government and Science*, Don K. Price went further by showing that in the United States the intolerability of life in an industrial city, which would have inevitably resulted from the unfettered exercise of Jeffersonian republican freedom, was countered by science-induced developments in legal theory and administrative machinery. These developments led to the evolution of a federal Constitution and a regulatory apparatus that works for modern society.

Nevertheless, and despite its cleanliness, tidiness and general municipal order, Aberdeen still has a thriving red light district. Hegel's dictum is often true: 'what experience and history teach is this – that people and governments never have learned anything from history, or acted on principles deduced from it.' Food safety is no exception – the recommendation of the Expert Group that butchers should be licensed was first made to the government by the Richmond Committee in 1989, many outbreaks of food poisoning ago.

A general principle governing the success and failure of regulatory regimes is that learning from past errors is a powerful and effective way to make progress. No doubt this was a thought that passed through the mind of the then Secretary of State for Scotland Michael

Forsyth when he set up the Expert Group. Its converse – that not attending to what is known is a source of failure – is well documented. A good example was the 1986 Chernobyl disaster. The design fault in the RBMK reactor control-rods which caused a transient but massive increase in power when they were suddenly inserted into the reactor to shut it off in an emergency – a positive scram – and which caused the reactor to blow up, was identified in Lithuania three years before, but no compensatory measures were taken and no information disseminated about it.

In contrast, a classical example of a regulatory system which became remarkably effective by learning from disasters was the nineteenth-century British Railways Inspectorate, established in 1840 by the Regulation of Railways Act. The Inspectorate was a branch of the Board of Trade, staffed by officers seconded from the Royal Corps of Engineers. It investigated accidents vigorously and in public and made recommendations – in contrast to food poisoning, where even now this only happens sporadically and where learning about rather than learning from incidents still predominates. By the end of the century it could be counted a success, because the probability of death in an accident on a train had fallen to 1/100,000,000 per journey.

The inspectorate emphasised self-regulation by railway companies. This was not entirely deliberate. Mid-Victorian judges, sympathetic to those who saw the activities of regulators as dangerous to individual liberty, often granted orders of *certiorari* to quash regulatory decisions, and when Parliament responded by including clauses to nullify these in legislation they made mandatory orders instead. Nevertheless, it is clear that a mixture of self-regulation and legally supported enforcement of prescriptive measures worked well in an atmosphere of unbridled capitalism and for an industry with enormous political power. The setting of the balance between these elements of regulation is a continuing issue today, and our report has stimulated a debate about it in Scotland and the rest of the United Kingdom.

The government is pressing ahead with plans to establish a Food Standards Agency. Academics played a significant part in providing information and advice to Professor Philip James while he prepared its blueprint for Tony Blair. It has much to do. Pressure of parliamentary time means that it will not be up and running before 1999. Until then, academics have a major role in making sure that food safety remains in the first rank as a public health issue.

In 1997 the Labour government accepted the recommendations of Professor Pennington's Expert Group and introduced a system for licensing butchers' shops in a bid to improve food hygiene.

Further reading

Advisory Committee on the Microbial Safety of Food, *Report on Verocytotoxin-producing Escherichia coli*, HMSO, London, 1995.

Armstrong, G. L., Hollingsworth, J., Morris, J. G., Emerging foodborne pathogens: Escherichia coli 0157:H7 as a model of entry of a new pathogen in the food supply of the developed world, *Epidemiologic Reviews* 18, 1996; 29–51.

Prevention and control of enterohaemorrhagic coli (EHEC) infections. Report of a World Health Organisation consultation, Geneva, Switzerland, 28 April–1 May, 1997, WHO, 1997.

Price, Don K., *Government and Science*, Oxford University Press, New York, 1962.

Rolt, L. T. C., *Red for Danger*, Pan Books, London, 1996.

Mad cows and Englishmen

Richard Lacey

Sadly, nearly twelve years on from the first case of mad cow disease or bovine spongiform encephalopathy (BSE) in England, the knowledge of the disease is scant indeed. In the popular imagination, there is horror at the way in which the disease spreads and fear created by half-truths and rumours. Is BSE passed from sheep to cows, and so then to people, causing a new variant of the progressive dementia, Creutzfeldt–Jakob Disease (CJD)? Is it the result of a new type of cannibalism, the eating of meat-eating cattle? Can it turn the brain soft and spongy? Will it become a mass epidemic, with millions of fatalities? What bits of the cow are the most fatal? The lack of hard facts about the disease has made the public only more confused and frightened.

Even among scientists, little is understood about the illness. This is partly because it is particularly difficult to develop tests for the disease. Unlike all other infectious diseases, transmissible spongiform encephalopathies (TSEs) – of which BSE is one form – do not provoke an immune response to the infection. Cells do not produce antibodies to resist the infection, as they do in the case of AIDS, and so tests based on antibody production cannot be set up. Unlike HIV, too, the chief cause of TSEs – what is known as the 'prion' – is incredibly resistant to heat, chemicals and irradiation. The infectious particle is truly a tough fighter. The other major problem with TSEs is tracking the disease. Like HIV infections, there is a long period of incubation prior to the final illnesses, and it is because of that long interval that

there is the opportunity for spread to new hosts. Unlike HIV, which has a predilection for one mammalian species, the causative prions of TSEs probably have the capacity to infect several different species of mammals. These difficulties in identifying and tracking the illness have led some people to deny that TSEs are infectious. It is tempting, especially for organic beef farmers, to suggest that the cause of the disease is organophosphorus chemicals rather than any infectious particle. But enough is known now to be sure that the disease is infectious, and strides in our knowledge of how the infection spreads are being made all the time.

For an infection to develop and spread, there has to be a means by which an increase in numbers of the infectious particle can occur. With all other micro-organisms, this replication is achieved by DNA or RNA, or both, within the particle. This enables nutrients from the parasitised host to be used to synthesise new copies of the infective agent. But the infectious particle of TSE does not seem to contain DNA or RNA, because these are relatively easily destroyed by commonly used disinfecting and sterilising methods to which TSEs are resistant. Two major scientific breakthroughs have solved this problem. The American Stanley Prusiner, winner of the 1997 Nobel Prize for medicine, suggested in 1982 that the cause of TSEs was a protein he called a prion which could, when in the cell, somehow cause further similar proteins to be produced. Since then, work in Zurich has proved that DNA is needed for the production of a normal protein and the prion then converts that normal protein into an abnormal one. So DNA and RNA *are* needed for the disease process to occur, but they are not actually in the particle itself.

The normal proteins, and the DNA responsible for their formation, vary between species and indeed within members of one species. Apparently, eighteen million people possess the right genes to have the potential to develop CJD, if infected. Humans are possibly protected by what is known as the 'species barrier'. The ability of the causative prions of TSEs to cause disease is influenced by the genes of their host and so they vary greatly in their properties, according to which animal they are infecting. This makes it more likely that prions will spread within one species and are less likely to infect different species. It means that either more infectivity or more time is needed for the disease to spread across species. However, the species barrier seems to vary in the extent to which it is insurmountable. So even *if* sheep scrapie did cause BSE (which it didn't), and assuming sheep scrapie did not infect mankind, it could not be assumed that BSE would not infect people, because the cattle genes could well have changed the prion. Although this information is pretty complicated, the experimental data was known in the late 1980s and explains why a few scientists said then that BSE presented a *prima facie* hazard to the human population.

Where did BSE come from? Although no similar research was performed in the UK – and this is a terrible indictment on the authorities at the time – American research was published in 1994 showing that sheep scrapie did not cause BSE. The BSE prion is even more durable than the scrapie prion and the rapid rise of BSE from 1988–92 was not associated with any increase in sheep scrapie a few years before. So sheep brains were not the cause of BSE. What was? We do not know for certain, but there are three possibilities.

One possibility, and I believe this to be the most likely, is that BSE is a variant of a rare similar cattle disease that was responsible for the earlier types of CJD in many countries. That BSE arose initially in the United Kingdom would then be a matter of chance, since cannibalistic cattle-feeding was widespread in the developed world. The second possibility is that BSE was derived from the remains of another mammal via the rendering plants and meat and bone-meal added to cattle feed. This could include domestic cats put down by veterinarians whose carcasses were disposed of in the rendering plants. TSE in cats does closely resemble BSE. However, the first TSE in a cat was not reported until 1990, making the direction of spread of infection more likely to be cattle to cats rather than the reverse. Third, it is just possible that human remains entered the rendering plants and so passed into cattle feed. It has been reported that human placentas were fed to Swiss cattle, and, if BSE was caused by CJD, it might explain the virtual identity of the new variant CJD and BSE. But I believe this explanation of the source of BSE is more theoretical than probable.

For several decades before the first BSE case, extensive research was performed on both natural and experimental transfer of TSEs. This research showed that infection could be transferred by a variety of routes, not just one. Infection can enter an animal through ingestion. It can pass directly from animal to animal (horizontal), for example through direct blood contact when the animal becoming infected has lacerations. Then, as expected with any persistent infection, TSEs can pass from the dam to her offspring before birth. This presumably occurs through maternal substances entering the umbilical cord of the foetus. Transfer by semen is theoretically possible, but not substantiated. However, CJD has been acquired by blood transfusion, grafts, transplants and contaminated hormones from the pituitary gland. It has also been suggested that mites may be a means by which environmental contamination might enter an animal's body. It is also possible that buried infected animals might contaminate water supplies on account of the durability of the prion. Experiments demonstrating this have not and cannot be done. Thus, the routes of acquisition of TSEs are varied, and many of these, notably feed, vertical and horizontal transmission and environmental contamination, accounted for the rapid rise of clinical BSE cases in 1988–92, with the exposure to the agent around four to five years prior to this.

Regrettably, little is known about how the BSE prion spreads within cattle to produce the final brain disease. However, by analogy with other TSEs, it is possible to paint a general picture that is, of course, highly relevant to predicting which organs or tissues might contain most infectivity. Most experiments are performed on rodents or sheep naturally infected with scrapie. Often, animals under experiment do not seem to be infected. It is difficult to decide whether this means that there is no infection or whether the particular animal under experiment is not vulnerable to the disease.

However, despite these experimental difficulties, we do know the following: first, that the greater the dose of infection entering the animal, the shorter the interval before the fatal brain damage; second, the way in which the prion enters the animal is not crucial for determining the course of the disease; third, the first cells which the prion attacks are those related to immunity, known as the reticulo-endothelial system. These cells are located in the guts, spleen, thymus and tonsils, which explains why these organs (together with the brain and spinal cord) were removed from cattle over the age of 6 months at slaughter in late 1989. However, these cells are also found in many other tissues, including liver, blood, bones, lungs and lymph nodes distributed throughout the mammal.

Suggestions have been made that prions are transferred to the brain as a result of entering and moving up nerves in a similar manner to the rabies virus or herpes. This is most unlikely, as the brain is uniformly affected. Although prions multiply in these non-nervous organs and are detectable about halfway through the period leading to the development of the clinical disease in the animal, they do not appear to cause much damage to these, except sometimes to the liver in patients with CJD. So the infection probably reaches the brain through the blood. Once in the brain, the nerve cells are gradually destroyed. Brain damage is inevitably permanent because nerve cells are incapable of repair or regeneration except in the foetus. Greatest infectivity is therefore found in the animal's brain after death, sometimes to such a degree that a single gram of tissue is capable of infecting ten thousand million mice.

One of the problems with investigating BSE is that, rather than calves being used in experiments, a breed of mouse has been used which is barely vulnerable to BSE. There is, in other words, a strong species barrier between cattle and these mice. The only cattle organs where infectivity has been demonstrated are the brain, spinal cord, optic nerve and intestines. This does not mean that infectivity is not present elsewhere in the animal. It just means that it cannot be detected elsewhere when experimenting on mice. Indeed, we think that infectivity is actually widespread within cattle with BSE. Since the disease is passed on from cow to calf in about 10 per cent of cases, it seems it must be passed through blood. And it is through blood, too, that the prion is thought to reach the cattle brain.

Were BSE to be simply an amplification of a defined existing malady, it might be possible to extrapolate the likely effects on the human population. But this would appear not to be the case. The crucial year was 1985. Prior to that date, TSEs under 'natural' conditions had been identified in only six mammals – mankind, sheep, goats, mink, elk and deer. Since 1985, TSEs have been shown to occur in thirteen new species, including zoo cats, domestic cats, antelopes and even ostriches. The most significant medical finding has been the detection of a novel type of CJD, actually referred to as new variant CJD. Whilst both the old and the new CJD are sporadic, and hence assumed to be acquired from animals, the diseases are different. With the old variant, the average age for the onset of the disease is 65 years, the length of final illness is 7 months and dementia occurs early on. With the new variant, the age of onset has been 16–52 years, the illness averages 14 months and dementia occurs relatively late. Moreover, the biochemical and microscopic changes in the brain are different in the two types. This does indicate very strongly that TSEs, including BSE, those in zoo animals, the domestic cat and the new type of CJD, are indeed new and probably transferred between these species.

It is remotely possible that the new CJD caused BSE, but the timing is wrong and it is difficult to see how a transfer took place. It is also theoretically possible that an as yet undefined source, other than cattle, caused the infection, but despite enthusiastic searching, none has been suggested. Thus the inevitable inference is that BSE causes new variant CJD, although it is much less certain how the disease was transferred. Direct spread from cattle is just possible. More likely might be the ingestion of beef products, particularly those containing offal. However, milk cannot be formally excluded, even though milk does not transfer the disease experimentally to mice.

How many people might succumb to new CJD and when? Despite enthusiastic efforts to predict future cases, the reality is that any figure is nothing more than a guess. One worrying long-term possibility is that some people may be incubating the disease, but appear healthy. However, such carriers might transfer the infection to others in ways comparable with the spread of HIV – e.g. blood products, surgery, transplants, sex. The uncertainty in making predictions is due to the length and variation of the incubation period. For example, if those already diagnosed with new CJD caught it in the early or mid-1980s when BSE was rare, we might expect many more cases to emerge soon in those exposed to the infection in the late 1980s and 1990s. If the incubation period were to be about 30 years, the omens would be gloomy. This estimate is based on the analogy with cattle, where by 1996 only 80 BSE cases out of around 160,000 (i.e. 0.05 per cent) were in animals aged less than 30 months. The average age of BSE cattle is around 5 years, and it would be reasonable to expect that the longer lived *Homo sapiens* would experience a much longer incubation period, particularly if the species barrier were to have any effect. As a result, it is terribly difficult to assess the risk for humans from infected cattle.

Because the infection causing TSEs can pass between animals in various ways, persist in the environment for years, and there is still no practical means of identifying which animals are incubating the disease, the only means of complete control is the slaughter of all infected herds and their replacement with BSE-free stock established in new territory. The policy of herd slaughter is adopted by countries other than the United Kingdom and is feasible because the problem is less extensive elsewhere. But it seems as if the potential cost and disruption of this policy, together with the inadequate facilities for disposal of unwanted cattle remains, all put it beyond our capability. The current policy of preventing the carcasses of cattle aged over 30 months of age from entering the food chain is evidently a com-promise. Even so, incinerator capacity is not adequate even for these carcasses, whether or not previously rendered.

It remains to be seen what the course of the disease will be. At pres-ent, there are strong suspicions that the dramatic drop in BSE cases over the last two years is partly due to reduced reporting of cases by farmers – hardly surprising since their livelihoods are threatened. Since it is thought that the infection is acquired in the animal around birth and that the infection passes from the dam to the calf before birth, it is difficult to see how the disease can be eradicated, when infected dairy herds are still breeding and there are no restrictions upon the movement of cattle or calves to other herds.

Avoiding eating beef from cattle aged over 30 months reduces the hazard of contracting new variant CJD considerably, but not com-pletely. Because infectivity can be acquired by the calf at or before birth, younger animals will carry some infection. Perhaps, small expos-ure to BSE prions in a person who had previously consumed a higher dose will not pose much additional risk, unless the hazard is indeed cumulative, like cigarette smoking or irradiation. Certainly, pregnant women, young children and people from abroad should avoid the risk altogether.

While some of the details of BSE remain disputed, the cause has to be attributed to intensive farming, centralised food production and the consumer demand for cheap, convenient dairy products and beef. Almost as soon as the disease was identified, its scale was such that the political and economic cost of attempting to eradicate it was beyond that of the government of the time. The message is simple: when centralised food production goes wrong, the consequences are devastating. This is the price which the urban dweller pays for cheap food.

My analysis is largely pessimistic. The beef lobby and its parliamen-tary supporters have come up with an alternative assessment which plays down the health risk of the disease and plays up the economic harm being inflicted on farmers and rural communities. The hysteria over BSE is not justified, according to their argument, and the real need now is to encourage the consumption of British beef, said to be the best in the world. In other words, according to their alternative assessment, BSE is a problem of consumer confidence. This view may or may not be correct. The point is that, at present, we do not know. Science has failed to deliver the facts. Scientists have failed us, and that failure shamefully has allowed the disaster to escalate and explode unchecked.

Further reading

Collinge J. and Palmer M. S., *Prion Diseases*, Oxford University Press, London 1977.

Gajdusek D. C., Unconventional viruses and the origin and disappearance of Kuru, *Science* 197, 1977; 943–60.

Lacey R. W., *Mad Cow Disease. A History of BSE in Britain*, Cypsela, Jersey, UK, 1994.

Prusiner S. B., *Prions, Prions, Prions*, Springer, New York, 1995.

Wilesmith J. H. W., *et al.*, Bovine spongiform encephalopathy: epidemiological studies, *Veterinary Record* 123, 1988; 638–44.

Setting food standards

Philip James

The recent crisis over British beef, and how it became contaminated with BSE, or mad cow disease, has sparked off much of the debate about how safe our food really is. In fact, however, criticism of food in Britain has been quietly rumbling for years. There was the campaign in the 1970s about food additives and colourings, which led to a reappraisal of the need for luridly coloured foods and the remarkably different amounts of additives in similar products. By the early 1980s the British public knew that many of their epidemic diseases, such as heart disease and cancer, had a dietary contribution. They also realised that industrial processing could profoundly change the nature of food by, for example, altering its fatty acid content. Manipulations in one direction could lead to improved health; in another direction to an early death. Food labelling became more complex. Then came the food irradiation debate, the incidence of food poisoning soared, Edwina Currie invoked the salmonella-in-eggs scare, a listeria panic followed and concern mounted about the heavy metal poisoning

of fish. More recently, there has been debate about probiotics, prebiotics, functional foods and genetically modified plants and animals. This long series of food scares has chipped away at consumer confidence in the food industry.

A perception appears to have developed that the British food chain is controlled by companies primarily concerned with profit, which, in conjunction with the United Kingdom's Ministry of Agriculture, Fisheries and Food (MAFF), and under the guise of deregulation, have short-circuited rigorous checks over the safety of food. People feel strongly that the Ministry's dual role in protecting public health, on the one hand, and promoting the food and agriculture industries on the other, has sometimes led to conflicts of interest. These conflicts have, to date, been handled within the Ministry, or in discussions with the Department of Health (DoH), and because of the secrecy of such decision-making it is often not clear how they have been resolved. But certainly MAFF is accused of having jumped too many times to the defence of farmers or food manufacturers.

The BSE crisis, and the inadequacy of some of the United Kingdom's controls on animal feeds and slaughterhouse procedures, have made the public question both the scientific competence and the priorities of the Ministry of Agriculture. During my assessment of policy needs I discovered that consumers felt that they had been treated to inept and condescending publicity campaigns over many years, which in practice, misled rather than reassured them. They believed that the Ministry concentrated on promoting the interests of companies whilst paying only lip-service to consumer and public health issues. This was an image not helped by MAFF's publications, which have, in the past, listed the promotion of the British farming and food industries as one of the Ministry's key objectives.

I became involved in the debate about the standards of British food on 6 March 1997, after an exchange between the then Prime Minister John Major, and Tony Blair, then Leader of the Opposition, about the alleged suppression of a report on MAFF's recently established Meat Hygiene Service. The immediate cause of complaint was that the report had not been sent to the committee investigating the fatal outbreak of food poisoning in Scotland in 1996 caused by the meat-borne bacterial toxin *E.coli* 0157.

On the evening of the parliamentary exchange, the Shadow Agriculture Minister, Gavin Strang, telephoned me. He had just met with Tony Blair, who wanted a clear definition of the Labour Party's commitment to a Food Standards Agency. Although many people accepted the principle of such an agency, it meant different things to different people. What was the most appropriate structure for such an agency? What should be its remit? The Conservatives had plans to appoint a food safety council, chaired by a food safety adviser, to provide the public as well as MAFF with advice. Most of the UK public interest groups had dismissed this proposal as totally inadequate since it continued the by now offensive assumption that the public was either over-anxious or ignorant about food.

Those eager to maintain the *status quo* argued that the growing epidemic of food poisoning was caused by public ignorance about good hygiene practices at home. They said that there was no need for any change in the food supply system and used the words 'food choice' incessantly in a bid to convey the value to the consumer of the abundance stemming from an increasingly free market in food, unfettered by outdated regulations.

On 7 March 1997, however, Tony Blair and I agreed that protecting public health was paramount. I would prepare a proposal for an independent Food Standards Agency and deliver it personally to him should Labour win the election. We also agreed that I would publish the report and make it available to whoever was in government after 1 May, 1997. The agency would need to be accountable to Parliament and report to ministers but it must be free of political and industrial pressures. It would separate the role of promoting public health from that of promoting business.

With less than seven weeks to go to the election the task seemed at first impossible. Yet within a week we were able to organise our first think-tank involving key representatives of the food industry: farming, medical, public health, microbiology, toxicology, novel foods and consumer interests. At that meeting we concentrated on two issues – how radical a reform was required and how broad a remit a new agency should tackle.

An amazing consensus emerged about the nature and extent

of consumer unease. Surveys conducted by the food industry, consumer organisations and various academics confirmed a widespread crisis of confidence in the UK system for ensuring food safety. It was clear that, contrary to the views of some in the food industry, educating a discerning member of the public about the issues relating to food safety increased rather than allayed their anxieties. To advocate education and reassurance was not the solution – fundamental structural changes in the management and monitoring of the food chain were needed.

On the question of how broad the new agency's remit should be, there was agreement that there were four big issues that needed to be addressed: food's microbiology, its toxicology, the manipulation of food by genetics and other processes and the nutrition of the nation (since people's health can be greatly influenced by what they eat). At that point there was little dissent over the range of issues to be handled – perhaps because those we consulted were the real experts in the complexity of the food issues involved.

Much later, however, we heard the view that really we should have dealt only with food safety, concentrating in particular on the variety of infections transmitted by food. The other issues should not have been included within our proposals for the agency's remit. This view is, of course, legitimate. If you think of food poisoning by bacterial toxins as the key issue in terms of risk to public health, then an agency for food safety with a limited remit could have been created. Some scientists, who do not routinely deal with food issues, feel more comfortable with this. They argue that the problems of microbiological food safety are difficult enough to handle without extending an agency's task into other areas.

There is also a view among some doctors that all that is needed in terms of improving the health of the nation is to educate consumers to make appropriate food choices. This view is usually accompanied by a failure to recognise that nutritional issues underlie most of our major health problems. Yet advice, from the DoH, for instance, on which foods are healthy or unhealthy always affects some British food or farming interest – potentially boosting or cutting sales. There is almost no nutrition or food policy analysis made either by the DoH or by MAFF which does not affect the food or agricultural industries.

Over the past fifteen years, the renaissance in the recognition of the nutritional basis for so many public health problems has resulted in changes in DoH policies. Goals for dietary change, however, have been limited either by the sense that, in practice, the British cannot be expected to change their food habits very much or by concern that some industrial sector – e.g. the sugar, dairy, oils, meat or salt-related industries – will make life difficult for the government. Despite making only modest proposals on dietary change, the publication of the last DoH report on heart disease led to press stories of ministers being called back from holiday by Prime Ministerial demand to be berated in private by the chairmen of the affected industries. There were also reports of civil servants being asked to leave the room while the issues were discussed. The publication of the Scottish Diet Action Report – started by Ian Lang when he was Conservative Secretary of State in the Scottish Office – was also systematically opposed by both DoH and MAFF ministers because it seemed too radical. This is a typical example of the fragmentation and lack of coherence in the current system, which suffers badly from overlaps and conflicts between the various bodies involved in food policy and monitoring and enforcing food safety.

Nutrition is a major political and industrial punch-ball. It is little wonder, therefore, that consumers and other public interest groups insist that it be part of the remit of an independent Food Standards Agency. These intense industrial concerns and pressures relate to multi-billion dollar markets. Furthermore, the economic impact of nutrition on health is of far greater importance than all the other food safety costs put together – including the BSE and *E.coli* 0157 crises. A Danish study concluded that the economic cost of inappropriate nutrition was three to four times that of all other food safety hazards.

One interesting aspect of my enquiries was the discovery that many organisations still regard 'consumers' as troublesome busybodies. Consumer organisations in Britain are, however, often very sophisticated. In effect, they can be unofficial think-tanks on food policy. These groups, together with other 'public interest' groups such as public health specialists, were adamant that the agency's remit should be food standards and not just food safety. They argued that the agency's role should encompass a wide range of issues, including food labelling, chemical contaminants, additives and questions of genetic modification. Public interest groups have also highlighted their concern about the way DoH policies are swayed by industrial concerns and MAFF interference. In fact, despite MAFF's introduction of consumer panels and its appointment of consumer representatives to some of its own expert advisory committees, I found that nearly all the public interest groups consulted wanted to transfer the agriculture ministry's powers over health or consumer protection to the new agency. I was bombarded with complaints about MAFF's secretive decision-making and its alleged bias in favour of industry's rather than consumers' interests. Whatever the truth of these allegations most respondents warned that the agency was doomed if public health was not seen to dominate its agenda.

With such sensitive subjects as food and health how was I to devise an appropriate system in a democratic society? Should the agency be completely independent of government, subject to no democratic control? This did not sit comfortably with an agency handling delicate issues of considerable economic and political impact. But if the agency were to be managed by ministers, it could become subject to political dogma and be driven by a need to protect political figures. As a compromise we turned to a governmental model which had proved successful: the Health and Safety Commission/Executive (HSC/E) which had been set up at a time of great concern about risky industrial procedures such as mining, North Sea oil drilling and nuclear safety. Our discussions with a group of social anthropologists confirmed the value of this model. Attractive features included the relationship between local authority enforcement and central enforcement of regulations and the combination of policy-making, monitoring and tough intervention based on legislation to stop malpractice. Politically, the split between a policy-based commission supervising an executive agency was also a clever device to maintain political interactions while still protecting the executive from political interference.

I devised a modified scheme including the best elements of the HSC/E but emphasising a new approach to the public. The Food Standards Agency should be governed by a 'commission' of about ten members with consumer and public interest nominees in the majority. The commission would advise ministers, and the chair would be the body's 'public face'. There would be enough support staff to ensure that all commissioners had the support needed to participate fully in discussions – a feature that has been missing from the HSC/E. Like the HSC/E, the commission would be supported by an operational arm – the executive. It is difficult to restore confidence in a system where discussions and decisions are made behind closed doors. After discussions with US, European and Australian officials, I knew that the ideal way through the interrelationships between government, Parliament, industrial concerns and the public would be to have a completely transparent system that allowed debate about difficult decisions to be in the public domain. Yet, there is opposition to such openness within the British establishment; it is a curious, cultural feature that seems to stem from the pre-war system of central decision-making by the educated elite. Nonetheless, a freedom of information act was promised by the Labour Party and I believed that on this point I should be quite radical. I therefore proposed that most, if not all, meetings of the commission and the committees that advise it should be held in public.

Such an agency could also transform debates on sensitive food issues, which currently are seen as being in too narrow a technical framework. The licensing work of the Pesticides Safety Directorate and the Veterinary Medicines Directorate, for instance, is funded by companies' application fees. These assessment processes are accused of developing their own culture, removed from wider social concerns about public health. Since my report was published, recommendations have been made for the inclusion of both directorates within the new agency and for opening up their discussions to a wider audience.

A host of developments emerged with the public debate on my proposals. One issue related to my observation that there was little communication between the veterinary and medical professions about matters such as the use of antibiotics on farms, pesticide safety and the highly complex issue of infections transmitted from plough to plate. This was seen as highlighting the dearth of veterinary public health knowledge in the majority of vets. The disparate nature of the organisation of veterinary surveillance throughout Britain was also debated. Competing laboratories and chaotic methods of gaining access to facilities for testing whether people, foods, factories, abattoirs or farms were infected with lethal organisms did not help. The enforcement of food law is also uneven throughout the United Kingdom because it competes with other local authority responsibilities – such as education and social services – for funding.

The government set about producing its White Paper on food standards using the internal resources of Whitehall and without setting up the Commission I had previously recommended. The understandable reason given was that a government elected with such a huge majority could not be seen to be anticipating the decisions of Parliament about whether or not there should be a Food Standards Agency in the first place.

The unfortunate effect, however, was that the usual Whitehall processes prevailed and the fundamental shift needed to bring the big issues into the public domain was delayed. Curiously, the most powerful vested interests, defending the *status quo*, were claimed to be scientists anxious to protect their directorates or committees from being transferred to the new agency – a move which would result in them losing their personal reporting systems to ministers. Many officials at MAFF were, by contrast, delighted with the notion of a new agency and the opportunity it gave them to shift into a dimension wherein the public did not regard them as the enemy.

While the White Paper was being drawn up, the nutrition debate raged behind closed doors. Some members of the food industry panicked, resorting to the argument that the task of ensuring that people eat proper foods would require a nanny or even a police state.

There were rumours of company chairmen again lobbying ministers and nobody knew the outcome.

To most people's surprise the White Paper eventually emerged, in January 1998, bearing a remarkable similarity to my proposals and with few seemingly contentious issues except for a new proposal to fund the agency by levying a fee on all food outlets, collected by local authorities rather than by the agency directly. The Pesticide and Veterinary Medicines Directorates retained their independence as did the Public Health Laboratory Service. The problem will be to ensure that nutrition is dealt with in a coherent way and that the many problems relating to BSE, *E.coli* 0157 and salmonella – ie the need to transform the safety of animal foods – can be resolved. The agency is going to have to build a strategy with a flair for innovation and communication which will signify a fundamental culture shift in the way in which we work.

Further reading

Consumers' Association, *A National Food Agency*, Policy Report, London, 1997.

Lang, T., Millstone, E. and Rayner, M., *Food Standards and the State: A Fresh Start*, Thames Valley University, London, 1997.

The 'yuk' factor
Derek Burke

Over the last couple of years, genetically modified foods have been entering supermarkets in Britain as a result of the regulatory decisions made by the Advisory Committee on Novel Foods and Processes, which I chaired from 1988 to 1997. The outcome has been mixed; some foods have been accepted without hesitation by the public: 'vegetarian cheese' and the paste made from genetically modified (GM) tomatoes are two examples. But others, notably the flour from GM soya beans and an insect-resistant corn, have caused considerable controversy, and the consequences have reached right up to the top levels of decision-making in the EU and in some of its member states. Why is this, and what is the cause of the public's concern? What can we do about it and how might the technology be applied and develop in the future?

'Vegetarian cheese', sold by the Co-op chain of stores, was the first genetically modified food to come to the market. For centuries, traditional cheese manufacturers used a crude preparation of the

enzyme chymosin, called rennet and made from the cow's stomach, to coagulate the milk. Nobody worried much about this, but the crude enzyme was variable in its effect and was gradually replaced by a similar enzyme made in bacteria, and then by an enzyme made by genetic engineering. This was possible because the gene for chymosin had been cloned, and the first preparation of chymosin made in this way was cleared as safe in January 1991, while two other sources of the enzyme, from different micro-organisms, were later also approved. Initially, the cheese was not labelled because the enzyme was identical in every way to that obtained from calves, but one retailer did decide to label the cheese. Since no animal product had been used in its manufacture, it could carry a 'V' label – suitable for vegetarians. This was welcomed by many shoppers. Vegetarian cheese was the first example of a modified food that offered an advantage to the consumer.

A second successful product was a tomato paste made from GM tomatoes. In tomatoes, as in many other foods, the enzyme polygacturonase is responsible for the breakdown of the cell wall and the plant pectin that leads to the softening and ultimately the disintegration of the tomato. In 1994, the committee received a submission for a tomato paste from a GM tomato in which synthesis of this enzyme had been slowed down. These lower levels of the enzyme enabled the fruit to ripen normally, but it softened less quickly. The tomato did not have to be picked so early, the fruit could be transported with less damage and, because of the higher levels of pectin, the paste made from the tomatoes was more naturally viscous. The company chose to market the paste, rather than the whole fruit, since in that way there were no complications about consumer concerns over eating the DNA from the tomato's seeds. The company also worked carefully with two supermarket chains (Safeway and Sainsbury's) to produce explanatory material for the consumer, labelled the tins and, crucially, offered the consumer choice – with tins of tomato paste from GM and non-GM tomatoes side by side on the shelf. Consumers were perfectly happy to buy the GM paste. They knew what they were buying, and they were being offered a choice. Indeed, they accepted both the GM cheese and the tomato paste. But, before either of these products reached the shops we had a less successful experience with a GM baker's yeast. This was developed by introducing two genes from a similar yeast, in order to increase the rate at which the bread rose. We, as members of the advisory committee, thought that this was a straightforward case. After all, the genetic change could have been brought about by the naturally occurring yeast-mating process. We could not see any safety problems, and therefore we issued a brief press release which announced that 'the product may be used safely'.

Reaction from newspaper commentators, however, was not enthusiastic. It varied from: 'Genetic yeast passed for use' in *The Times*, through 'Man-made yeast raises temperature' in the *Independent*, to 'Bionic bread sales wrapped in secrecy' in *Today* and 'Are the boffins taking the rise out of bread?' in the *Star*. The Consumers' Association said: 'We think all genetically altered foods should be labelled.' The general reaction was so negative that the modified yeast has never been used.

As a result of this setback, a number of changes were made to the way in which our committee worked. A consumer representative and an ethical adviser joined committee members, and a number of steps were taken to open up the regulatory process and make it more transparent. The committee has produced an annual report since 1989, held an annual press conference and produced press releases before and after each committee meeting, as well as after ministerial approval of each product or process. We learned the hard way that when decisions involve the public being exposed to any risk that is not of its choosing, they must be taken as openly and publicly as possible. This principle is now being widely applied across government, and will be crucial for the success of the new Food Standards Agency.

In 1990 the committee was asked whether meat from genetically modified sheep could enter the food chain. These sheep carried the human gene for Factor IX, a protein needed for the treatment of haemophiliacs. However, it often takes a hundred animals to be reared before one animal is produced which yields Factor IX in high quantities. We were asked about the animals which either contained no gene, or only an inactive gene or part of a gene. Could they be eaten? We could not think of any reason why animals without any foreign DNA should not be eaten. But were newspapers going to run the headline: 'Failures from genetic engineering in your supermarket'? What about the animals containing an inactive human gene? Was this just a stretch of DNA like any other? Or was it special, because it came from a human being? Would eating sheep meat containing a single human gene even be regarded as cannibalism by some? Would Muslims or Jews be concerned about pork genes in lamb, and vegetarians about animal genes in plants? We did not know, but decided that it was probably a wider issue than one of pure technical safety, and suggested to the then Conservative Minister for Food John Gummer, that there should be wider consultation. Mr Gummer agreed and a small committee was set up with the Reverend John Polkinghorne, Fellow of the Royal Society, in the chair.

We found that the Christians were divided on the issue. Some had no objections, but many had an uneasy concern, a feeling shared by others, which has been termed the 'yuk' factor. The Jewish reaction was more straightforward; 'If it looks like a sheep, then it is a sheep', was their comment. Muslims and Hindus were much more opposed, as were the animal welfare groups and the vegetarians. None of the groups was moved when we pointed out that there was effectively no chance of their eating the original human gene, for it was hugely diluted in the processes of genetic manipulation, and the gene inserted into the sheep was more correctly called a 'copy-gene'. They said they would be concerned even if the gene was completely synthetic. They were also concerned by the 'slippery slope' argument. These sheep had only one human gene in 100,000 sheep genes. But what if the ratio were 50:50? Then all of us would be anxious. They were worried, too, about labelling, and wanted consumers to have choice. There was obviously quite widespread unease. The committee made a series of recommendations, which were accepted, with the result that not even the animals with no foreign genes will enter the food chain. Consumer concerns, even if they do not appear to have a rational basis to scientists, must be taken seriously and not brushed away.

In plants, the first genes to be manipulated were those which made crops capable of resisting herbicides, so that chemicals could be sprayed on fields to kill weeds without damaging cultivated crops. This development has been criticised, and is often put down to a 'plot' by the companies concerned to increase their sales of herbicides. It is true that in discussions that I was involved in in the early 1980s, when I was working in a company, we were aware of that opportunity. However, the main reason these genes were selected for manipulation was that they are single genes and therefore much easier to isolate and alter than the multi-gene complexes responsible for such crucial traits in plants as the ability to grow in salty or very dry soil. Possible science is done before more difficult or impossible science.

A number of products from several herbicide-resistant plants were approved by the advisory committee. Many of these were quite straightforward, but difficulty did arise over a line of soya beans from the US chemical and biotechnology company Monsanto, which were altered so that they could resist the herbicide glyphosate. Glyphosate works by inactivating an enzyme in the plant which is essential for the production of complex amino acids, thereby preventing growth. By introducing a gene from a bacterium into a commercial variety of soya beans, the beans were able to withstand the herbicide's effect.

The committee had no safety concerns over the product, which is the soya bean flour rather than the beans, since the DNA is degraded during the production of the flour. Nor did the product need to be labelled, although information was provided, on a voluntary basis, by the retailer – as was done in the successful launch of the paste from GM tomatoes earlier in the year. However, with soya, the retailers were not able to offer customers choice, because the GM soya was not segregated from the 'normal' soya at source.

Soya is grown in the US Middle West over a wide area. Farmers normally sow the different types of soya plant in their fields, often in the same field. So segregation would mean complete separation from start to finish: cleaning out the harvester between harvesting the different types, using separate trucks to separate elevators, using separate and identifiable rail wagons to the ports and then complete separation in the ships, and in all the stages in Europe after docking. Soya is a commodity crop, bought and sold like oil, and it is difficult, although not impossible, to follow a particular shipment. Even if these crops were to be harvested separately, there remain very substantial practical difficulties in maintaining separation throughout all of the subsequent stages of primary and secondary processing, food manufacture and distribution. This would require either separate batch operations or duplicate plant and equipment at every one of the stages. Then, too, would it be possible to offer alternatives – with and without GM soya – for all the 600 or so products in any supermarket that contain soya?

However, this explanation of the difficulty involved in trying to separate GM from normal soya was not accepted by consumer groups, who organised a series of demonstrations and boycotts. It is clear that consumers want to make their own, informed decisions about what they buy and eat. Following a decision by the Labour Minister for Food, Jeff Rooker, in 1997, food processors and retailers are now responding with much more extensive labelling of the contents of their products. Meanwhile, retailing organisations are working on an agreement with American farmers' organisations and distributors to ensure that GM soya coming to Britain is separately packaged and labelled.

It is extremely unfortunate that Monsanto took the approach it initially did, largely ignoring consumer concerns, and it is likely that the way in which its product was introduced has set back the commercial development of plant genetic manipulation. The company does not seem to have realised that consumer reactions in Europe are not the same as in the United States. European consumers do not see why they should lose their ability to choose whether or not to buy a product about which they may have concerns, simply to put money into the pockets of farmers and companies.

More recently, there has been concern about genes which make antibiotic treatments less effective in genetically altered plants. Are such genes at all likely to be transferred to bacteria in the guts of animals which eat genetically altered plants, and if so, does it matter? The advisory committee recommended approval of the modified tomato, despite the fact that it contains an antibiotic resistance gene, because the gene was controlled by a plant promoter, and therefore could not work in gut bacteria, and because the antibiotic, kanamycin, was not of great clinical significance. In contrast, a modified maize, developed by the company Ciba-Geigy, contained, in addition to a bacterial gene (the Bt gene) that confers resistance to the European corn-borer insect and a gene that confers resistance to the herbicide glufosinate-ammonium, a third gene that confers resistance to the antibiotic ampicillin. This third gene has been the source of much trouble, for it has a bacterial promoter in front of the penicillinase gene (which means that the gene could work in bacteria but not in plants). In addition, a high copy number plasmid was used, while the gene in question produced a particularly active penicillinase. The antibiotic resistance gene was a residue and served no useful function in the plant.

The committee was concerned as to whether there was any risk of transfer of this antibiotic resistance gene into the bacteria in animals' guts when the maize was used for animal feed in an unprocessed form. The technical risk was certainly small; the consequential risk could have been large. The advisory committee did not recommend that this product be approved, but our decision was later overruled in Brussels, the EU committees ruling that the possibility of a transfer of the gene from plants to animals and humans, thereby reducing the effectiveness of antibiotic medicines, was remote. They did not consider, therefore, that the risk constituted a sufficient reason for a ban. However, this decision by Brussels has since been challenged by several EU countries, notably Austria.

Why do consumers want to make their own decisions? Basically, I think because they have lost confidence in what they hear from politicians and, to a lesser extent, from regulators. And what are the reasons for this loss of consumer confidence?

Scientists, and the processes whereby products are approved by 'experts', are no longer trusted as they once were. The 'man in the white laboratory coat' no longer recommends washing powder; the consumer does. As an article in the science journal *Nature* (26 June 1997) pointed out: 'In an increasingly complex world, it has been said that trust is a functional substitute for knowledge ... in the absence of trust, perceived risks and moral dangers proliferate and appear greater.' Also, I think the public is largely unaware of the development of careful scientific methods of assessing risk, such as the use of hazard analysis, to come much closer to an 'objective' evaluation of risk. But it is also true that scientists have great difficulty explaining, and the public understanding, what is meant by different degrees of risk. Our National Lottery – with its slogan of 'It could be you' – does not help either; the message is clear: even what is very unlikely may happen. It has been pointed out that one is more likely to die while watching the National Lottery than win the jackpot, but that doesn't stop people buying tickets; someone has to win! So even if the risk from a new product is very low, maybe it will be me.

Risks are assessed differently according to the context. We will accept quite high risks when we are seriously ill, but will not tolerate much risk at all with food, as the outcome of the 1996 Eurobarometer survey showed clearly. According to this survey, conducted in each EU country, and involving 16,246 people, many Europeans are 'uneasy' about new genetic technologies. Although people see all biotechnology applications as potentially useful, those involving crop plants and food production are seen to involve risks, with 74 per cent of respondents indicating that they thought GM food should be labelled as such.

One explanation for the conflicting views of the public and scientists is that they work from different value systems. Scientists and technologists see novel applications of new discoveries as logical and reasonable – and characterise all opposition as unreasonable. 'If only they understood what we are doing', they say, 'the public would agree with us.' Scientists are used to an uncertain world, where knowledge is always flawed; they can handle risk judgements relatively easily, and are impatient of those who differ from them. The public's reaction is quite different. It includes outrage – 'how dare they do this to us?' and dread.

Scientists are regarded as arrogant, distant and uncaring. They are also condemned by some for playing God. The public asks, 'how do scientists know that they are not going to release a new plague?' Scientists reply that they see living systems as a unity, knowing that cells, from bacteria to man, work in much the same way. So of course, say the scientists, it's all right to move genes around – all we have to do is explain the scientific process clearly, and people will be reassured.

I think this type of scientific response is too glib in the late twentieth century. There are important technical issues to be talked about, particularly environmental issues. Will plants' resistance to herbicides spread to weeds, will genes rendering antibiotics ineffective transfer from plants to man through gut bacteria? The situation needs careful watching, and concerns have been expressed that the 'case-by-case' approach used by the British government's Advisory Committee on Releases into the Environment (ACRE) does not tackle the incremental effect of the series of individual decisions it has taken about releasing GM substances into the environment.

There are other issues too. There is the natural/unnatural issue. Some think that it is unwise, even unethical, to disturb the natural world – and that genetic modification is unnatural because it crosses species barriers. Others believe that BSE resulted from the 'unnatural' feeding of an animal foodstuff to a herbivore; so, in their view, BSE is a sort of Divine Judgement for upsetting the natural order of things. Personally, I do not accept that all that is natural is best; fungal infection of crops with production of the ergot alkaloids is certainly not for the good of those who eat crops. But to go back to the beginning: why were the people we consulted so resistant to the idea of eating a human gene even when it was totally synthetic?

Partly, I think, because they do not know where to draw the line between one gene and a thousand. Is this the start of a slippery slope? Surely we must be able to draw a line somewhere? I believe that we certainly have to try. We already do so in other cases, for example in the case of experiments on very early human embryos.

Is there a concern about what science is doing to our perception of humanness? People are loving, caring, choosing human beings, with deeply held beliefs and values, many of which are central to their view of what a human being is. They do not accept the theory that we are no more than a bunch of genes. They believe that there must be something special about human genes, that genes should not be treated merely as chemical entities. Is this a reaction to reductionism? A rejection of the idea that we are nothing but a bunch of genes? The concern of the public is not lessened by the aggressive determinism of some modern biologists.

In stressing the underlying simplicity and order of the complex world which modern molecular biology reveals, and in stressing the power and effectiveness of modern technology, we must also stress its limits. Scientists, I believe, must be less assertive, less arrogant than is currently sometimes the case. For, too often driven by their love of new technology, scientists are unaware of the dehumanising effect of their innate reductionism.

So, what is biotechnology likely to produce in the future? In my view, the most straightforward developments will be a whole series of new and improved enzymes for food processing and for the modification of existing foods, for example modifying foods containing high amounts of fat. The science is straightforward, and there seems to be little consumer concern.

In plants, I think we will see the following changes:

- continued development of methods to identify genes (genetic typing) to speed conventional plant breeding systems – this will lead to the pinpointing of genes responsible for desirable traits, and their transfer to other species, for example between cereals;
- continued development of GM plants resistant to herbicides, viruses, bacteria and fungi, reducing the financial losses due to these agents;
- continued development of fruits and vegetables with longer shelf lives capable of being transported long distances undamaged;
- modification of fatty acid synthetic pathways to produce oils containing more suitable fats and starches for either dietary or industrial use;
- improvement of the flavour, texture and nutritional content of fruit and vegetables through genetic modification; conversely, the elimination of genes for toxicants and allergens;

- isolation, and utilisation of more complex genetic systems such as those controlling plants' ability to thrive in salty soil and withstand drought, making possible the growth of plants in a wider variety of habitats;
- isolation of the genes that control plant development, making it possible to start to manipulate flower shape, and colour for the horticultural industry – for example, antirrhinums can now be made to flower to the tip, and recently a gene has been identified that makes stressed grass stay green longer;
- isolation of the genes that control plants' response to day length perhaps making it possible, by modifying these genes, to produce plants that come to maturity more quickly, and so push north, for example, the boundaries for growing rape in Canada, with a huge economic impact.

Developments in animals, apart from those leading to the production of high value/low volume drugs from transgenic animals will be slower, for public concerns are much more serious. But some predictions are possible:

- development of rapid genetic typing techniques will revolutionise animal breeding, enabling identification of the genes critical for elite stocks and their transfer by conventional breeding to others;
- the identification of genes for undesirable traits will accelerate our ability to remove those traits from breeding stock;
- better understanding of infectious disease pathogens should lead to the ability to breed animals with increased resistance to disease;
- genes could be introduced to enable cows to produce milk that is much closer in its composition to human milk for feeding to babies;
- a similar approach could be used to produce transgenic animals with, for example, less body fat. However it will, I think, be some time before such animals are acceptable for food.

What lessons can we draw from this to guide us for the future? Let me suggest four criteria for the development of a new product: it must be technically possible – and it is now true that almost anything is possible; it must offer the consumer an advantage, and not just the producer; the regulatory process must be rigorous, open and universal; and the consumer must be offered choice, at least for an initial period. Technical skills will not be sufficient on their own to turn this exciting and powerful new science into products and processes; scientists will have to take the public with them.

Further reading

The Genetics Forum, *Spilling the Genes* (report), London, 1996.
Hobbelink, Henk, *Biotechnology and the Future of World Agriculture*, Zed Books, London, 1991.
Organisation for Economic Co-operation and Development, *Biotechnology, Agriculture and Food*, OECD, Paris, 1992.
Lord Soulsby (ed.), *Genetic Engineering in Food Production*, Royal Society of Medicine Press, London, 1997.

Cooking with kids

Prue Leith

It is now almost impossible for a child in this country to learn to cook. Once, perhaps, children learnt at mother's knee. But mother's knee is out working. Or they learnt at school, but the cost of teaching cooking and the low status of anything to do with non-academic subjects has led to cooking being either optional or so academic as to bear little relationship to real cooking.

Last year, at the Royal Society of Arts, we staged an event to raise the whole debate about cooking in schools. It included a practical demonstration. While the theoretical debate went on upstairs, downstairs some famous chefs – Caroline Waldegrave, Anton Edelman of the Savoy and Albert Roux of the Gavroche – helped thirty 9-year-olds from an inner London primary school cook dinner for the two hundred people in the audience.

Caroline taught them to make vegetarian samosas filled with curry, filo parcels of pumpkin with ricotta and spinach. And they made a 'marble salad' by scooping cucumber, melon, apples and Edam into balls. Anton taught them how to make tagliatelle from scratch, mixing it, rolling it and cutting it into ribbons on a pasta machine. They also made meat balls and a pepper sauce, a green salad and dressing. Albert had them mixing, proving, kneading and baking real bread, and making bread-and-butter pudding.

While the children hugely enjoyed the event, they also learnt a lot more than simply how to make supper. Caroline had them doing mental arithmetic. If five of them needed to make fifty samosas between them, how many would they each have to do? And how much filling would they need for ten samosas? In Albert's corner the children learnt that it was the gluten in the flour that became stretchy and elastic as they kneaded the dough and allowed the air bubbles to

be caught in the dough as it rose – an elementary chemistry lesson. He explained that the air bubbles were produced by the growing yeast which was a living thing and multiplied like crazy when given the four living things need to grow: sustenance, warmth, moisture and time. That was a biology lesson. Anton's salad dressing was a lesson in physics – the making of an emulsion out of oil and vinegar. His meatballs, starting tough and ending tender, could have been a lesson on the gelatinising effect of heat on the collagen in connective tissue, but (since these were only 9-year-olds) I don't think he went into that.

None of the chefs set out to do more than teach cooking. But if you want to explain what's happening in cooking, you end up explaining why. Had there been time, those children could have got into geography: where do the spices come from? History: did Marco Polo really bring back pasta from China? Religious studies: why is Hindu India mainly vegetarian? Economics: how much did the meal cost per head? And so on.

Homo sapiens is the only species ritually to prepare and eat its food. All other species eat it as and where they find it. This community preparation, cooking and eating as a family or tribe is common

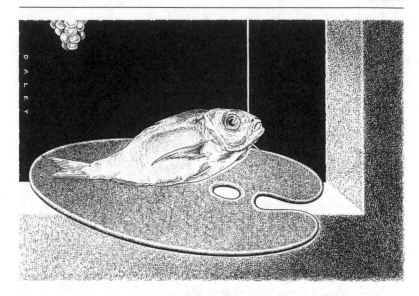

to every civilisation in every country in the world, from the dawn of man to the present generation in the developed West. We lose these cooking and eating rituals at our peril.

Lack of time and the pressures of advertising, as well as the loss of cooking skills, have played their part in the erosion of the kitchen-centred society. Cooking and eating occasions provide much of the glue that sticks society together. We all know that close contact breeds respect, tolerance, understanding and affection. But the alien and unknown is feared, scorned, ignored. How are the generations to have respect and affection for each other if they never meet; if they snack on the hoof, pass each other at the microwave; sit in silence in front of the telly? Cooking and preparing meals provides the opportunity for people to talk to each other, something children today rarely do face to face. They spend many hours a day passively watching television, perhaps an hour or so communicating with a computer game, CD Rom or the Internet, and hours and hours on the telephone to their mates. But none of that is the sort of real inter-personal communication that you need to be good at to get a job, to get on in life and to be happy.

Then there is the question of nutrition. If you are poor, conveni-ence foods mean junk food. If you cannot cook, you have to buy convenience foods. You are not going to risk something you have made being a disaster or being rejected by the children. So, under-standably, you go for what is acceptable to them and that means junk. If, on the other hand you are poor and you can cook, you can eat, if not well, at least less appallingly. Even if you are not among the poorest of the poor, if you know nothing about cooking, food or nutrition, you are unlikely to be very healthy. Good health tends to go with awareness of nutritional needs and an interest in diet. I believe that teaching cooking in schools could give a future generation that awareness – and save the National Health Service a fortune.

It is true that cooking has improved immeasurably in the last twenty years – for the rich. For the upper and middle classes who dine out, who can afford private cookery schools for their children, who buy cookbooks and who come from families with a tradition of knees-under-tables, eating is more exciting than it has ever been. And if they don't want to cook, or cannot cook, they can hare down to the local supermarket and help themselves to fresh pasta, ready-made pasta sauces, ready-washed salad, ready-sliced pineapple and eat very well indeed without cooking. But the poor have become relatively poorer and the poorest have become absolutely poorer. And they are the ones who cook the least and whose diet is most heavily dominated by fat and sugar: fat and sugar are cheap.

It is also true that there have never been more mainstream cooking programmes, reaching an audience of thousands. But they are watched as entertainment, for fun, and the take-up of fact-files and recipe books is comparatively slight. Almost everyone who buys a cookbook can already cook.

There are other, economic reasons why children should like food. In the restaurant industry there are worthwhile and satisfying jobs for those who want them; tourism and the national coffers will gain if Britain has a better reputation for good food. The French take the whole matter of food very seriously. They are terrified that a global tide of McDonald's will sink for ever the great French tradition of gastronomy. They are right to be concerned. For the last ten years, McDonald's has been the biggest restaurateur in France. So the French have developed a programme, under the heading *Semaine de la goût* under which chefs visit schools to conduct tastings, teach and cook. Children go into restaurants, cheese farms, bakers and *chocolatiers*. A similar initiative in Britain three years ago was called Kids in the Kitchen. *Academie Culinaire* provided the chefs, and the *Guardian* newspaper matched them with the schools. The degree of interest can be gauged from the fact that seven hundred schools instantly contacted Matthew Fort, the *Guardian*'s food and drink editor, asking for a visiting chef.

In France gastronomy is now officially one of the fine arts, which status allows a chef to get artist-in-residence funding in a school, for example, and work with children to improve their knowledge of food and cooking. So, what is wrong with the British system? Well, cooking in schools, though far from well, is still – just – alive. Before the announcement of the National Curriculum, a lot of cooking went on in primary schools. But now it features, if at all, as part of the design and technology syllabus, which requires all children to work with materials such as paper, card, dowel, fabric and food. Not all schools do anything with food, though they are meant to. When they do, lessons are often confined to some mixing and to hygiene.

At secondary school there is home economics or food technology. Once, I guess, children learnt cooking at school, but since this sounded rather low status, it was called domestic science. Then someone must have decided that too was low status, and called it home economics. You can still do home economics at school, if the school offers it, which they don't have to. Few do, for the understandable reason that hands-on cooking is expensive to teach (trained teachers are needed, the equipment is expensive, so are the ingredients and the safety and hygiene regulations are draconian). Schools, in their thousands, have torn out their food rooms and kitchens to make way for computer centres. It is understandable. Many more subjects can be taught on a computer than on a cooker.

Food technology is a non-compulsory option of design and technology and is, unsurprisingly, a very popular one in schools that offer it. But the course was never intended to provide life skills, or indeed much hands-on cooking. Like science, maths and the rest of the National Curriculum, it is essentially academic. Students may design and evaluate a chilled meal intended for sale in a supermarket, concentrating on the packaging, design, nutritional content, cost and marketing of the product. They may make it, and they may taste it in simulated factory conditions, but the hygiene regulations will not allow them to share it with their mates in the playground. Personally, I find the idea of children going home to show Mum their pizza topping designs, done via Computer Aided Design, profoundly depressing.

The other reason for the lack of cooking in schools is the paucity of trained teachers. Generally, food technology and home economics are taught by the same people and many are leaving the profession to work in more rewarding jobs in the food industry or in private schools. If you were a trained cookery teacher, would you want to spend your day teaching the theory of omelette-making rather than making omelettes? I have met many home economics teachers and I have never met one who did not want to do more hands-on cooking with their students.

To my mind, there are two viable ways forward. I'd like to see them both happen. First, if I was a politician responsible for education,

I'd try to get real cooking into British primary schools and leave the secondary schools pretty much alone. The food technology course in secondary schools does give students a taste of industry, and if home economics courses were more widely available and included more hands-on cooking, that would be as much of a revolution as a crowded curriculum could maybe stand. But I would go for real cooking in primary schools, with classes in school time, if not compulsory. What about a fully equipped cooking bus, maybe sponsored by the private sector, that goes from school to school with a trained teacher on board? What about getting some sense into the hygiene regulations so that students can cook in the school canteen, which is generally empty after 2 p.m.?

The benefits of an hour a week of real cooking would be enormous. Very young children could be introduced, while doing something they really love doing, to something that they mostly think they will not enjoy – maths and physics and chemistry, etc. Moreover, doing something creative, actually making something oneself, is the fastest way to self-esteem, confidence and the willingness to take risks – all qualities without which one cannot survive in a competitive world. If you get children young enough, when they are still open to new ideas (and before puberty and peer pressure combined have made them horribly conservative) you can introduce them to new flavours, other peoples' cultures, give them a taste of experiment and enquiry. And, of course, one cannot cook without learning to work in teams, to communicate, to co-operate. On top of all that, the children will learn to cook.

I would like to track my primary school cohort for the next ten years and see if they eat more healthily than their peers; if they still cook at the age of 15; if they are more adventurous about eating; if the boys still cook as much as the girls. A lot could be learnt from such an experiment.

Another possible route for improving the nation's ability to cook is the after-school club. What about a cookery club where parents and children cook together, under the guiding eye of a teacher, or at least with guidelines and workbooks to follow? Some excellent after-school cookery clubs exist and all of them provide enjoyment. But if Granny is teaching the class nothing more nutritious than the rock-buns and lardy-cake she learnt in domestic science, then it is a bit of a wasted opportunity. Could not the cookery club communally make supper in the canteen kitchen and then all the families taking part could have supper together? That way, ingredients would not be thought of by parents as expensive extras.

When it comes to higher and further education, there is another cogent argument for cooking. And that is simply that there is a crying need for cooks. The restaurant and leisure industry is the country's largest. Thousands of foreign workers are imported to British kitchens every year, while thousands of young British people join the dole queue. Universities and colleges have always rather looked down their nose at practical cooking and waiting skills. But hotel and restaurant managers cannot be trained exclusively in lecture rooms and on computers.

Education is the only business I know that appears to accept that its product does not satisfy the customers. Large numbers of them vote with their feet. Someone should publish a league table of which classes are ducked and which are attended. I bet the participating classes in schools, such as drama, art, design, music and sport, do better than the academic ones. I bet there is less truanting from GNVQ classes than from GCSE ones. And if proper cooking, with real food at the end of it, was taught, I'd lay my life it would come top of the league.

But mostly, of course, I want children to learn to cook for the sheer pleasure of it. There is nothing so instantly gratifying as serving supper to your friends and family and watching them wolf it down. It is a pleasure that very few of our children will ever have. Over half of them have never boiled an egg. Shouldn't we do something about it?

Further reading

Bastyra, Judy, *Cooking with Dad!*, Bloomsbury, London, 1997.
Harvey, Gill, *Starting Cooking*, Usborne, London, 1995.
Laurie, Jo, *Pot Luck – Cooking and Recipes from the Past*, A. N. C. Black, Cambridge, 1991.
Leather, Suzi, *The Making of Modern Malnutrition. An Overiew of Food Poverty in the UK*, Caroline Walker Trust, London, 1996.

A recipe (for 4 people)

Bread and butter pudding

2 slices of plain bread
30 g/1 oz plain bread
30 g/1 oz butter
30 ml/2 tbl currants and sultanas, mixed
10 ml/2 tsp candied peel
2 eggs and 1 yolk
15 ml/1 rounded tablespoon sugar
290 ml/½ pint creamy milk

vanilla essence
ground cinnamon
demerara sugar

Cut the crusts off the bread and spread with butter. Cut into quarters. Arrange in a shallow ovenproof dish, buttered side up, and sprinkle with currants, sultanas and candied peel.

Make the custard: mix the eggs and yolk with the sugar and stir in the milk and vanilla essence.

Pour the custard carefully over the bread and leave to soak for 30 minutes. Sprinkle with ground cinnamon and demerara sugar.

Heat the oven to 180°C/350°F/gas mark 4.

Place the pudding in a roasting pan of hot water and cook in the middle of the oven for about 45 minutes or until the custard is set and the top is brown and crusty.

Taken from Leith's Cookery Bible by Prue Leith and Caroline Waldegrave, published by Bloomsbury.

Banana bills

David Bederman

Cultures have always debated what to eat and how much, the timing and rituals of meals, and how nourishing and healthy food should be. How we talk about food has also, recently, become a subject of legal regulation: a matter of interest for agribusiness and food conglomerates, health advocates, legislators, lawyers and judges. It is not a happy development. Recent events both sides of the Atlantic show that when we use coercive legal restrictions to regulate public debate about food, the result is often intolerance and misinformation. The debate rapidly becomes as unwholesome as the food it is intended to edify.

In the United States, the move to restrict public debate about the safety of certain kinds of foods can be traced to a 1989 broadcast by the TV news programme *60 Minutes*. The broadcast described the use of *daminozide* (also known as Alar), a chemical sprayed on apples to regulate their growth. Based largely on *Intolerable Risk: Pesticides in Our Children's Food*, a Natural Resources Defense Council Report, the broadcast discussed the health risks and potential carcinogenic effects of Alar. Following the item, the Washington apple industry lost millions of dollars as consumer demand for apples fell sharply. A group of Washington State apple-growers, representing some 4,700 growers across the country, filed suit against CBS. After years

of litigation, a federal appeals court dismissed the action. The court ruled that, under the common law, in order for the apple-growers to establish a claim of product disparagement (or trade libel), they must show that CBS disseminated a knowingly false statement and intended such a statement to harm the growers' pecuniary interests. The appeals court also ruled that it was up to the growers to prove the falsity of the disparaging statements and that the Washington apple-growers had failed to carry that burden of proof.

The problem with the apple-growers' case was that it did not fit into the common law's basic model of trade libel suits, whereby one provider of goods or services claims that a competitor tried to steal business by disseminating false information. Where the speaker is a media outlet or an advocate of public health rather than a commercial rival, the rationale for trade libel is less compelling. Just as importantly, the court found that CBS's report was, on the whole, balanced and objective. The broadcast did not assert that Alar causes cancer nor that the risk of cancer is especially great in children. Instead, the report simply disclosed the results of scientific investigations which raised a concern that Alar could be a carcinogen in animals. The growers were thus obliged to argue that the studies themselves were not reliable indicators of the effects of suspected carcinogens in humans, and that CBS had been irresponsible in disseminating inconclusive evidence to the public.

The court, in rejecting the suit, believed that CBS's report could not properly be construed as disparaging. 'Because a broadcast could be interpreted in numerous, nuanced ways,' the court wrote, 'a great deal of uncertainty would arise as to the message conveyed.' The court recognised that allowing the growers' suit to go forward would risk stifling journalistic speech. Scientific uncertainty over food safety risks should not be made actionable and should be aired in a climate of openness and free speech.

Traditional, common law principles of trade disparagement thus proved unavailing to the Washington apple-growers. It is no surprise, therefore, that many agribusinesses then expressed a desire to achieve by statute what had eluded them under the common law: the creation of a tailor-made cause of action for agricultural disparagement. The Alar case sparked the passage of the first of several agricultural disparagement statutes across the United States.

To date, thirteen American states have passed strikingly similar laws, making it an actionable tort unjustifiably to criticise food produced in those jurisdictions. Comparable laws have been proposed in nearly a dozen other states. The basic thrust of these statutes – known variously as 'vegetable disparagement laws', 'banana bills' and 'food slander laws' – is to make it civilly actionable to disseminate 'false' information about food products. What makes particular information 'false', and how one goes about proving that, is at the crux of the constitutionality of these laws.

The First Amendment to the US Constitution provides that 'Congress shall make no law . . . abridging the freedom of speech'. This provision applies both to the federal and state governments in the United States. The First Amendment alone may not make food libel laws unconstitutional. But there are also other grounds for objection, such as US Supreme Court Justice Oliver Wendell Holmes's metaphor of the 'marketplace of ideas'. According to Holmes, freedom of speech requires 'breathing space' in order to have fair competition of ideas within a free and open society. Occasionally, the need to protect the competition of ideas will require the courts to 'protect some falsehood in order to protect speech that matters'. In order to provide this protection, states may not heavily regulate the marketplace of ideas. Yet these newly enacted agricultural disparagement statutes do just that: they place severe restrictions on the so-called marketplace of ideas.

In my opinion these food libel laws are fundamentally flawed. First, they violate the First Amendment by making actionable speech that is protected. Second, they do not provide for 'fault', a constitutionally necessary requirement in product disparagement cases.

Legal actions for product disparagement may not be brought for statements disseminated to further public safety. Statements concerning issues of grave public concern are protected under American law. The US Supreme Court, in a case called *New York Times Co.* v. *Sullivan*, considered state defamation laws in the context of the First

Amendment right to free speech. The Supreme Court held that a public official must demonstrate that an [allegedly defamatory] 'statement was made with "actual malice" – that is, with knowledge that it was false or with reckless disregard of whether it was false or not'. Three years later, the Supreme Court extended this standard beyond public officials to all 'public figures' seeking recovery for libel. This rule has arguably been expanded to cover reporting on any matter of public concern. Every journalist in America knows that this is the standard that guides their search for truth and the conduct of investigative reporting.

Food safety is, quintessentially, a matter of grave public concern. In order to promote a robust public debate on food safety issues, American courts are likely to extend the fullest possible protection. At a minimum, this will mean that those seeking to sue media outlets or health advocates for providing controversial food safety information will have to prove that the statements were made either in 'reckless disregard' of whether they were true or false, or knowing that they were false.

Whether these food libel laws will have the effect of suppressing the debate on food safety remains to be seen. Recently, a report published by an environmental watchdog organisation, the Environmental Working Group, identified twelve of the most popular fruits and vegetables consumed in the United States as posing extraordinary risks of pesticide ingestion. Publication of the report inspired activists in Arizona to challenge farmers or the state to sue them under Arizona's food libel statute.

Public debate has also raged about the health consequences for humans of consuming beef from cows stricken by BSE, or mad cow disease. In May 1996, Texas cattlemen filed the first agricultural disparagement statutory action in the United States when they sued Oprah Winfrey, her syndicated television show, and one of her guests, Howard Lyman, who claimed that a large portion of American herds were at risk from infection with BSE.

The matter went to trial early in 1998. In the middle of the trial the judge found that the cattlemen had failed to prove one of the elements of Texas's agricultural disparagement law and dismissed that part of the case. The case then proceeded on a theory of common law business disparagement – just like the Alar controversy – and the jury gave a verdict for Oprah Winfrey, finding that she had not falsely defamed the cattlemen.

In any event, the cattlemen's loss has not deterred other agricultural interests from filing their own suits. Emu ranchers have sued for a statement made in a humorous automobile advert, likening their product to pork. And when a large egg producer was caught by a public-interest group repackaging eggs which had passed their expiry date, it counter-sued under a veggie libel law.

At stake in this frenzy of litigation is scientific certainty in an uncertain and unpredictable world. Legal restrictions on statements about food safety are an attempt to regulate the marketplace of ideas in that grey area where scientific investigation, economic protection and public safety overlap. The underlying thrust of food libel statutes is to regulate speech by encouraging certain kinds of exchanges and punishing others. I think such an approach is profoundly misguided. But it would be folly to ignore the powerful interests that support restrictions on statements about food safety.

Agribusiness is big business. The agricultural sectors of our national economies are no longer marginalised and backward. Vast food conglomerates, able to command extraordinary production, market access and political power have emerged. Farmers, growers and herders have always wielded disproportionate political power in the United States (and to a lesser degree in the United Kingdom), but now that power is combined with immense political influence, as well as corporate muscle.

In an integrated global economy, dissemination of information can produce quick shifts in the market. Some of these are unpredictable and can hardly be subject to legal remedies – news of corn withered on the stalk by drought or a reported outbreak of swine fever. But many in the agricultural community believe that speculation about food safety, if prematurely disclosed to the public, can have unwarranted effects on demand and prices, and, thus, should be controlled. And if such information cannot be suppressed, the next best thing is to punish civilly the authors of damaging disclosures.

In the United States at least, there has always been fear of too-robust speech. When neo-Nazis demonstrate in Jewish-dominated neighbourhoods (or, for that matter, Orangemen march through Catholic villages in Ulster), many believe that there must be limits to free speech or the civil society that makes such freedoms possible is placed at risk. And while disseminating information about food safety can hardly be seen to rise to the emotive level of Nazis in Skokie, Illinois, restrictions on such disclosures can be seen as part of a movement reminding those who use free speech rights that they have correlative responsibilities to society. Just as tobacco companies have argued that smokers have a right to choose to smoke and thus, in making that choice, should be responsible enough to bear the consequences of that decision, so too should those who disseminate information resulting in adverse market effects. If free speech is a right, so the argument goes, then it must come with responsibility; if you are wrong in what you say, then you must bear the costs.

The effort to suppress free speech about food has become part of a larger backlash against science and the scientific method. The campaign against 'junk science' has become a rallying cry for those who oppose government funding for science as much as it has been for those seeking reform of America's civil tort system. Science has been dichotomised into 'good' and 'bad', 'responsible' and 'irresponsible'. Foetal tissue research is ethically suspect and 'immoral'. An unscrupulous trial lawyer's use of unverified data to prove that a new drug is dangerous is labelled 'junk' and cannot be presented to jurors.

What legal regulation of food safety speech means is that courts will ultimately decide what is responsible science and what are justifiable disclosures of food safety concerns to the public. An adversarial system of justice culminating in a decision by a judge or jury is a lousy way to seek scientific truth and secure public health. Moreover, the two mechanisms that society has come to rely upon to assess risks in a progressively more complicated world – peer review among scientists and robust public debate – will no longer be available. If food libel laws succeed in punishing disclosures that are later proved to be wrong, scientists will alter their research agenda and the media will simply abstain from reporting controversial food issues.

Imagine a scientist who hypothesised ten years ago that there was a link between eating meat from cows suffering from BSE and contracting Creutzfeldt–Jakob disease, the neurological disease affecting humans. A decade later, such a conclusion would be largely vindicated. But at the time it was made, such a deduction would have been at the leading-edge of scientific inquiry. It would have also been quite actionable under the food libel laws passed in the United States, and also under the common law of libel in the United Kingdom.

An outlandish result? Perhaps. But that is the nature of scientific inquiry. Someone always has to be first: the first to hypothesise; the first to fashion a study; and the first to publish results and begin the process of building (or dismantling) scientific consensus through peer review. And that is precisely the evil of regulating disclosures on any subject of public health or safety (whether it is about the food we eat, the drugs we use, or the cars we drive). The legal process distorts scientific inquiry and public debate by replacing one standard of proof for another and by not allowing time and the advance of human knowledge to take its course. Health dangers that may not be acknowledged at one time, may be universally accepted later. Think about lead, PCBs, and yes, finally, tobacco.

Libel suits and agricultural disparagement statutes represent a legal attempt to insulate an economic sector from criticism. They also reflect a curious mixture of interest group politics and industry protectionism. In this respect, they may be strikingly successful in chilling the speech of anyone concerned about the food we eat. Freedom of speech, always precious, becomes ever more so as agricultural industries use previously untried methods from exotic pesticides and growth hormones to radiation and genetic engineering on our food supply. Scientists and consumer advocates must be able to express their legitimate, even if unproven, concerns. Food libel quells those voices. Any restriction on free speech about the quality and safety of our food is dangerous, unconstitutional and undemocratic.

Further reading

Bederman, David, Christensen, Scott M. and Quesenberry, Scott Dean, Of banana bills and veggie hate crimes: the constitutionality of agricultural disparagement statutes, *Harvard Journal on Legislation* 34, 1997; 135.

Holt, Tom, Could law suits be the cure for junk science?, *Priorities* 7, 2, 1995; 14.

Scrochi, Julie J., Must peaches be preserved at all costs? Questioning the constitutional validity of Georgia's Perishable Product Disparagement Law, *Georgia State University Law Review* 16, 1996; 1223.

Semple, Megan W., Veggie libel meets free speech: a constitutional analysis of agricultural disparagement laws, *Virginia Environmental Law Journal* 15, 1995–6; 403.

A vegetarian philosophy

Peter Singer

Over the next twenty years eating meat could follow smoking into disrepute. Like smoking, the heavily meat-based diet followed by most people in affluent countries has been shown to cause cancer and heart disease. On top of that, the BSE scare hurt the beef industry, not only because of the risk of contracting the disease itself, but because consumers learnt that today's cattle eat abattoir by-products.

While cattle in developing countries are more likely to eat grass, the grassland is often felled rainforest, taken after tribal people have been pushed off their land. The destruction of the rainforest carries implications for global warming that threaten the lives of millions of people farming low-lying land in regions like Bangladesh and Egypt. Pollution of streams and ground water by toxic animal wastes is another major problem for the meat industry. And the animal movement is convincing growing numbers of people that our treatment of animals is grounded on a prejudice against taking seriously the interests of beings who are not members of our species. No wonder that the number of vegetarians and near-vegetarians continues to grow.

Issues around eating meat were highlighted in 1997 by the longest trial in British legal history. *McDonald's Corporation and McDonald's Restaurants Limited* v. *Steel and Morris*, better known as the 'McLibel' trial, ran for 313 days, and heard 180 witnesses. In suing Helen Steel and David Morris, two activists involved with the London Greenpeace organisation, McDonald's put on trial the way in which its fast food products are produced, packaged, advertised and sold, as well as their nutritional value, the environmental impact of producing them, and the treatment of the animals whose flesh and eggs are made into that food.

Admittedly, even if McDonald's had lost on every point, producers of animal products by organic farming methods could justifiably have claimed that the decision was irrelevant to what they were doing. So the trial was not a test of the morality of eating meat. But for the majority of consumers, whether they eat at McDonald's, at a rival fast food chain, or just pick up their meat at a supermarket with an eye more to its cost than to the manner in which it is produced, the morality of the meat they are eating was on trial.

The case provided a remarkable opportunity for weighing up evidence for and against modern agribusiness methods. The leaflet 'What's Wrong with McDonald's' that provoked the defamation suit had a row of McDonald's arches along the top of each page. Two of these arches bore the words 'McMurder' and 'McTorture'. One section below was headed 'In what way are McDonald's responsible for torture and murder?' The leaflet answered the question as follows:

> The menu at McDonald's is based on meat. They sell millions of burgers every day in 35 countries throughout the world. This means the constant slaughter, day by day, of animals born and bred solely to be turned into McDonald's products. Some of them – especially chickens and pigs – spend their lives in the entirely artificial conditions

of huge factory farms, with no access to air or sunshine and no freedom of movement. Their deaths are bloody and barbaric.

McDonald's claimed that the leaflet meant that the company was responsible for the inhumane torture and murder of cattle, chicken and pigs, and that this was defamatory. In considering this claim, Mr Justice Bell based his judgment on what he took to be attitudes that were generally accepted in Britain. Thus for the epithet 'McTorture' to be justified, he held, it would not be enough for Steel and Morris to show that animals were under stress or suffered some pain or discomfort:

> Merely containing, handling and transporting an animal may cause it stress; and taking it to slaughter certainly may do so. But I do not believe that the ordinary reasonable person believes any of these things to be cruel, provided that the necessary stress, or discomfort or even pain is kept to a reasonably acceptable level. That ordinary person may know little about the detail of farming and slaughtering methods but he must find a certain amount of stress, discomfort or even pain acceptable and not to be criticised as cruel.

By the end of the trial, however, Mr Justice Bell found that the stress, discomfort and pain inflicted on some animals amounted to more than this acceptable level, and hence did constitute a 'cruel practice' for which McDonald's was 'culpably responsible'. Chickens, laying hens and sows, he said, kept in individual stalls suffered from 'severe restriction of movement' which 'is cruel'. He also found a number of other cruel practices in the production of chickens, including the restricted diet fed to breeding birds which leaves them permanently hungry, the injuries inflicted on chickens by catchers stuffing 600 birds an hour into crates to take them to slaughter, and the failure of the stunning apparatus to ensure that all birds are stunned before they have their throats cut. Judging by entirely conventional moral standards, Mr Justice Bell held these practices to be cruel, and McDonald's to be culpably responsible for them.

It was not libellous to describe McDonald's as 'McTorture', because the charge was substantially true. What follows from this judgment about the morality of buying and eating intensively raised chickens, pig products that come from the offspring of sows kept in stalls, or eggs laid by hens kept in battery cages? Surely that, too, must be wrong?

This claim has been challenged. At a conference dinner some years ago I found myself sitting opposite a Buddhist philosopher from Thailand. As we helped ourselves to the lavish buffet, I avoided the various forms of meat on offer, but the Thai philosopher did not. When I asked him how he reconciled the dinner he had chosen with the first precept of Buddhism, which tells us to avoid harming sentient beings, he told me that in the Buddhist tradition it is wrong to eat meat only if you have reason to believe that the animal was killed specially for you. The meat he had taken, however, was not from animals killed specially for him; the animals would have died anyway, even if he were a strict vegetarian, or had not been in that city at all. Hence, by eating it, he was not harming any animals.

I was unable to persuade my dinner companion that this defence of meat eating was better suited to a time when a peasant family might kill an animal especially to have something to put in the begging bowl of a wandering monk, than it is to our own era. The flaw in the defence is the disregard of the link between the meat I eat today and the future killing of animals. Granted, the chicken lying in the supermarket freezer today would have died even if I had never existed; but the fact that I take the chicken from the freezer, and ignore the tofu on a nearby shelf, has something to do with the number of chickens, or blocks of tofu, the supermarket will order next week, and thus contributes, in a small way, to the future growth or decline of the chicken and tofu industries. That is what the laws of supply and demand are all about.

Some defenders of a variant of the ancient Buddhist line may still want to argue that one chicken fewer sold makes no perceptible difference to the chicken producers, and therefore there can be nothing wrong with buying chicken. The division of moral responsibility in a situation of this kind does raise some interesting issues, but it is a fallacy to argue that a person can do wrong only by making a perceptible harm. The Oxford philosopher Jonathan Glover has explored the implications of this refusal to accept the divisibility of responsibility in an entertaining article called 'It makes no difference whether or not I do it' (*Proceedings of the Aristotelian Society*, 1975).

Glover imagines that in a village, 100 people are about to eat lunch. Each has a bowl containing 100 beans. Suddenly, 100 hungry bandits swoop on the village. Each bandit takes the contents of the bowl of one villager, eats it, and gallops off. Next week, the bandits plan to do it again, but one of their number is afflicted by doubts about whether it is right to steal from the poor. These doubts are set to rest by another of their number who proposes that each bandit, instead of eating the entire contents of the bowl of one villager, should take one bean from every villager's bowl. Since the loss of one bean cannot make a perceptible difference to any villager, no bandit will have harmed anyone. The bandits follow this plan, each taking a solitary bean from 100 bowls. The villagers are just as hungry as they were the previous week, but the bandits can all sleep well on their full stomachs, knowing that none of them has harmed anyone.

Glover's example shows the absurdity of denying that we are each responsible for a share of the harms we collectively cause, even if each of us makes no perceptible difference. McDonald's has a far bigger impact on the practices of the chicken, egg and pig industries than any individual consumer; but McDonald's itself would be powerless if no one ate at its restaurants. Collectively, all consumers of animal products are responsible for the existence of the cruel practices involved in producing them. In the absence of special circumstances, a portion of this responsibility must be attributed back to each purchaser.

Without in any way departing from a conventional moral attitude towards animals, then, we have reached the conclusion that eating intensively produced chicken, battery eggs and some pig products is wrong. This is, of course, well short of an argument for vegetarianism. Mr Justice Bell found 'cruel practices' only in these areas of McDonald's food production. But he did not find that McDonald's beef is 'cruelty-free'. He did not consider that question, because he drew a distinction between McDonald's responsibility for practices in the beef and dairy industries, and those in the chicken, egg and pig industries. McDonald's chickens, eggs and pig products are supplied by a relatively small number of very large producers, over whose practices the corporation could quite easily have a major influence. On the other hand, McDonald's beef and dairy requirements came from a very large number of producers and in respect of whose methods, Mr Justice Bell held, 'there was no evidence from which I could infer that [McDonald's] would have any effective influence, should it try to exert it'. Whatever one may think of that view – it seems highly implausible to me – the judge, in accepting it, decided not to address the evidence presented to him of cruelty in the raising of cattle, so that no conclusions either way can be drawn.

This does not mean that the trial itself had nothing to say about animal suffering in general. McDonald's called as a witness Mr David Walker, Chief Executive of one of their major United Kingdom suppliers, McKey Food Services Ltd. In cross-examination, Helen Steel asked Walker whether it was true that, 'as the result of the meat industry, the suffering of animals is inevitable?' Walker replied: 'The answer to that must be "yes".'

Walker's admission raises a serious question about the ethics of the meat industry: how much suffering are we justified in inflicting on animals in order to turn them into meat, or to use their eggs or milk? To answer this question we need to depart from Mr Justice

Bell's presuppositions and ask whether conventional moral views about animals are defensible. The prevailing Western ethic is still essentially pre-Darwinian. It shows this even in the language it uses, which, by contrasting 'humans' and 'animals', denies that humans are animals.

The twin roots of the Western ethic lie in Aristotle's idea that the world is a hierarchy in which the less rational exist in order to serve the more rational, and in the Judaeo-Christian teaching that humans have 'dominion' over animals, and a God-given right to make use of them. Whether or not people still believe that humans alone are made 'in the image of God', most do think of animals as distinctly 'lower creatures'. The assumption is that human beings are infinitely superior in moral status to all forms of animal life, and that they are in some way meant to serve our ends. With the exception of concerns about endangered species – which are not really concerns about the interests of individual animals at all – the general view is that if our interests conflict with theirs, it is always the interests of the animals that have to give way.

Since the rise of the modern animal liberation movement in the 1970s, this view has been under attack. Animal liberationists question the right of our species to assume that our interests must always prevail. They want to extend the basic moral ideas of equality and rights beyond the species barrier. If, they ask, we reject racist or hierarchical ideas about human beings, and instead insist on the equality of all humans, what is it that entitles us to put non-human beings outside that sphere of equality?

Obviously, this view does not mean that animals should have equal rights to vote, or to free speech. The kind of equality which animal liberationists want to extend to animals is equal consideration of interests. The basic right that animals should have is the right to equal consideration. If an animal feels pain, the pain matters as much as it does when a human feels pain – if the pain hurts just as much, and will last just as long, and will not have further bad consequences for the human that it does not have for the non-human animal. Pain is pain, whatever the species of being that experiences it.

The principle of equal consideration of interests does not imply that it is as wrong to kill a chicken as it is to kill a normal human being. The interest that beings have in continuing to live will depend on the capacities that they have. In what ways can they enjoy their lives? Do they know that they have a life to lead? Are they aware that they exist over time, have a past, and could have a future? Do they have desires to do things in the future, which they will not be able to do if they are killed? All these questions are relevant to the wrongness of killing. What is not relevant, according to the principle of equal consideration of interests, is the species to which the being belongs. Species membership may be an indication of the capacities a being has, but it is the capacities themselves, not the species membership, that is ethically significant.

The principle of equal consideration of interests is not absolutist and does not require vegetarianism in all possible circumstances. A person shipwrecked on a desert island may be justified in eating meat to survive. A little more relevant to most of us is the claim made on behalf of organic farmers that there are ways of rearing animals that fully respect their interests throughout their lives. If the animals do have good lives, and do not have sufficient self-awareness to have desires for the future, it could be argued that killing them painlessly for food would not be wrong. The issue is a complex one, leading into some of the most baffling questions in ethics. Is it wrong to kill animals because it deprives them of the future life they would have enjoyed, even if they know nothing of it? Perhaps it is; but what if we can then replace that animal with another, who will have as good a life? 'If all the world were Jewish, there would be no pigs at all', Leslie Stephen once argued in an attempt to refute vegetarians. But can we justify ending the life of one animal by conferring benefits on an as yet non-existent animal?

These questions are philosophically intriguing, but of minor practical significance. We must not lose sight of the larger picture. The case for vegetarianism is at its strongest when we see it as a moral protest against our use of animals as mere things, to be exploited for our convenience in whatever way makes them most cheaply available to us. Only the tiniest fraction of the tens of billions of farm animals slaughtered for food each year – the figure for the United States alone is nine billion – were treated during their lives in ways that respected their interests. Questions about the wrongness of killing in itself are not relevant to the moral issue of eating meat or eggs from factory-farmed animals, as most people in developed countries do. Even when animals are roaming freely over large areas, as sheep and cattle do in Australia, operations like hot-iron branding, castration and dehorning are carried out without any regard for the animals' capacity to suffer. The same is true of handling and transport prior to slaughter. In the light of these facts, the issue to focus on is not whether there are some circumstances in which it could be right to eat meat, but on what we can do to avoid contributing to this immense amount of animal suffering.

The answer is to boycott all meat and eggs produced by large-scale commercial methods of animal production, and encourage others to do the same. Consideration for the interests of animals alone is enough justification for this response, but the case is further strengthened by the environmental problems that the meat industry causes. Although Mr Justice Bell found that the allegations directed at McDonald's regarding its contribution to the destruction of rainforests were not true, the meat industry as a whole can take little comfort from that, because Bell accepted evidence that cattle-ranching, particularly in Brazil, had contributed to the clearing of vast areas of rainforest. The problem for David Morris and Helen Steel was that they did not persuade the judge that the meat used by McDonald's came from these regions. So the meat industry as a whole remains culpable for the loss of rainforest, and all the consequences of that, from global warming to the deaths of indigenous people fighting to defend their way of life.

Environmentalists are increasingly recognising that the choice of what we eat is an environmental issue. Animals raised in sheds or on feedlots eat grains or soy beans, and they use most of the food value of these products simply in order to maintain basic functions and develop unpalatable parts of the body like bones and skin. To convert eight or nine kilos of grain protein into a single kilo of animal protein wastes land, energy and water. On a crowded planet with a growing human population, that is a luxury that we are becoming increasingly unable to afford.

Intensive animal production is a heavy user of fossil fuels and a major source of pollution of both air and water. It releases large quantities of methane and other greenhouse gases into the atmosphere. We are risking unpredictable changes to the climate of our planet – which means, ultimately, the lives of billions of people, not to mention the extinction of untold thousands of species of plants and animals unable to cope with changing conditions – for the sake of more hamburgers.

A diet heavy on animal products, catered for by intensive animal production, is a disaster for animals, the environment, and the health of those who eat it. The scale of the disaster will be multiplied many times over if the trend for other countries to copy Western diets and methods of production continues. It is already happening in the more successful economies of East Asia, and it seems bound to spread further as the sphere of prosperity widens. One billion Chinese, eating a Western diet produced by intensive farming methods, would dwarf the contribution to global warming and pollution now made by the agribusiness industries of the entire European Community.

There is an urgent need for a concerted effort to halt the spread of our disastrous diet. This will require an interdisciplinary effort, bringing together the best scientific studies from experts in nutrition, public health and environmental science, along with philosophers working on the ethical issues involved in our treatment of animals and the environment. One sign that this kind of work may be getting under way is the establishment of the Centre for a Livable Future, under the direction of Dr Robert Lawrence, of the School of Public Health at Johns Hopkins University in Baltimore. The centre's aim is not more research into the harmful effects of a diet that is already high in animal products – there is already ample evidence of that – but rather to find ways of changing people's attitudes so that they do not want this diet.

University teachers of philosophy should be playing a role in bringing about this change. Food must be seen as one of the most profound ethical issues we face. When we consider how much attention is paid in ethics courses to issues that students rarely (if ever) confront (for example euthanasia), it is extraordinary how we neglect the ethics of an issue that we face three times a day. Of course, the question of the ethics of our treatment of our animals is now a part of many ethics courses and that makes a welcome contrast with the situation that prevailed until about twenty years ago. But the ethics of what we eat brings in other considerations as well, and it should be the subject of a more focussed discussion.

In the end, the example that we in the developed Western nations set to the rest of the world will probably be more influential than anything we tell them. For that reason it is important that we start thinking about the ethics of our diet. Challenging our students with some of the issues outlined above is a good place to begin.

Further reading

Eisnitz, Gail, *Slaughterhouse*, Prometheus, Amherst, New York, 1997.
Johnson, Andrew, *Factory Farming*, Blackwell, Oxford, 1991.
Rifkin, Jeremy, *Beyond Beef*, Dutton, New York, 1992.
Singer, Peter, *Animal Liberation*, 2nd ed, Pimlico, London, 1995.
Vidal, John, *McLibel – Burger Culture on Trial*, Macmillan, London, 1997.
Wynne-Tyson, Jon, *Food for a Future*, Thorsons, Wellingborough, 1988.

A recipe

This recipe is vegan, very simple, nutritious and tasty. It's also eaten by hundreds of millions of people every day.

Dal

1 cup red lentils
3 cups water
1 onion, chopped
2 cloves garlic, crushed

2 tbsp oil
1 400 g tin of tomatoes or equivalent chopped fresh tomatoes
1 stick cinnamon
bay leaf
1 tsp medium curry powder or to taste
50 g creamed coconut or half cup coconut milk (optional)
Juice of 1 lemon (optional)
Salt to taste.

In a deep frying pan, heat the oil and fry the onion and garlic until translucent. Add the lentils and fry them for a minute or two, then add the water, bay leaf, cinnamon stick and curry powder. Stir, bring to the boil, then let simmer for twenty minutes, adding a little more water from time to time if it gets dry. Add the can of tomatoes, and simmer another ten minutes. By now the lentils should be very soft. Add the creamed coconut or coconut milk, lemon juice and salt to taste. Remove cinnamon stick and bay leaf before serving.

The final product should flow freely – add more water if it is too stodgy. It is usually served over rice, with some lime pickle and mango chutney. Sliced banana is another good accompaniment, and so too are poppadams.

Feeding humanity

Tim Dyson

Sitting on a crowded bus, as it jerked its way through London's traffic back in 1991, I saw an article by Lester Brown in *State of the World*, the annual report of his influential Worldwatch Institute in Washington, USA. Reading the article altered my life, because Brown was making some arresting claims. Specifically, he asserted that the growth of the world's population had been outpacing the world's production of cereal since the early 1980s, and therefore that world per capita cereal production was falling. Furthermore, according to Brown, the global downturn in per capita cereal output reflected similar downturns in each region of the world. Writing in the 1994 version of the same report, Brown highlighted a 'dramatic slowdown' in world cereal yield growth after 1984.

These claims have been used to argue that – because of environmental degradation and unprecedented demographic growth – the world's food outlook is grim. Moreover, Brown's claims seem straightforward, making them all the more difficult to dispute.

Assessing the world food situation and, still more, humanity's food prospects is a daunting task. It touches on so much – natural resources, agriculture, economics and politics – that nobody can claim particular expertise.

On the one hand, the relationship between population growth and food production can be approached in relatively simple terms: there are measures of food output (e.g. cereal production) and measures of population, and changes in both can be compared. This simple approach is nicely illustrated by the Chinese characters which, taken together, correspond to the English word for 'population':

A person appears on the left. An open mouth, needing food, appears on the right. This simple approach chimes well with Malthus's initial characterisation (in his *Essay on the Principle of Population* of 1798) of the growth in the output of food being 'arithmetical' at best, while population growth is potentially 'geometrical'. It is this approach which frequently occupies the public mind – and which facilitates the idea that we might actually 'run out of food'.

On the other hand, it is obvious that populations and their food supplies are also linked in many complex ways. For example, many people in Africa and Asia still cultivate, gather or catch much of the food that they eat. But, in countries like Britain most of us have little contact with – or, sadly, knowledge of – the original source of our food. Instead, a trip to the local supermarket is sufficient to reveal a huge choice of foodstuff – transported from all around the world.

The complexity means that if people are threatened with food shortages then there are usually several possible responses. It may be feasible to purchase additional food supplies, or increase the land area planted with crops, or substitute one type of food for another, or draw on stocks (both animal and vegetable). If things get really difficult then people may migrate in search of employment and food. Moreover, people's nutritional requirements depend partly upon their experience of infectious disease and their level of physical activity – both of which are generally declining in the modern world. With rapid urbanisation, obesity is fast replacing under-nutrition as the main food problem in many countries. So while the simple approach to the relationship between population and food is certainly required – e.g. for purposes of exposition – the complexity of the relationship – which allows for a range of adjustments – must never be forgotten.

As a demographer I had to familiarise myself with agricultural data before I could examine Brown's claim about world population growth outpacing the world's production of cereal but, once I had done this, it took only a short time to conclude that it was both oversimple and misleading. It is true that world per capita cereal production has fallen since the early 1980s. But the explanation has little to do with population growth or environmental degradation. Instead, it is important to appreciate that in the 1980s – largely because of the subsidised overproduction of cereals in North America and Europe – the world price of cereals was falling rapidly, and cereal stocks (which are costly to maintain) were rising to unprecedented levels. These facts led the United States – which produces roughly a fifth of the world's harvest – to withdraw very large areas of land from cereal production under a variety of commodity and conservation schemes. Many farmers in other major cereal exporting countries – like Australia and Argentina – simply found it unprofitable to grow grain for export at the low prevailing prices. Nor could the EU avoid the logic of the world market situation for long – although the cumbersome Common Agricultural Policy certainly delayed its response. From the late 1980s land set-aside and changes in agricultural support led to significant reductions in EU cereal production. Finally, the collapse of communism had a major additional effect. As recently as 1990 the former Soviet Union (FSU) had a near-record cereal harvest of 227 million tons, but by 1993 the constituent countries of the FSU harvested only 153 million tons.

So the explanation for the fall in world per capita cereal production lies mostly in policy changes in North America and Europe – comparatively developed parts of the world, with relatively slow-growing populations. By contrast, per capita cereal output has generally been rising in the world's largest developing regions – South Asia (including India) and the Far East (including China). Together, these regions contain 56 per cent of humanity. In both there are also grounds to believe that diets have generally been becoming more varied. The evidence on this is particularly strong for China – where there have been sharp increases in the per capita production of sugar, fruit, vegetables, eggs, edible oils and meat (especially pork).

This said, the meagre level of per capita cereal production in sub-Saharan Africa has been falling since the 1970s. Many factors have contributed to this – not least, widespread socio-political instability and a general neglect of agriculture by governments. The decline has been partly offset by increased imports. But it is hard to discount the view that extremely rapid demographic growth – with populations commonly doubling in less than twenty-five years – has not helped matters. The Middle East is another fast-growing region which has experienced a decline in per capita cereal output. Around 1990 this region was importing grain equivalent to roughly one-third of its total consumption – although most of the Middle Eastern countries could afford the costs. For the water-scarce Middle East these cereal imports can be seen as a form of 'virtual water' – because they are the product of water used for agriculture elsewhere in the world (especially North America).

However, looking at trends in world food production, the general impression is certainly one of modest improvement. Today per capita cereal output in the developing world as a whole is significantly higher than in the past. And the same is true of per capita food production more generally. There is good evidence that most people in most regions have a more varied diet now than was the case, say, twenty-five years ago. Famines are relatively rare events, usually more closely related to politics and warfare than to natural calamity, and largely confined to sub-Saharan Africa. Even in Africa the chances of someone dying in a famine have recently been described as 'vanishingly small'. Indeed, to use the word 'famine' to describe most contemporary food crises is to change its meaning from that of earlier times.

This said, the global food situation is hardly rosy. Sub-Saharan Africa's predicament is particularly lamentable, but there are many millions of undernourished people elsewhere too. The fact that the world's worst-fed regions are generally experiencing the greatest volumes of population growth is acting to help maintain the absolute number of hungry people (though this number is probably diminishing). Many poor people are unable to purchase enough food – even where supplies are available. And many farming families live in poverty precisely because they are unable to grow enough food. Poverty and meagre food production are often two sides of the same coin. Another disturbing trend is a general rise in harvest variability in sub-Saharan Africa and North America. The trend in North America is crucial because of its key cereal exporting role. The USA has now experienced fairly extreme weather-induced cereal production declines in 1983, 1988, 1993 and 1995.

Nevertheless, the fact that past trends in world food production have not been as bleak as they are often portrayed makes it easier to paint a more hopeful – if far from glowing – picture of the future. So (using cereals as an indicator because of their central place in the human diet), what can we say about the world's food prospects?

Ultimately, the answer to this question boils down to two quantities. The future of world food demand will largely be a matter of population growth. And the future of world food supply will largely be a matter of crop yields.

In every decade since the Second World War the main reason more cereals have had to be grown has been the simple expansion of human numbers (rather than any increase in the amount of cereals consumed per head). Moreover, the role of population growth in determining the increase in world cereal production has become stronger with each passing decade.

In 1950 the world's population was about 2.5 billion. By 1990 it had reached 5.3 billion. And in 1997 it was 5.9 billion. Because demographers have a pretty good record of projecting the world's population over time-horizons of about twenty-five years, we can be reasonably confident that humanity will number about 7.9 billion in the year 2020.

Virtually all of this population growth will happen in the world's developing regions, most of which have – and will continue to have – comparatively low levels of per capita food consumption. Thus the United Nations estimates that between 1990 and 2020 South Asia will experience the largest population addition (of 800 million) and sub-Saharan Africa the second largest (590 million).

So what is the growth of cereal demand to the year 2020 likely to be? If we assume that levels of per capita cereal consumption will remain constant in each world region at the levels prevailing around 1990 (when the annual world cereal harvest was about 1.9 billion tons) and adopt the United Nation's population projections, then it can be shown that world cereal output will have to rise to roughly 2.65 billion tons in the year 2020.

However, this figure is probably an underestimate because it makes no allowance for likely future increases in per capita cereal consumption – especially in the Far East, the Middle East, Latin America and South Asia, regions which have experienced rising levels of per capita cereal consumption during recent decades. These upward trends will probably continue in the coming decades as average incomes rise and – with the exception of vegetarian South Asia – there is increased consumption of livestock products (currently about 39 per cent of all human cereal consumption is 'indirect', i.e. in the form of feed fed to livestock in order to produce meat or dairy produce). Allowing for these considerations suggests a 'ball-park' global cereal production requirement of roughly 2.9 billion tons in the year 2020.

On this scenario a 50 per cent rise in the world's population between 1990 and 2020 must be matched by a 50 per cent rise in cereal output. Therefore world per capita cereal production would remain constant – even though per capita cereal consumption in four world regions would increase significantly. The explanation for this apparent anomaly is simple and important: because of very different rates of population growth, the regional composition of humanity is changing fast – towards those regions with relatively low levels of per capita consumption.

But is 2.9 billion tons of cereals a realistic target for the world's farmers in the year 2020? Yield growth is the main engine of increased world food output. Since the early 1950s roughly 90 per cent of the rise in the global cereal harvest has been due to increases in yield, and only about 10 per cent has been due to increases in the area of land harvested. Or to make the point another way: in the mid-1990s the world cereal harvest was considerably greater than it was in the early 1980s, but the total area of land harvested of cereals worldwide has been significantly reduced (mainly because of the deliberate withdrawal of land from cereal cultivation).

There are no obvious signs of a 'dramatic slowdown' in the world cereal yield. On the contrary, since 1981 it has been increasing at about 42 kilograms per hectare per year – close to its long-run average increment. The upward march is impressive. If the average yield continues to rise by 42 kilograms annually, then by 2020 it will reach almost 4 metric tons per hectare. And this yield on the 703 million hectares of land that was being harvested of cereals worldwide in the years around 1990 would produce 2.81 billion tons of grain –

leaving only a minor shortfall compared with our projected demand figure of 2.9 billion tons.

What this means is that, given some relatively modest expansion of the global harvested cereal area (e.g. through reduced set-aside), world cereal supply and demand probably will broadly match in the year 2020. We can be reasonably confident of this – particularly given the various adjustments that are inherent in the complex relationship between population and food. Moreover, it seems likely that – mainly for health reasons – there will be a continuing shift towards reduced meat consumption in rich countries – a trend which will also inject some flexibility into the situation. This said, of course, the preceding calculations are very simple! So let's add just four of the many caveats which need to be made.

First, if the analysis is conducted at the world regional level, then it becomes clear that in some parts of the world there will be an increasing degree of mismatch between the expansion of demand and the capacity to supply that demand. In only a few regions – notably North America, Europe (including much of the FSU), Australia, Argentina and probably Brazil – is it likely that future yield growth will generate an increasing grain surplus for export. So most developing regions will become increasingly dependent upon imports to meet their consumption. For example, in the Middle East imports could easily rise to 50 per cent of cereal consumption. In the Far East (including China) the percentage will be much smaller than this, but the absolute grain import requirement will be significantly larger. In sub-Saharan Africa some countries may be able to finance cereal imports, but others will experience growing 'food gaps'. Between 1990 and 2020 the volume of interregional transfers in cereals could well treble. Population growth will act as the principal engine behind the future expansion of the world grain trade.

Second, in terms of natural resources, water for agriculture will be the biggest single problem. Many countries are already seriously affected by water shortages. Today about 17 per cent of the world's cropland is irrigated – and this irrigated land produces almost 40 per cent of the world's entire harvest. Both China and India produce more than half their food from their irrigated cropland – and, understandably, they will maintain a strong commitment to expand irrigation (and build dams) in the coming years. This said, there is little doubt that world agriculture is highly inefficient in its use of water; this is particularly true of large-scale government-run irrigation schemes based on gravity flooding. So water must be used more efficiently – and this will often involve raising its price to farmers. Water markets, and related legal and regulatory frameworks, will become much more prominent in the years ahead. Land and soil issues will be less important. It is hard to find evidence that land degradation is seriously restricting yield growth in the world's major food-producing areas.

Third, in the coming decades farmers are going to have to become increasingly reliant upon information-intensive farm-management procedures. This development will extend far beyond greater efficiency in water use. A host of decisions – including those relating to soil maintenance – will become increasingly tailored to the requirements of individual fields. As in the past, so in the future, the basis of increased world food output will be extremely broad. It will encompass the fruits of agricultural research (both high- and low-tech), but it will also reflect many other developments – for example, in transport, electrification, synthetic material and, not least, farmer education.

Fourth, it is inevitable that because of continuing demographic growth, the world is going to become even more heavily dependent upon synthetic nitrogen for its food supply. Few supermarket shoppers are likely to appreciate the staggering fact that roughly half of all nutrients currently incorporated into the global harvest come from the application of synthetic nitrogen fertilisers. The world would be a very different place without the Haber-Bosch process for the synthesis of ammonia! Sometimes there will be scope for greater efficiency in nitrogen use. However, given the pace of contemporary population growth, many developing countries have little option but to increase their use of synthetic nitrogen in agriculture. I estimate that by 2020 humanity's use of nitrogen must roughly double. Fortunately, this increase in nitrogen production is feasible – probably at reduced cost per unit. But there is no practical alternative to much greater use of nitrogen fertilisers if yields are to be increased at the necessary speed.

According to my calculations the world's medium-term food prospects are not as bad as they are often portrayed. Humanity will probably be somewhat better fed in the year 2020 than it is today – although significant food problems will remain. This, however, is not the sort of message that grabs the headlines. And it can be portrayed, quite wrongly, as complacency.

Of course, it won't be easy to raise yields (it never has been easy). And there are significant environmental implications which stem from the need to increase the production of food – including adverse effects from greater nitrogen use. Given the recent rundown of world cereal stocks and the increased variability of harvests in the United States, we may well face a future of greater world cereal price volatility – which will be troublesome for poor importing countries. Resources must be spent on the supply side of the equation – e.g. agricultural research. And efforts on the demand side – especially making modern contraception accessible to people everywhere – are equally vital.

It is hard to hide some exasperation with an environmental lobby which sometimes so devalues its message by so overstating its case. The topic is too important for that. But at least reading Brown on the bus got me absorbed in the subject. With a billion extra people being added to the world every twelve years, population growth is arguably the most important dynamic of the modern era. Yet, worldwide, the amount of serious forward-looking research directed at estimating and handling the enormous implications of this growth is remarkably thin and scattered. This situation needs remedying. Demographers – and many others – should become more concerned with research on the future.

Further reading

Alexandratos, N. (ed.), *World Agriculture: Towards 2010, an FAO Study*, J. Wiley and Sons, Chichester, 1995.

Islam, N., *Population and Food in the Early 21st Century*, International Food Policy Research Institute, Washington, DC, 1995.

Mitchell, D., Ingco M. and Duncan, R., *The World Food Outlook*, Cambridge University Press, Cambridge, 1997.

Unequal health

Ann Ralph

'It's the rich wot gets the pleasure, it's the poor wot gets the blame', goes the old refrain. Unpalatable as it is, the shaming reality at the end of a century of enormous gains in wealth is that there remains a great divide between the health of different social classes. It was spelt out very clearly way back in 1980 in the report by a UK research working group chaired by Sir Douglas Black on *Inequalities in Health*. Although general health was improving, a clear differential was emerging between social groups, both in terms of infant mortality and in terms of adult death rates from chronic disease.

Viewed as a legacy of a defeated Labour administration, the Black report was consigned to Whitehall oblivion. An indifferent Thatcher government released a limited number of copies on August bank holiday 1980 with an almost palpable air of disdain. What should have been the turning point in addressing the nation's health became a

distant milestone forgotten by succeeding ministers throughout the years the Conservative government was in power.

Not that their advisers failed to remind them of the reality. Recognition that the risk factors of heart disease and stroke – namely high blood pressure, diet, stress, smoking, obesity and physical inactivity – were not just symptoms of poverty, but of inequality came from Sir Donald Acheson, the UK government's Chief Medical Officer from 1983 to 1991. He wrote in 1995 expressing his concern that while the health of the nation as a whole was improving, the inequalities between social groups were widening.

The late 1990s Labour government has gone full circle to return to the original premise of the Black report. Health ministers Frank Dobson and Tessa Jowell hope to find ways of tackling this health divide, the origins of which are complex. Diet has always been considered a risk factor for health, although the classic diseases of a deficient diet, such as scurvy, goitre and rickets, are rare in Britain. In these days of the welfare state, free education, an abundance of cheap food in supermarkets and a decade of health education messages, we might assume that no one is going short of food, and everyone knows what they should be eating.

We have cars to get to the supermarket, or, if we are lucky, perhaps there is even a nearby market with fresh local produce. We don't have to watch every penny, so can afford to try new things, buy our favourite varieties of cheese or wine or exotic fruits and vegetables. Perhaps we have gardens where we can grow some of our own food. We probably have freezers to stock up on seasonal foods, bargains and a variety of prepared meals. We have kitchens with a range of cooking equipment and a selection of cookery books. We prepare different dishes from those our parents and grandparents cooked. We sample them abroad, see them demonstrated on TV programmes by enthusiastic chefs. We can eat out or get a take-away. Of course, many of us have ethical concerns so we may wish to avoid certain foods, buy organic produce, or become vegetarian. Most of us are able to make an informed choice about what we eat. These choices depend on knowledge, access to a variety of foods and money – requisites that are not readily available to the poor.

Many people in the lower socio-economic groups are young, single parents or the elderly. Surveys of these groups reveal that the poor claim to know what they should be eating but find it difficult to do so. Many young people today probably never learned to cook either at school or at home. They know or care little about different cuts of meat, types of fresh fish, or how to use vegetables and fruit. They were reared on widely advertised, processed food. A lot of children, especially in Scotland, can probably name about fifty varieties of sweets, but only half a dozen vegetables. Older people may at least know how to buy for and cook economical dishes such as soups or stews from cheap cuts of meat and root vegetables, but they too have difficulties in shopping for food.

A single parent on income support or a low wage, living on a large housing estate, is unlikely to have a car to get to the supermarket which may be several bus rides away. In some rural communities it may be a journey of 50 miles to a supermarket. More than a quarter of greengrocers have closed since the mid-1980s and there has also been a decline in the number of food shops. Local shops, particularly in deprived areas, stock a limited range of long shelf-life goods costing up to 30 per cent more than supermarkets, while fruit and vegetables are limited, and often not very fresh. Tins and economy-size packs are heavy and difficult to carry with kids and push-chairs. Kids won't eat things they don't like, so hard-up parents buy what they will eat, so there is no waste. What they like is probably highly flavoured with salt or sugar. To cook quickly, it is fried in fat or cheap oil. It may be easier just to go round to the local chippy where everything is deep fried. Vegetables are not served with most take-aways – a bit of salad with a burger perhaps, but not much. Fruit is not nearly as filling or comforting as a cake or bar of chocolate.

Several recent in-depth studies of food poverty have highlighted the problems. The Low Income Project, part of the Nutrition Task

Force set up belatedly by the Conservative government in 1994 to improve the nation's health, identified some complex issues surrounding low income and healthy eating. It recognised the existence of inner city food deserts and the irony that in some rural areas, cheap, healthy food is virtually unobtainable. It also looked at local initiatives set up to deal with them.

Suzi Leather, in the Caroline Walker lecture of 1996, introduced the idea of modern malnutrition resulting from food poverty in the United Kingdom. This and other studies by the National Food Alliance – an organisation that represents public interest bodies working at all levels to influence policies and practices that enhance public health – go a long way towards exploding the often-quoted myths about food and the poor, such as: 'If they don't eat a healthy diet it's their own fault', or 'Healthy food isn't expensive'. New definitions of food poverty are emerging. One of the best is: 'The inability to acquire or consume an adequate quality or sufficient quantity of food in socially acceptable ways.'

The annual household food survey gives details of expenditure on and consumption of food and nutrients by region, family composition, social class and income group. The statistics show that compared with the highest income group A (gross weekly income of the head of household over £790), low income groups D and E2 (with less than £140 per week) have a less healthy diet. They drink more milk but less of it semi-skimmed, eat more meat and meat products, including higher fat products such as pies and sausages, more fats, sugar, preserves, potatoes and refined cereal products. They eat fewer fresh vegetables, fruit and high fibre products such as wholemeal bread.

The poorest 10 per cent of the population spend 29 per cent of their disposable income on food, while the richest 10 per cent spend 18 per cent. Contrary to popular myth, the poor spend more efficiently in certain respects. A carrot may be cheaper and healthier than a chocolate bar, but it has fewer calories. This is the problem: high calorie foods based on fat and sugar are much cheaper per calorie than foods rich in protective micro-nutrients, and much more satisfying in the short term. Mainstream healthy food options are likely to cost an extra 10 per cent, so poor people are buying calories which are cheap, not vitamins and beneficial nutrients which are more expensive, and tend to come in foods that are low in calories.

This results in a lower intake of many vital nutrients (calcium, iron, magnesium, the B vitamin, folate – think of foliage and green leaves – other B vitamins, and particularly vitamin C) among low income groups. While their vitamin intake may not be low enough to cause the classic deficiency symptoms, such as scurvy, there is now clear evidence that higher levels of certain nutrients do play a protective role in many diseases. Vitamins A, C and E are known as antioxidants and protect us from so-called free radical damage – a natural phenomenon with some beneficial effects, but also thought to be responsible for aspects of heart disease, ageing and cancer – possibly through damage to the DNA of genetic material.

Even between lower income groups there are disparities. Households in group D spend less on food than those on income support in group E2. Loss of benefits such as free school meals may push group D further into the poverty trap. One in five income support claimants has compulsory deductions for rent or fuel, so their spending on food is very restricted and their diet falls far below the recommended intakes for iron, calcium, dietary fibre, vitamin C and folate. The intake of these micro-nutrients is even lower for smokers who actually require more antioxidants than non-smokers.

Over the past fifteen years our total food consumption has fallen, reflecting an increasingly sedentary lifestyle requiring fewer calories from the macro-nutrients fat, protein and carbohydrate. But as total food intake declines, it is more difficult to obtain sufficient micro-nutrients, the essential vitamins, minerals and other nutrients.

Our diets need to become more rich in these micro-nutrients to compensate. Not surprisingly, the well-off have been better able to make this adjustment than the poor. The consumption of fruit, vegetables, carotene (a form of vitamin A, found in carrots and other red, yellow and orange plant foods) and vitamin C has declined in both groups, but for everything except vitamin C, the differences between rich and poor are greater now than fifteen years ago.

We have clear evidence that the lower socio-economic groups are eating a diet lacking many essential nutrients, and that access to healthy food is restricted by a variety of circumstances. This poor diet has health consequences that can be seen at all ages.

In pregnancy, smoking and lack of adequate nutrition both result in premature, low birth-weight babies. Diets low in folate predispose to shorter pregnancy, low birth weight, and defects such as spina bifida. Lack of the special fats (known as omega-3 fatty acids) present in oily fish like herring, sardines and mackerel not only limits growth of the foetus, pregnancy duration and the function of the placenta, but can also affect brain development. This limited foetal growth is linked with adult chronic diseases such as high blood pressure, abdominal obesity, diabetes and heart disease. The poor have more adolescent pregnancies and premature deliveries of low birth-weight babies who are immediately at a disadvantage.

Breast-feeding is increasingly recognised as fundamental to the long-term health of the baby. It benefits the mother too, yet the breast-feeding rates of the poor are only half those of the better off. Numerous factors in breast milk help the development of the intestine and increase immunity, limiting diarrhoea, chest infections, diabetes, eczema and asthma until adulthood. Premature babies who are breast-fed develop higher IQs. Low iron intakes can lead to anaemia in mother and child, with the situation made worse if babies drink unmodified whole cow's milk before reaching the age of twelve months, although small amounts may be used to mix up foods after six months. Low iron stores at a critical time may affect the brain permanently, resulting in lower intelligence.

Weaning is a critical time to establish dietary tastes. If toddlers are not introduced at an early age to vegetables and fruits and given water to drink, but are given sweets, highly seasoned crisps, biscuits and soft drinks, they learn to expect these foods. Often they are given as rewards, despite the fact that they lead to dental decay and high blood pressure at an early age. Inadequate vitamin intakes can affect the immune system in children (and the elderly), making them more susceptible to recurrent infections.

Schoolchildren face further problems. Once girls start to menstruate they lose iron, and are susceptible to anaemia. Iron is best obtained from a diet including red meat. Vegetarian sources of iron are less well absorbed but uptake is better if eaten along with vitamin C in the food. Non-meat eaters require a very well-balanced diet to avoid anaemia. Physical activities such as walking or dancing, as well as sport, are also important to develop strong bones, which, along with adequate calcium from milk , cheese and yoghurt, reduce the risk of later osteoporosis. Diets low in calcium are made worse by diets high in phosphate, particularly the acid form in cola type drinks, which not only limits bone accretion but causes calcium to be resorbed from the bone and lost in the urine. So the junk food habits of teenagers may have consequences other than the risk of heart disease.

Heavy smoking and diets low in vegetables and fruits (low in antioxidants) can damage the DNA in young men's sperm and may increase the risk of cancers in their offspring. Adolescent girls entering pregnancy with inadequate intakes of iron, calcium, folate and the special unsaturated fats from fish, vegetables and nuts or quality vegetable oils, are then at risk of having premature low birth-weight babies. So the intergenerational cycle of disease and social disadvantage continues.

Obesity, high blood pressure, diabetes, heart disease and stroke were once known as the diseases of affluence, and they still are in developing countries, but they now particularly affect the poor in Britain. A diet rich in animal fats raises cholesterol levels in the blood which contributes to heart disease. A diet low in vegetables and fruit, such as the diets of the poor and average diets in Scotland, Wales and Northern Ireland, also contributes to heart disease through low antioxidant levels. Low intakes of folate increase the chemical homocysteine in the blood – a risk factor for heart disease, stroke and other circulatory problems. Trans-fatty acids, found in the hydrogen-ated hard margarines used in cheap bakery products, also contribute to thrombosis and low birth weights because the placenta cannot transfer them normally. Higher salt intake, often found in the diet of the lower social classes, increases blood pressure and the risk of stroke, while a diet rich in potassium from fruits and vegetables has the opposite effect. The often mentioned special unsaturated oils from fish and nuts also limit sudden death from cardiac arrhythmia.

Obesity, particularly of the abdomen, is twice as prevalent in women in the lower social class groups in Britain. This type of abdominal obesity has been linked to poor foetal growth conditions and to long-term stress. Obesity is not only uncomfortable in itself, but is associated with a wide range of other health problems. These include diabetes, heart disease, some cancers, breathlessness, men-strual disturbances, pregnancy complications, back pain, arthritis, skin disorders and varicose veins. The causes of obesity are complex, prob-ably have a genetic component, but include lack of exercise and a high fat, energy-dense diet.

Most cancers, except for breast and bowel cancer, are more preval-ent in the lower social classes. Survival from breast and colon cancer certainly is positively related to social class, but the precise links with diet are uncertain. In October 1997, a report on *Food, Nutrition and the Prevention of Cancer*, the outcome of a four-year review of scientific literature by sixteen scientists from all over the world, made dietary recommendations suitable for use on a global scale to reduce the risk of many common cancers. These included advice to choose mainly plant-based diets, to eat 400–500 g of vegetables and fruit daily and 600–800 g of cereals, to limit red meat to less than 80 g per day, and to ensure that fats and oils provide less than 30 per cent of your daily energy requirement.

Old people are particularly vulnerable to a poor diet, whether at home or in hospital or residential care where lack of resources and staff time may mean that they do not always get well fed. Lack of adequate nutrition leads to general weakness, inactivity, risk of acci-dents, osteoporosis and a weak immune system, which is why old people and the very young are so susceptible to *E.coli* and other infections. Poor vision and cataracts are now linked to diets low in fruit and vegetables and antioxidants.

More than 13 million people, and one-third of all children live in households with incomes of less than £120 a week. Poor diet affects the health of the socially disadvantaged from the cradle to the grave, but the potential for improved health through a better diet is enormous. A low-quality diet, lack of exercise and smoking are a lethal triad for the lower social classes, leading to an intergenerational spiral of ill health and handicap. Modern nutritional and sociological research is now providing a basis for action to break this cycle.

Further reading

Barker (ed.), D. J. P., *Fetal and Infant Origins of Adult Diseases*, BMJ Books, London, 1992.
The Health of the Nation 1996: Low Income, Food, Nutrition and Health: Strategies for Improvement. A report by The Low Income Project Team for the Nutrition Task Force, Department of Health, London.
James, W. P. T., Nutritional disorders affecting the heart, in Julian, D. G., Camm, A. J., Fox, K. M., Hall, R. J. C. and Poole-Wilson, P. A. (eds), *Diseases of the Heart*, W. B. Saunders Co. Ltd, London, 1996; 1442–58.
James, W. P. T., Nelson, M., Ralph, A. and Leather, S., The contribution of nutrition to inequalities in health, *British Medical Journal* 314, 1997; 1545–9.
Leather, S., *The Making of Modern Malnutrition. An Overview of Food Poverty in the UK*, Caroline Walker Trust, London, 1996.
Nelson, M., Mayer, A. B. and Manley, P., The food budget, in Bradshaw, G. H. (ed.), *Budget Standards for the United Kingdom*, Aldershot, Avebury, 1993.
World Cancer Research Fund, American Institute for Cancer Research, *Food Nutrition and the Prevention of Cancer: A Global Perspective*, Washington D.C., 1997.

The British as a whole, and academics in particular, hate being told what to eat, distrust most official advice and have their own special theories about food. So here is some totally unofficial advice, which the poor are unable to follow:

* Eat plenty of starchy basic foods, such as bread, potatoes, rice or pasta with every meal.
* Eat at least five portions a day of vegetables and fruit – fresh, frozen or even canned. Try to include green leaves for folate, citrus for vitamin C, and yellow/orange, e.g. carrots, for carotene.
* Eat oily fish such as herrings, sardines, mackerel, trout or salmon twice a week.
* For cooking and salad dressings use olive oil or quality vegetable oils such as sunflower oil.
* Use butter or margarine sparingly – 500 g polyunsaturated margarine and 250 g of butter lasts two of us about a month.

- If you eat meat, choose lean cuts or remove fat, but eat in moderation (2–3 times a week) and cook carefully.
- Eat meat products such as sausages, pies, pâtés sparingly (once a week) and choose low-fat varieties.
- Drink semi-skimmed milk and use lower-fat cheeses.
- Ideally, drink water when you are thirsty – drink it with your children.
- Enjoy a glass of wine or beer with your meal.
- Eat with family or friends.
- Limit to once or twice a week: chips, crisps, salted or smoked foods, sweets, cakes, biscuits, cream, ice cream, sweet soft and fizzy drinks.

Waist not, want not

David Booth

The sciences of food, eating and nutrition could make major contributions to protecting people's health in the Western world. Yet they are largely failing to do so. The problem is not so much academic snobbery about cooking, shopping or farming. Rather, most damage stems from our ignorance about the effects of the ways in which, on a daily basis, people choose to eat the foods they do.

It is way beyond the capacity of molecular biology or brain research to identify the patterns of food choice that subsequently affect people's physical health and quality of life. Nor are biologists and neuroscientists capable of measuring the huge variety of influences on beneficial eating habits in different cultures. Without detailed scientific study of the effects of what people eat, what we are left with is mere supposition: no more than abstract theories about nutrient intakes. Such theories include the notion that overeating and obesity can be explained as part of our evolutionary heritage, a legacy of our past as hunter-gatherers when we needed to store fat because the next meal might be, literally, days away.

The neglect of behavioural science in food and nutrition is truly fatal. Almost half the British population suffers from excess fat around the waist, an affliction which could well be causing more premature deaths in the West than smoking, alcohol misuse or unsafe sex. Yet we have no firm evidence about what precisely we are doing to cause this unhealthy condition.

A waistline bigger than the hipline in men and a waist measurement which is more than 80 per cent of the circumference of the hips

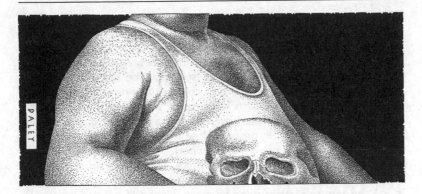

in women increases the risk of heart disease, stroke, diabetes and certain cancers. Recent analysis indicates that staying lean for life almost halves the chance of heart disease. Even being 10 per cent overweight (2–3 kg or half a stone for many of us) is a clear statistical risk to health and longevity. Obesity is a killer.

Obesity is not directly caused by genes, or hormones, or an unluckily efficient metabolism or the fats or other chemicals hidden in our foods. For each of us, whatever our biological endowment, getting fat is the result of what we choose to eat and drink and how we choose to move around. Nobody should be fooled by high-tech researchers' and drug companies' enthusiasm for fat-burning medications, leptin, lean gene engineering or the like. Magic from molecular medicine can never bypass 'fat physics' – the Law of Conservation of Energy applied to the human body: if any of us eats more calories than he or she spends, the excess energy must be stored. Maybe one day our fatty tissues will be genetically engineered to help tune down our desires for food or even to make us crave exercise. Yet we would still have to eat regularly, and many of us would have to sit down much of the day to get our work done.

It is obvious, then, that, to lose weight, a person must eat less and/or be more active than at present. Only slightly less obviously, the individual's lower food intake and greater activity must be sustained indefinitely; otherwise, the weight will go back on again. So, there is no point in starting to change eating and movement habits unless the changes are permanent.

What is less obvious is a fact that most weight control and obesity research enterprises have never faced up to. Patterns of eating and food choice are so complex that nobody yet knows what any particular change in a person's eating pattern does, either to that individual's total accumulated energy intake or to the medium-term difference between energy taken in and energy spent. Likewise, working out the long-term impact of a particular change in an individual's activity pattern is a complicated calculation far beyond existing knowledge and quite possibly never feasible.

Another relatively straightforward but poorly understood point is that weight loss reduces the energy spent by the body (and weight gain increases it). As a result, any change in eating or movement habits has diminishing returns in terms of weight change. Once the initial decrease in weight has levelled out, another effective change in behaviour is needed in order to lose more weight.

It follows that we need hard evidence as to the exact choices which actually do reduce energy intake or increase energy output and which can be sustained indefinitely. Moreover, the least (and most) fattening practices need to be described in practical terms by anybody with a weight problem. Without such evidence, dieticians and doctors can only guess which recipes, eating patterns and physical activities to recommend. Clinical psychologists also simply don't know which behaviours they should advise a fat person to modify.

As a result, most dieters try and fail with one remedy after another, even when they are following expert advice. When overweight patients fail to follow prescribed diets or exercising regimens, they are sometimes dismissed as idle and stupid. This is unjustifiable because the advice they receive is not founded on controlled studies demonstrating its efficacy. Despite Britain's strength in clinical research, the need for evidence-based intervention on behaviour has been ignored.

Experts from around the world have been meeting since the 1970s to argue about the latest drug or diet which might aid weight loss; yet they totally neglect the practical choices ordinary people need to make in order to reduce their weight for long enough to improve their health prospects. Every dietary, pharmaceutical and psychological treatment for obesity is followed by a general regain of the weight lost. Yet no psychosocial research in the United Kingdom, the United States or elsewhere has been commissioned to identify the exact food and activity habits that would be most effective at preventing unhealthy weight gain.

Strange events result from this long-standing dismissal of research into the actual behaviour which causes obesity. Some years ago, the Department of Health was so ill-advised as to set a target of reducing the prevalence of obesity among adults in England by at least one quarter within little more than a decade. Ministers should have been told that nobody knows how to bring down the calories in a nation's food choices to stay in line with increasingly sedentary lifestyles – indeed, no research has ever been funded on the issue. So, when Professor Philip James was asked to co-ordinate expert opinion

about how this target might be met, he had to persuade the government to let the report be published under a title like 'Slowing the
Rise in Obesity', as opposed to 'Cutting Obesity'.

The mechanisms influencing human food intake were clear in outline by the mid-1970s. The implications for weight control were spelt
out at that time to medical practitioners and research investigators.
Since then, however, obesity research has focused on the brain,
particularly on research into neurotransmitters and gut hormones.
Alternatively, it has succumbed to genetic or metabolic determinism,
instead of facing the brute fact of thermodynamics that eating more
than is spent means getting fatter. As a result, we still have nothing
specific which is widely recognised as likely to prevent unhealthy
weight gain. All that the recent report on obesity did was to reiter-
ate long-standing pleas to eat less fat and to take more exercise.

A basic logical mistake in many research reports arises from
neglect of the fact that weight reduction requires action from a
thinking, feeling individual. The putative slimmer will have preferences for different strategies and may well act on them, affecting
any controlled trial of a diet or exercise regimen. Psychologists have
pointed out that this invalidates the established criteria for clinical
trials, according to which patients have no particular opinions
about different treatments. When the assigned treatment can be
affected by the patient's (or the clinician's) perceptions or actions,
fully disguised ('double-blind') experimental control is impossible
and randomisation into comparison groups is likely to be vitiated
during the trial, if not at its start. This means that there is no way to
evaluate the effectiveness of a weight-control procedure (or any
other healthy eating strategy) without having a decent theory of the
processes by which it might work and then using those hypotheses
to track each individual's potentially relevant beliefs and responses to
them. This combination of experimental and observational designs is
well established in applied social psychology, but is disregarded by
medical experimenters, epidemiological statisticians and food product developers alike.

The case against neglect of behavioural research into obesity is
evident. What a person eats is a matter of what he or she thinks and
feels – about the particular food materials available, the body they
go into, and the personal and social meaning of each eating and
drinking occasion. Yet the only data relating food choices to risk of
disease are based on estimates of the total weights of nutritive chemicals that groups of the population usually swallow each day. These
estimated nutrient intakes are based on inevitably biased records or
memories of which foods were eaten in what amounts and when.
All the other scientifically usable information about food and drink

consumption is routinely thrown away in order to calculate daily doses of fat, carbohydrate, sodium ions, vitamin E and so on. This ignores the dependence of any one food's physiological effects on the amount consumed on any specific occasion, on what is eaten with it or at what time of day – all data included in standard dietary records or readily added to them.

These are material patterns of food choice. It is another task to relate them to eating decisions as consumers describe them within their own social context. Psychologists have shown that respondents to dietary surveys could easily record other details relevant to their eating decisions such as cultural factors or family eating patterns.

Dietary guidelines around the world have recently been rewritten in terms of foods, instead of in terms of the nutrients on which the medical evidence is based. However, food-based advice contradicts the fundamental principle that it is not a food which is healthy or unhealthy but the way it is used within the individual's overall dietary pattern. What is needed therefore are dietary guidelines about culturally embedded food choices, directly based on evidence from nutritional social psychology.

The United Kingdom's official medical advice on food policy since the early 1980s has been to give priority to cutting back on all fats. This was recently reiterated, although with a more positive spin: advice to increase the intake of starch, the other main source of energy in food. However, the epidemiology of heart disease indicates that lowering of dietary fat needs to be focused on the saturated fats found most in lard, and even more on the partly hydrogenated fats from vegetable oils. Indeed, modest amounts of oils which have not been chemically stiffened, like corn oil and olive oil, and the polyunsaturate-rich oils (soya, sunflower), as also a little alcohol, are a positive help to health.

There is another reason for this switch from cutting fats to boosting starch. Despite being in operation for most of two decades, the anti-fat policy has had zero impact on the average of UK citizens' intake of fat as a fraction of total calories. Surveys need to include psychological measurements of respondents' strategies for avoiding 'fatty foods', especially while they are recording their food intake or reporting what they recall eating recently. Such research has yet to begin, even though new methods of measuring energy expenditure has confirmed the suspicion that fatter people under-record their intake of energy-containing foods. The exclusion of behavioural considerations has probably contributed to the failure to reduce this nation's fat intake. A primary pillar of the policy has been the requirement to list fat and other nutrient contents on food packets. Yet some years before those lists came to the United Kingdom,

psychologists were unsurprised to find that they had no specific impact on food consumers' choices. The consumer undoubtedly has a
right of easy access to such information, but there is no basis for the
belief that access to such information will change behaviour.

A more realistic strategy of the anti-fat campaign has been to
encourage food businesses to provide foods correctly claiming to be
'low fat', for those consumers who are persuaded by the propaganda on the risks of eating fat. However, this strategy neglects the
economic behaviour of agricultural producers and our almost total
ignorance of the sensory physiology and psychology of the appreciation of fats in foods. As a result, we have myriads of skimmed
milk products (where lack of cream can be disguised for some
consumers), sold alongside products made from the extra butterfat,
while as much fat as ever is eaten in meat products and in bakeries
which contribute more fat to the British diet than dairy products do
anyway.

One of the best reasons for cutting down on fats is their contribution to obesity. Fats tend to be in rich foods. So do sugar and starch.
A major problem for weight control is that we actively overeat
energy-rich foods. This fact arises from two influences on our eating
decisions.

First, we eat foods by volume – how big the portion is to look at
and also, less directly, how much it fills the stomach. After all, we
can't sense the energy content of a food as we eat it. Many psychological experiments of the 1970s refuted the idea that the number
of calories in a particular food influences how much we eat. This fact
is beginning to be acknowledged by nutritionists. Nevertheless, even
psychologists persist in converting food intake into energy units and
assuming that energy intake is physiologically regulated: biologically
oriented eating research is dominated by the empty question how
good or bad the 'compensation' is at test meals for a given type of
excursion from a supposedly regulated level.

Second, the later in the meal that the rich recipe is eaten, the less
effective it is at inducing moderation on that menu in future. So,
rich main courses could be less fattening than rich desserts: lots of
easily digested carbohydrate (or perhaps fat) can train the appetite
to go easy on dessert and reduce the volume and calories in the
meal. This is especially helpful to the waistline at the last meal of
the day: it is often the largest and the least capable of influencing
the amount eaten at the next meal. If easily digested starchy foods
like bread and rice are to help in weight control, they need to be in
the early courses of full meals. Fortunately, the cooked multi-course
meal is still remarkably common, even though under pressure from
late twentieth-century Western lifestyles.

More and less fattening habits may vary among lifestyles and environments. It is reasonable to hope that strong commonalities will emerge from the overlapping diversities of eating patterns and food materials now available in the more affluent parts of the world. However, sophisticated handling of the data on material and cultural patterns of food choice is required to establish evidence-based weight control. The potential for confusion is illustrated by the term 'snacking'. On the basis of theory of food intake control, it was proposed that frequent ingestion of even small amounts of energy in and with drinks between substantial eating occasions is particularly fattening – bad news for lovers of tea and biscuits, or cola and crisps! This is quite different from the theoretically unrationalised idea that frequent eating helps reduce weight or other health risk factors: British nutritionists recently reviewed the evidence from the superficial eating pattern analyses carried out thus far and found no solid support for this idea. By contrast, the hypothesis about frequent drinks being particularly fattening has been empirically confirmed by appropriate behavioural research, three times in the United Kingdom and once so far in Germany. Less specific methods used in the United States have yielded similar findings. However, earlier British data show that in this country the fattening pattern of tea and biscuits or cola and crisps is not thought of as a 'snack'; so, cutting back on 'snacking' did not result in a reduction of these fattening extras.

In conclusion then, there are powerful research methods for discovering which eating choices actually are healthy and how foods and drinks can be enjoyed in a healthy diet. The methods range from controlled experiments to observational analysis in everyday physiological and cultural contexts, providing both conceptual and numerical information on the cognitive mechanisms organising our physical and social behaviour. Choosing foods comes as naturally as anything in life. Our personal experience forms a rich and yet seamless whole. This can make it difficult to see how psychology can objectify the processes by which a person performs such mental tasks and subsequently to measure the influences – material or symbolic – on our thoughts, feelings and activities. Some are appalled by causal analysis of eating and drinking. Others find it hard to believe anything not produced by brain scanners or laboratory instruments. Yet for 150 years (twice as long as biochemistry and three times longer than neurophysiology), the scientific discipline of psychology has been dedicated to working out the quantitative processes by which individuals operate in their cultural contexts. Its research-based practitioners help to solve personal and social problems by collaborating with other professions in similar roles. Food businesses and medical services would do well also to cultivate applications of psychology to eating.

Further reading

Angel, Aubie, *et al.* (eds), *Progress in Obesity Research*, John Libbey, London, 1996.

Blair, Alan J., *et al.*, The relative success of official and informal weight reduction techniques, *Psychology and Health* 3, 1989; 195–206.

Booth, David, *Psychology of Nutrition*, Taylor and Francis/Psychology Press, London, 1994.

Department of Health, *Reversing the Increasing Problem of Obesity in England*, Wetherby, 1995.

Lewis, Vivien J., *et al.*, Outcome of group therapy for body image emotionality and weight-control self-efficacy, *Behavioural Psychotherapy* 20, 1992; 155–66.

Coded messages
Mary Douglas

I first got interested in the ritual aspects of food around the age of five or six. We had been sent home from Burma to be brought up by my grandparents who had retired to live in a bungalow in Devon (I and my younger sister, aged three). This was where I learnt to read off the day of the week from the lunchtime menu. Sunday lunch was a roast: a chicken, leg of lamb or beef or pork. It must have been a big roast, or we had very small helpings, as it served for the next three days as well: Monday, cold with salad; Tuesday, shepherd's pie with cabbage or sprouts; Wednesday, rissoles with bubble-and-squeak, or curry. On Thursday, a fresh start with liver and bacon, Friday was fish, Saturday was fishcakes, kedgeree or sausages and mash, then we were back again on roast.

There was no need to ask why. The principles were obvious: the celebration of Sunday, and then the left-overs and other frugal items for the rest of the week, fish fitting in with Friday abstinence, and the easy-to-serve cold meat accommodating the extra housework and laundry of Monday. The system of the laundry was more difficult. 'Why are the sheets dirty on Monday, Granny?' My grandmother was flummoxed, as she would have said. She might have answered that the seven-day week is a co-ordinating principle for household activities, and, on being pressed further, that it is an arbitrary

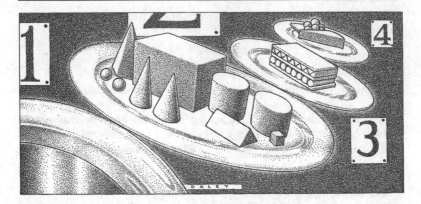

convention from the point of view of the bedding, but founded in history and tradition. I did not understand her answer, so the problem of arbitrary convention has remained with me all my life and the experience of living in an orderly household was the beginning of my interest in the coding of material objects.

The 1960s were a great period for communication studies and linguistics. In anthropology the study of communication blossomed in structuralist studies of myth, led by Claude Lévi-Strauss who applied linguistic analysis to South American Indian food systems. The idea that food is a system of communication was much touted in the early 1970s. But no one tried to work out exactly how food communicates. So when Michael Nicod was looking around for a topic for a Master's thesis in the anthropology department of University College, London, where I was then teaching, I suggested that he study the rules governing food in working-class London families. He would study human food habits, just as ethologists study the eating habits of chimpanzees. Unlike the ethologists, he would have to eat the same as the research subjects in whose homes he lived, and they would have to know what he was doing. He was interested in the project, mentioning only that he would have preferred to study French food, and preferably middle-class food, but he stayed with the plan and in due course produced a remarkable report.

The idea of grammar was fashionable at the time. Roland Barthes' great book on fashion (*Le Système de la mode*, 1967) was a linguistics approach to dress as a system of communication. Nicod planned to work on the grammar of food. Instead of asking: 'What does this particular item of food mean?' he was interested in the system of rules. For example, if a person I hardly know invites me to dinner at his house, what does it mean when baked beans on toast appear on my plate? It might mean that I am counted as an intimate friend entitled to homely food, or it might mean that I am a despised guest, unworthy of a decent dinner. It depends on the convention.

Roland Barthes never made a grammar of any particular dress code, he only showed what might be done about the system of dress. Instead of words (or phonemes), he had items of dress, defined by the fashion trade. Instead of words matched to objects, he had sequences of dress items matching events in the world: garden parties in summer, barbecues and so on. Grammar has sequencing rules, for example for putting adjectives before or after nouns, or verbs before or after their subjects. Likewise for the dress code: the human body itself gives a sequencing principle – gloves for hands, hats for heads. The seasons make another sequencing – different clothes for different times of the year. The point is that items of clothes have no meanings in themselves, only in their sequencing and assembly. By the way they are grouped and separated they give the meanings to events. So when big hats are seen this year at Ascot, it is not the hats but the races at Ascot that get a new meaning as a fashion focus for a new set of race-goers. Barthes' clever trick was to have found a way of looking at fashion and clothing as systems which respond to things happening in the world.

Following this simple grammatical model, Nicod aimed to find the sequencing rules for the food of the families he was studying, through the day, through the week, through the year, and also the rules connecting items of food with each other, like roast potatoes with beef, but chips with fish. He found a strongly rule-bound system. For instance, a meal is not a dinner unless it figures potatoes; hot food is dinner, cold food can be for tea; sweet (with custard) is after not before savoury. He also found an aesthetic principle governing the structure of a meal and of meals through the day, a principle of diminishing heat, moisture and size and increasing sculptural qualities. The ideal celebratory meal had a structure that started off with an appetising hot and messy dish of gravy over meat and potatoes (on one big plate), and became more of an architectural achievement as it went on through pudding (on a smaller plate), and tea with an optional small coloured biscuit (on a still smaller plate). Who says the French meal system is more structured than the English?

In those days anthropologists' projects depended on comparisons of culture and Nicod was on to a method for saying for sure whether one domain of living was more structured than another. But the research was never published. Partly, perhaps, it was so original that, apart from the French tradition of semiology, it did not fit into received patterns of ideas. Partly, the department was small and diversified, so that to everyone except the biological anthropologists his project was bizarre. Another important reason may have been the timing: the early 1970s witnessed horrifying world famines. At such a time, work on a grammar of food could seem quite inappropriate.

It must be important to know that even the simplest foods in the most economically hard-pressed households are subject to elaborate aesthetic judgements. Famine-relief workers have reported starving persons choosing to die of hunger rather than go to a clinic without being decently dressed. It is something fundamental to do with being human, something about cognition. But it is difficult to name the immediate pay-off for food research which offers no advice for nutritionists or welfare agencies. Once Nicod tried to explain his objectives to an incredulous radio interviewer: 'Do you seriously mean to tell me that you are studying the place of the biscuit in the English food system?' Someone I met later, joking about the ludicrous jargon of sociologists, quoted Nicod's term 'food event' to crown it all: 'What's wrong with the good simple English word, "meal"? And what is the point of calling dinner a "potato event"? It takes the biscuit! Ha, ha!' Well, the project did not need terms laden with middle-class cultural values. It needed terms that explicitly linked the eating to the events of social life.

The Minister for Education was challenged in a parliamentary question to justify student grants being spent on frivolous research into the meaning of biscuits. I think it was answered with reference to the freedom of the universities, but I am grateful to Huntley and Palmers for the box of biscuits they sent me for bearing the brunt of the attack.

The main trouble was that Michael Nicod's thesis looked like research into food, but was actually research into a philosophical subject – classification – that had shifted from its central position. In the 1970s Marxist anthropology was mobilising feminist studies, colonial studies, ethnicity and everything to do with oppression and vulnerability. With post-modern anthropology, the structuralist interest was channelled into the arts, literature and other people's religions: what you might call 'leisure pursuits' if you were thinking of asking a parliamentary question. Claims to objectivity were suspect: a witty colleague asked me on this subject why I still indulged in 'physics envy'.

When Aaron Wildavsky invited me to develop research on culture at the Russell Sage Foundation in 1977 I chose food complexity as the central theme. Aaron was shortly to be dismissed after only six months as President, and I fear that my topic did not help his arguments with the Foundation's hard-nosed Board of Trustees. But I was obstinate, I felt that it was very important.

The whole world is turned upside down by agribusiness, but no one can say that the powerful demand that it responds to is triggered by physical need. It is not hunger that calls forth exotic passion fruit, fresh mangoes and dates, nor fear of starvation that delivers huge hard tomatoes, sturdy asparagus and very solid 'soft fruits', strawberries specially bred to travel long distances all the year round. 'Is your journey really necessary?' was on posters at railway stations in the war. We may wish to protect the environment, but its problems start at our hospitable tables. 'Is your avocado pear really necessary?' No ascetic movement is round the corner threatening the collapse of the food trade routes, nor any angry caricaturist cruelly satirising us in our restaurants. Even so, it must be important to understand the social pressures we are making on the food industry.

The first step was to go on from Nicod's insights to develop a general method of comparing degrees of structuredness in meals. I was lucky to find Jonathan Gross, a mathematician who was interested in complex structures in the perspective of information theory. Complexity is the combination of variety with logical order. A dietary system that responds to changes in some other process, like Roland Barthes' dress system responding to the world, or like my grandmother's menu responding to the days of the week, would score more for complexity. A dietary system that changed according to who was present at the meal – sorry, no, at the food event – would have another dimension of complexity.

Three teams of American anthropologists who had been studying food habits in distinct ethnic communities came together and collaborated in working out a common programme of research. William Powers and Marla Powers were studying the Oglala Sioux Indians; Judith Goode, Karen Curtis, and Janet Theophano, the Italian American community in Philadelphia; and Tony Whitehead was investigating a Southern American community.

We wanted to know why some people give themselves so much trouble over elaborating their food. The Americans were determined not to impose their own culture on their research, yet they wanted to make comparisons. They gave the term 'food event' as much of a bashing as Nicod had given to the term 'meal'. If three or more people gathered round a vending machine to eat and converse together, did that count as a 'food event'? The Oglala Sioux Indians snatched handfuls of berries off bushes as they rode by and shared them: did that count? Some households never gathered round a table anyway; did it count as a food event if the mother announced that the food was ready and each person took what they wanted back to whatever they were doing? Eventually, with guidance from Jonathan Gross, they constructed a scale of complexity they could all use.

Jointly, we produced a book, *Food in the Social Order*, in which each team gave a summary of the situation of the ethnic group it was studying, and tried to explain the gamut between the most modest, hasty, unceremonial moment of the food-taking series (usually breakfast) and the grandest festivities. There were several suggestive results. One was that people's behaviour in the complexity dimension tends to be consistent. If some households were used to making formal and complex distinctions in their food every day, they tended to do so even more on their big occasions. The opposite was also true: those who normally went for simplicity celebrated the big occasions with increased volume, not increased complexity. So what? Does this abstruse information make any conceivable difference to anyone?

Well, you could be interested in social integration. The more that everyone in the community is likely to drop in on everyone else, the less complexity. Conversely, the more complexity, the fewer random arrivals at the table. This applied to the very poor families in North Carolina who used each other's kitchens as support networks when they had no food in the house. If the shopper has little idea about who will be present for the meals, perishable fruit and vegetables will be forgone. The same for festivities, when every woman contributes her best dish to the church lunch, there is no scope for making it all into a logical pattern. Obviously, elaborate meal structures, with value set on the right sequence – soup before the solids, the pudding before the cheese, or whatever, and the right sauces and garnishes for each thing – go with a different kind of society. The more that food is ritualised, the more conscious of social distinctions are those who eat it. This is a long way from the television programmes that call on us to rejoice in more and more refinements of taste. It casts a slur of bad taste on the extravagances extolled by the food-writing industry.

There ought to be a connection between the way that people spend their money, how they dress, furnish homes, use their time and the way they eat. The complexity of the food should be a clue to everything else that is going on. We have brain-washed ourselves into thinking that everything we need to know about food habits can be gathered as statistics of family size, social class and education. This suggests a funny set of judgements about why people eat what they do. Some households are traditionalist in everything they do. Some households are strivingly mobile and busily networking all over the place; presumably it is they who make the demand for kiwi fruit and strawberries out of season. Some households are severely moralistic in their diet and demand exotic spices to flavour otherwise bland vegetarian foods. The cultural bias has little to do with money, and it does not depend on social class or income, though it has something to do with occupation.

Volumes have been written about cultural theory that explains why people eat what they eat. It is partly to signal that they are not like the other people who eat whatever it is – meat, blood, pig, beef; partly it is to build up a satisfying model of the order of the day and the year, keeping or rejecting the traditions of the older generations. Subsequent work on the comparison of household cultures puts traditionalist complex food systems into the same group as regular routines, own places at table, fixed times for washing clothes, traditional ingredients and saving for holidays. It sounds just like my grandparents' house in Totnes, and it is true that not many people dropped in there at odd times for a meal. But it had other merits: stability, predictability and readiness to adopt grandchildren.

I am sadly aware that the comparison of food rituals and lifestyles is still a conversation that has not gone far beyond the descriptive stage. Nutrition studies would be more informative if they could sometimes shake off the habit of expecting differences in social class, income and education to explain what is interesting about eating. It is important also to understand how food fits into the social order in the home. One of the key questions is turning out to be the seating arrangements: does each person have a known, fixed time for eating, do they expect to eat together, do they wait until everyone is assembled before they start? The answers make a cluster around other habits: the control of the budget, the celebration of special events, who comes to parties and what gets on the menu.

Between the famine relief end of the research spectrum and the competition for five-star restaurant ratings at the other end, the uses of food are not being recognised or studied. If we wanted to correct the ignorance that flourishes around the topic of food, research on consumer habits would have to change very fundamentally. A form of false innocence flourishes in this empty space in our knowledge of ourselves.

Further reading

Dake, Karl and Thompson, Michael, The meanings of sustainable development: household strategies for managing needs and resources, in Wright, Scott, Dietz, Thomas, Borden, Richard, Young, Gerald and Guagnano, Gregory, (eds), *Human Ecology: Crossing Boundaries*, The Society for Human Ecology, Fort Collins, Colorado, 1993.

Douglas, Mary, Food as a system of communication, in *In the Active Voice*, London, Routledge, 1982; 81–118.

Douglas, Mary (ed.), *Food in the Social Order, Studies of Food and Festivities in Three American Communities*, Russell Sage Foundation, New York, 1984.

A recipe

From *The Radiation Cookery Book* for use with the Regulo New World Gas Cookers, first edition 1927, quoted from p. 280 of the 1955 edition published by Radiation Group Sales Ltd.

Custard sauce (economical)

¼ oz cornflour
1 pint milk
1 oz sugar
1 egg

Mix the cornflour to a smooth paste with a little of the milk. Boil the rest of the milk and add the cornflour, stirring well. Add the sugar, bring to the boil, and boil for 3 minutes. Allow to cool slightly. Beat the egg, stir it into the milk and cornflour and stir over a low flame until the egg cooks and thickens.

Do not allow the sauce to boil after the addition of the egg, or it will curdle. Serve hot.

The nation's diet

Anne Murcott

At the beginning of the 1990s, there were reasons enough to suggest that Britons were perhaps more 'food conscious' than at any previous point in the nation's history. Interest in the population's eating habits was accelerating both as a matter of vast and competitive business, and as an integral element of public health policy and efforts to reduce heart diseases, the main cause of premature death. And to these concerns the recent memory of salmonella and listeria scares had been conspicuously added. If these were not social changes enough, around the edges were others, including, at times, faintly unlikely straws in a British culinary wind: cookbooks were said to be occupying an even greater share of non-fiction sales; vegetarianism was losing its cranky public image; ever more inventive TV food programmes were proliferating; sacks of barbecue charcoal heaped up outdoors at the petrol station were becoming as familiar as the cartons of semi-skimmed milk on sale inside. And never mind Cuban cafés in Islington – a Mongolian restaurant was spotted in a South Wales valley.

All this and more provided the rationale for the first research programme on food choice that the Economic and Social Research Council (ESRC) had ever mounted. It is a rationale which, if anything, has even more force towards the end of the decade now that BSE has been added to so many Britons' vocabulary, has raised another set of significant public health concerns and has had drastic consequences for the economy and the nation's standing in Europe and beyond. The council's research programmes aim to address scientific topics of strategic and national importance. Food choice had become just such a topic, though it was one which had yet to receive extensive, systematic study across a range of social sciences. All the more reason for the ESRC to grant approval in 1990 for the programme that became known as 'The nation's diet'. The six-year, £1.6 million, multi-disciplinary programme was launched a couple of years later. Organisational factors operating when the programme was formulated have meant that it had a greater emphasis on the consumption/demand side than on the production/supply side of food choice, although no one expected that a programme on so comparatively modest a scale could ever be comprehensive. All the same, the sheer volume of material will, in time, provide all manner of landmarks and baselines for the examination of British food choice in the 1990s.

From the outset, one question aroused everyone's curiosity: 'Why do people eat what they do?' Everyone – from dentists to caterers, schoolteachers to community dieticians, food manufacturers and supermarkets, civil servants to journalists, not forgetting 'ordinary' members of the public – seemed intrigued, despite differing, and at times, of course, conflicting, interests in the nation's eating habits. Accordingly, this question was placed at the centre of the brief to be addressed by each of the programme's eighteen studies, although each displays a different, sometimes strongly contrasting approach.

'Change' in some guise or another runs through a good many of the studies. This is not simply a reflection of the fact that changing food habits feature so prominently in the 1990s dietary landscape. Certainly, contributing to documenting the nature of such change is inevitably one of the programme's tasks, and addressing, for instance, the need for dietary change required by public health policies is part of the programme's purpose. More than that, it is that fixing on change is a convenient analytic strategy, exposing to investigative view forces that are otherwise likely to remain concealed in the ordinary run of things. Apart from anything else, all of us, at times more often than we should like, find ourselves faced with one sort of dietary change or another.

Many of us, for instance, will recognise the headache presented to parents whose small children flatly refuse to eat any but the most limited diet. This is not just a problem for the hapless parent, but since it is often presumed that the eating patterns established in childhood might be set for life, trouble could be stored up for the child who will not eat, say, fruit and vegetables – the very foods modern nutritional science shows are especially important to promote health. But Fergus Lowe and his colleagues (University of Wales, Bangor) are able to reassure parents, teachers and child-minders that what children eat is a matter of learning – and is thus amenable to change. With parents' co-operation and approval, they mounted a set of bold studies in experimental psychology. They found that after using a combination of video-taped stories of 'goodies' and 'baddies' incorporating suitable food-related storylines and associated rewards (badges, caps, tee-shirts and the like), 5–7 year-olds who had previously turned their noses up at apples or avocado, peas or kiwi fruit simply took to eating them. Moreover, this was not a one-off. 'Fussy eaters' were still eating the fruit in question when reassessed two months and again six months after the rewards and stories had been discontinued.

Other changes, though, are more benign facts of life. Some, like a couple's first setting-up home together, are no doubt welcome, but also, of course, mean readjusting. Early results from Annie Anderson, Debbie Kemmer and David Marshall's (Universities of Glasgow and Edinburgh) small-scale 'before' and 'after' study suggest a reassuringly familiar picture. Although the young (heterosexual) couples they interviewed did not seem to organise their menus with health concerns primarily in mind, their eating none the less became more orderly, and their shopping trips more regular and planned. The evening meal turned into a specially important part of the day which couples nurtured as a symbol of their newly created life together. For the most part, however, even though both were out at work or studying, the young women were that much more likely than their partners to bear the main responsibility for buying the food and cooking the meals.

It is sometimes claimed that one of the social changes affecting food choice is the erosion of the convention that women are to do the cooking. But results from other parts of the programme run along similar lines to those reported from this Scottish study. It seems that the social arrangement tying women to domesticity dies hard. To be sure, Pat Caplan and her team (Goldsmith's College, London) found that in an inner-city area of London younger people thought they ought to share tasks such as shopping. But it did not altogether work out like that in practice. Even when men, especially if not currently in employment, did go to the shops, they were still likely to be equipped with a list that their (employed) partner had written out for them. It also meant that for summer visitors to rural West Wales, in the second part of Caplan's anthropological study, holidaying in a hotel was 'relaxing', the 'treat' that gave wives a break from the routine of family catering. Granted, the evidence still needs to be rounded up, never mind counterbalanced with a closer look at those cases where couples are firmly committed to domestic equity. At the moment, however, it looks as if the picture is both varied and complicated by the sometimes quite dramatic changes in both men's and women's employment patterns, together with the continued need for someone to hold domestic arrangements together.

This last is well illustrated in a study of possibly rather less welcome domestic change, in which Spencer Henson and his colleagues (University of Reading) coupled qualitative work with a survey. What happens at home, they wondered, when someone's diet alters? How does the rest of the family react to a unilateral declaration to turn vegetarian? What about everyone else's meals if someone is trying to lose weight, or comes home from hospital armed with a diet sheet? After all, there can be a surprising number of immediate practical consequences; new nutritional information may need to be collected, studied and learned – accommodating to diabetes is an obvious instance. Buying different foods may mean finding different shops as well as spending more money; adopting different cooking techniques may need to be remembered as well as practised.

All this could threaten a fairly major domestic upheaval. What appears to happen however, is that instead of overturning existing routines, the change of diet is assimilated into them. Broad findings so far indicate that it was the woman who orchestrated the smooth adoption of the change. She also tended to be the family 'authority' about food. As a result, she played a central part in determining the manner in which everyone else responded. She generally also bore the brunt of all the new tasks involved, although there were some cases where they were shared. Yet, by and large, doing it all was not thought to pose any problem. Indeed, it was reported that incorporating the changes into the normal routine of meal preparation was accomplished with relative ease, even when it was clear that quite significant additional effort was needed. Few of us would be surprised to discover that medically advised dietary changes were readily adopted, but easy adaptation is found to apply in the case of diet change for other reasons as well. Though it is no more than speculation at this stage, it may be worth pondering on the nature and quality of family bonds. Perhaps they mean that most of us would rise to the occasion, most of us strive to ensure dietary change is made more welcome than it could at first appear.

Other changes are unequivocally less welcome. Psychological stress, which has important implications for various aspects of health, is a common feature of modern life. It is also possible that stress affects food choice. The tired cliché 'comfort' food includes people reaching for the chocolate when faced with a difficult period in their lives. Equally, we have long been familiar with the idea that, when unhappy or under pressure, people may not feel like eating anything at all. Since there was little psychological research on the topic, Andrew Steptoe and his team (St George's Hospital Medical School) elected to pursue it, not in the laboratory, but under naturalistic conditions. University students were studied at points during the normal academic year and then again a few days before major exams. And shop workers in a large department store were assessed four times over the six months that included the sales or the Christmas rush, covering periods of both high and low workload.

These studies show that psychological stress does affect both the amount that is eaten as well as the choice of food. That said, however, the precise dietary patterns vary with the type of stress and also according to the characteristics of the individual. For instance, it was found that students displayed increased levels of emotional disturbance in the days before the exams. But food intake only altered among those who were anxiety-prone and were comparatively socially isolated. The results also show that, broadly, where the selection of foods changed, an increased fat intake was likely. The upshot is that although food choice can indeed be affected by stress, the effects are not uniform but depend on a person's temperament or social circumstances. As Steptoe observes, the results are important, for they are not about less frequent if major disturbances of life events like bereavement or being made redundant, but revolve around the ordinary, daily difficulties of work or home life to which everyone is exposed.

Working out how to avoid succumbing to adverse dietary effects of stress still lies ahead. In the meantime, though, national targets for the public to reduce their intake of fat, or to be sure of eating their 'five-a-day' fruit and vegetables, have still to be achieved. It is already quite firmly established that the majority of the population is very well aware of modern nutritional advice – which throws the spotlight onto converting the advice into practice. This provided the point of departure for Mark Conner and his colleagues (Leeds University and Reading) to investigate what part ambivalence might play in formulating people's attitudes to attempts to alter what they usually eat, especially since it is well known that, in the case of 'healthy eating', members of the public are more than a little scep- tical of experts who seem to keep changing their advice. Conner's study starts not only to confirm that people do indeed display am- bivalence towards changing their diet, and that, yes, those who are found to be more ambivalent do seem to be less likely to reduce their fat intake or increase the number of helpings of salad they report eating. His work takes us a little further, too, in suggesting that ambivalent feelings have different degrees of force at different stages of people's decision-making about dietary change.

There are several well-trodden paths in the general field of en- quiry about changing food choice, particularly when it comes to discussion of food, health and safety. One is to despair of a well- informed public that apparently continues to be unwilling, too weak or too stupid to eat what is advised as good for health, fitness and physical well-being. Another heavily worn path is to berate the mass media for sensationalism about food safety, which links to a third which blames a gullible public for believing everything in the news- papers. Sally Macintyre, John Eldridge and their colleagues (Univer- sity of Glasgow) argue that persistently sticking to these paths is to risk oversimplification and undue selectivity about the evidence. They started off from the conundrum pointed out years ago by Charlie Davison. He remarked that the response to media coverage of food and health was apparently minimal if the item was all about the risk of too much fat and heart disease, but seemingly immediate and drastic if the item was about salmonella in eggs. Macintyre demon- strated that, far from being passive, the public is more likely to be discriminating and thoughtful about media output. She showed too that, in contrast to 'healthy eating', which is more commonly dealt with by the features sections of the newspapers, so-called scares about food safety fall into the fiefdom of news/current affairs editors when- ever journalistic suspicions of 'cover up' are aroused.

Mongolian restaurants? Cuban cafes? The nation is ethnically diverse and so too is its diet. With this in mind, Rory Williams (Uni- versity of Glasgow) and his team tackled the unexpected facts that South Asians and Italians in Britain have, respectively, high and low levels of coronary heart disease. Both groups originate from a peasant-based economy. But it might be expected that South Asians would be less influenced by the 'majority culture' and so would have preserved the benefit of the low-fat diet of such economies more completely. These are, however, also economies in which women may specialise more exclusively in household roles and food preparation, and where there may have been a history of food scarcity, both of which may predispose migrants to view elaborate cookery and hospitality and large body shapes as signs of success.

Among his conclusions are the salutary reminders that minority communities have very different diet and exercise patterns, and, further, that these vary between migrant and the British-born members. Health promotion efforts need to be devised accordingly. The retention of healthy eating patterns in Italian migrants suggests that cultural factors can be harnessed to encourage and preserve Mediterranean diets. But where hospitality conventions are strong, substitution of ingredients is the most promising health strategy, and exploration of possibilities should be encouraged in the South Asian and wider food retail industry.

No matter how well equipped people are with information, no matter how low their ambivalence score or how eager they are to adopt a nutritionally advised diet, they cannot make changes if they are hemmed in by other constraints. Financial constraints – low income and high prices – represent obvious limits. Selecting a particular corner of the market that has noticeably changed over the last twenty years and more, Trevor Young and his colleagues (Manchester University) mounted a short study into the economics of the decline in the sales of meat. Yes, more people proclaim they are becoming vegetarian and that no longer signifies their 'lifestyle' is 'alternative'. But perhaps there is something far more basic going on, like changes in meat prices and shifts in income. Young found sure signs of other reasons besides cost for the decline in meat sales. Those who have steadily given up buying meat are younger householders who are in employment, have more educational qualifications and have no dependent children at home. Those who have not only continued buying meat but spend more on it than others who have also kept on buying it, are not just likely to be older, but also to own a freezer and tend to live in metropolitan areas.

All of which ties in to Ben Fine and his colleagues' work (School of Oriental and African Studies), which, departing somewhat from orthodox economics, starts by confirming that there are distinct patterns of food choice, with food purchases varying systematically according to socio-economic characteristics (age, income, class, etc.). It goes further. For these patterns tend to vary according to the type of food. And this in turn reflects, even depends on, the nature of a separate production chain for each group of foodstuffs, meat, sugar, dairy products or whatever. In these terms, we may better appreciate the irony that purchases of low-fat food products are increasing, even though purchases of cream and high-fat dairy products are not decreasing but remaining steady.

Examining the nature of the food supply was picked up in the second phase of the programme's work, drawing further attention not only to the manner in which suppliers create a range from which the public selects, but also to the remarkable changes in the structure of the food supply during the 1990s. Moreover, faced with growing consumer awareness, governments at the national and European level have sought to reshape the ways in which food standards are regulated. A nationalised system of food regulation is now in place, based on a more consistent system of hazard analysis, implemented at local authority level. Preliminary findings from the study run by Terry Marsden and his team (University of Wales, Cardiff) show that although this system is indeed applied throughout the retailing sector, the Environmental Health and Trading Standards officers 'on the ground' have developed differential patterns of regulatory practice. With the big supermarkets, officers act as external auditors of quality control. This is because these 'superleague' retailers have become increasingly responsible for their own regulation. But with the more diffuse independent sector, officers are advisers and educators, striving to maintain baseline standards.

It must be emphasised that while none of the research I have described denies that there are economic constraints sometimes shaping people's food choices, it also demonstrates that the financial is not the only limit to 'choice'. The word choice in the present context can be deceptive. It is not neutral. It can mould analytic thinking about what people eat in terms of little more than the consequence of individual decisions, autonomously expressing some desire, like or dislike. This way of thinking, it should be noted, is enjoying widespread currency in industrial sectors and much public health discussion. Of course, the reason why someone eats something may appropriately be accounted for in terms of personal likes or dislikes. But to be sure that it can safely be explained in this manner, other possibilities – the collective, the cultural – have to be ruled out on the basis of evidence rather than by dint of merely being overlooked.

Threaded through the programme's findings are example after example of social, non-financial constraints on food choice. Alan Warde and Lydia Martens's (Lancaster University) survey revealed an intriguing instance. More than half of their 1,001 city-dwelling respondents claimed to have had no say in where they went the last time they ate out – their companions decided. And it is not as if eating out was a rarity; excluding holidays and workplace eating, this sample of people went out for a meal of some kind on average once every three weeks. Again, Marlene Morrison and Bob Burgess's (University of Warwick) detailed ethnographic study of four schools found that the essential organisational requirements of keeping the day's activities on schedule meant that the watchword in the dinner hour had to be 'eat up', hurrying children through to the playground to let the second lunch sitting start on time. Stopping to use the occasion to encourage children to gain some informed understanding about what they should eat had to compete with this and other exigencies of school life. As a result, a wedge was driven between the educational commitment to 'healthy eating' and the reality of school-based eating.

Overall, then, 'The nation's diet' findings both confirm predictions and open out new lines of enquiry. They also provide a better informed, social scientific basis for tracking quite why we eat what we do.

Further reading

Murcott, Anne (ed.), *The Nation's Diet: The Social Science of Food Choice*, Longman, forthcoming.

The programme's publications: listed on its web page http://www.sbu.ac.uk/~natdi.

The prawn cocktail ritual

Alan Warde and Lydia Martens

No subject that we had previously researched was ever found so immediately fascinating in casual conversation. Even divulging the topic of our research was enough to raise a smile: dining out. And no, we were not allowed to use participant observation methods! A study not only about food but also mostly about pleasure is quite a departure for social scientists, who are usually more concerned with the sources of misery and suffering.

Never before had so many people been convinced that they already knew the answers before we told them. What proportion of household food expenditure does the average British household devote to eating out? How often do people eat out? What proportion of the population has not visited a restaurant specialising in ethnic cuisine in the last year? Please estimate before reading on . . .

At the outset of our investigation there was almost no systematic social scientific research on the nature and experience of eating out. After the project began, the National Food Survey reported for the first time in some detail, but, previously, only inaccessible market research reports and occasional historically oriented campaigning books by food connoisseurs reflected on eating away from home. Yet, as a proportion of food expenditure, spending on meals out increased from about 10 per cent to about 21 per cent between 1960 and 1993, equivalent to between 3 and 4 per cent of all household expenditure.

In autumn 1994 we conducted in-depth interviews in thirty households in and around Preston. Then, in April 1995, 1,001 people aged between 16 and 65 were interviewed in three cities in England – London, Bristol and Preston. We asked questions about the frequency with which interviewees ate out, the types of outlet visited and their attitudes to eating out; we also went into quite a lot of detail about what they actually ate.

Meals eaten out, either on commercial premises or in someone else's home, were the focus of our investigations. Excluding holidays and eating at the workplace, on average the respondents to the survey ate a main meal in a pub, restaurant, café or similar establishment about once every three weeks. We found that 21 per cent ate out at least once a week and 7 per cent claimed never to eat out. Frequency of eating at someone else's home was about the same, except that a much larger proportion of people (20 per cent) never did so. People who ate out often were likely to have a high household income, be highly educated, younger and single. Housewives were unlikely to eat out often.

Sociologists have often commented on the way that social status is registered by means of consumption. Style of life is part of a system of reputation, wherein definitions of good taste result in members of different social classes systematically picking some items in preference to others. Some tastes are more prestigious than others. The survey offered evidence of this phenomenon because different social groups chose different eateries.

A marked proportion of people in our survey avoided ethnic restaurants altogether: 48 per cent had never eaten in such a restaurant in the previous year, while 27 per cent said they had never eaten an ethnic take-away. The factors associated with liking ethnic food suggest that it carries a certain level of class-based cultural distinction. Customers of ethnic restaurants were particularly likely to have higher incomes, to live in London, to have qualifications from higher education institutions, to have attended private school, to have a professional or managerial occupation and to have a middle-class father. Familiarity with ethnic cuisine seems to be a contemporary mark of refinement.

We also uncovered a 'metropolitan mode' of dining out, with people eating out most frequently in London, where the range of venues visited was also more diverse. Whereas in the two provincial cities around 40 per cent of respondents ate their last main meal out in a pub, that was the case for only 10 per cent of Londoners.

Though partly a function of the distinctive social and household composition of the capital, the peculiarity of the metropolitan mode is sufficient to justify a warning – beware of the generalisations of food journalists based in London!

The sparse analytic literature in this area tends to be highly critical – condemning restaurants for the quality of the food they serve, for the standardisation accompanying mass-production techniques and for being oppressively inauthentic contexts for social interaction. By contrast, one remarkable feature of our survey of English urban populations was the great sense of pleasure and satisfaction that people claim to derive from eating out. Of these respondents, 82 per cent agreed with the proposition 'I always enjoy myself when I eat out', with only 7 per cent disagreeing. Aspects of sociability were the most likely to be pleasing, with over 95 per cent of people saying they liked both the company and the conversation the last time they ate out. But 94 per cent said they liked the food, 87 per cent the service, and the same proportion thought they had received value for money.

Almost everyone considers eating out to be special – with some people even saying that they would not want to eat out more often because it would lose this particular appeal. Eating out is not yet routine, and perhaps it would be surprising if the expectation was not one of potential pleasure. If a person makes a special journey, invests discretionary income in order to eat a substantial meal, on a special occasion, in the company of others and not involving personal toil, then he or she might anticipate physical and emotional gratification. Whether the expectation is so high that diners become reluctant to admit disappointment is uncertain, but our research suggests justifiable anticipation.

Certainly, our qualitative interviews revealed more evidence of critical reflection, though rarely were the reservations, even in situations where something went grossly wrong, grave enough to lead interviewees to deny that they enjoyed the occasion. Thus, one interviewee reported a 'bar-type' lunch where the food 'was so salty I couldn't eat it', 'some had finished their meal before the others were served' and a faulty jukebox had played for fifteen minutes – yet still she said 'we quite enjoyed the meal on the whole'.

Although pleasure was almost universal, the means by which it was achieved varied widely. Some people preferred to stay at home unless the quality of the commercial alternative was of the highest order; others were committed to the pursuit of variety, apparently treating eating out as a perpetual experiment. As one of our interviewees put it, 'every time we go out we tend to like to go somewhere different and try a different meal and things like that. We get a bit of variety.' Yet others seemed to pay very little attention to the food at all, the social event being the most important part of the experience.

But why do people eat out? This wasn't a question, we discovered, with one simple answer. Reasons behind decisions to eat out are complex. It is not merely a matter of ability to pay or degree of convenience, important though these factors are. It is also a matter of the texture of social relationships in the home, familial perceptions of treats and luxuries, and sets of values and judgements about food and eating in public.

The extraordinary levels of satisfaction with commercial provision which we found were yet surpassed by enthusiasm about invitations to eat at someone else's home. Comparative evaluations of public and private outings were primarily couched in terms of the difference between the formality of a public occasion and the possibility of being more relaxed in the company of friends in private. Despite the shift of restaurant service towards greater familiarity and friendliness, most people sought to avoid feeling uncomfortable in restaurants they considered too formal. However, the threshold of formality varied enormously between interviewees, with the young working class having the lowest levels of tolerance for formal atmospheres.

While eating out is good for the psyche it may be less beneficial for the waistline. Probably because they consider eating out to be special, people suspend normal restrictions governing food consumption. Over 40 per cent of respondents to the survey agreed with statements like: 'When I eat out I like to eat more than I do at home' and 'I am not as concerned with the healthiness of the food served when I eat out.' Differences between men and women in those attitudes were insignificant and in other respects there were greater similarities than might have been anticipated. For instance, men made up a third of the numbers expressing concern about weight, while 40 per cent of the vegetarians in our sample were male. Nevertheless there were some differences in food taste: men liked red meats, while women chose fish and chicken as main courses. Women were particularly likely to want to eat out often.

The range of food eaten was extensive. The most popular dinner menu was prawn cocktail for starters, then roast meat, peas, carrots and chips, with gâteau to follow. Roast meat was served when being entertained at someone's home on 40 per cent of occasions; pasta and curry dishes each appeared on less than 10 per cent of plates. While there was more diversity of main courses in the commercial sphere, steak was the most popular single dish.

We were unable to corroborate the hypothesis that the nature of the domestic division of labour would influence the decision to eat out. We had initially speculated that it might be members of those households where men had to cook regularly who would go out most often! But this was not so. Many aspects of household organisation influence people's decision to eat out, including the employment patterns of household members, the presence of children, the current state of personal relationships, the appeal of other leisure activities and the character of domestic decision-taking in the food field. But the gendered division of labour within the household is not of direct causal significance, partly because food preparation continues to be overwhelmingly women's work.

One intriguing feature of the survey was how little control individuals had over the decision about whether to eat out because of the tendency to eat in company. Only 45 per cent of respondents claimed to have been involved in deciding the last time they ate out. Nor need one be consulted about where to eat: to the question 'Did you have any say in the decision to eat there?' 20 per cent said 'No'. While popular impressions of eating out are couched in terms of consumer choice, in fact freedom is circumscribed. Availability of resources, systemic inequalities of power in decision-making, shared cultural and aesthetic judgements, and views of what it is appropriate to do in given situations, all constrain the individual even in this, one of the apparently most discretionary of consumer activities. As sociologists are inclined to observe, the rewards associated with social participation often outweigh personal inclinations. Sometimes, for the sake of companionship, you just must have a prawn cocktail.

Further reading

Beardsworth, Alan and Keil, Teresa, *Sociology on the Menu: An Invitation to the Study of Food and Society*, Routledge, London, 1997.
Finkelstein, Joanne, *Dining Out: A Sociology of Modern Manners*, Polity Press, Cambridge, 1989.
Mennell, Steven, *All Manners of Food: Eating and Taste in England and France from the Middle Ages to the Present*, Blackwell, Oxford, 1985.

Ask the family

Roger Dickinson and Simon Leader

For some time there has been a tendency for journalists and social commentators to announce (and lament) the decline of the family meal, and with it the decline of the family. 'The family started falling to pieces in 1962', wrote Matthew Fort (*Observer*, 10 November

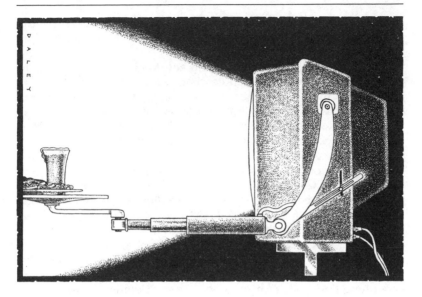

1996). 'That was the year Batchelors launched the Vesta range of Ambient Ready meals, the descendants of which now cram fridges and freezers all over the country.' One reason for the success of convenience foods, Fort argues, is that they have given us more time to watch television, but this means that we have less time for, and are less inclined to keep up with, the tradition of the family meal as a time when everyone in the household shares not only food but also conversation.

A few months earlier in *The Times* (17 June 1996), Roger Scruton was warning us:

> People are acquiring the habit of eating distractedly before a television screen, replenishing their bodies in the street, or walking around their workplace with a sandwich in their hands. This means that the most important moment of social renewal – on which families depend for their inner self-confidence, and on which serious friendships are built – is of increasingly marginal significance . . .
>
> [Consider] the traditional Chinese meal, in which the family and guests sit around a single dish, lifting small portions into their mouths. The communal dish forbids both gluttony and faddishness. The focus here is on hospitality and conversation, while the body and its needs are hidden from view. Such meals are spiritual achievements and occasions of social renewal. Contrast them with the snatched meals in an American diner, in which conversation barely exists, and the

silence is filled by mindless pop music, and you will understand the danger to which young people in our society are now exposed.

The link between television, eating and family decline was made explicit more recently by Nicholas Roe, who, writing in the *Independent* reported: 'A survey for market analysts Key Note recently found that two-thirds of Britons eat their evening meal in front of the television and the trend is increasing. The family meal is dying on its sofas. All those end-of-day catch-ups; all that witty banter. Gone.' (25 September 1997).

It's a bleak picture. Between them, television and convenience foods seem to have brought the family to its knees. Can this really be true? Is the fabric of social life really so flimsy? The study of social life being the province of sociologists, you would expect them to have some answers to these questions. They do, but, and perhaps this is predictable, they don't all agree. Often, as in Nicholas Roe's case, popular pronouncements on our eating habits are triggered by the publication of market research data, whose details are sketchy, and whose designs are, at least for some sociologists, ourselves included, methodologically dubious. It should be said, however, that not all sociologists are immune to the attractions of the snap-shot analyses of marketeers. Nearly twenty years ago, for example, the French sociologist Claude Fischler, weighing the evidence from a marketing survey of American eating habits, announced the decline of the organised, ritualised meal in Western societies. The finding that American urban middle-class families could have as many as twenty 'food contacts' a day led Fischler to conclude that the increase in 'snacking and nibbling' was ushering in the 'empire of snacks'. 'Meals,' he wrote, 'are being increasingly eroded by or reduced to snacks. Eating is becoming less of a social, and more of a strictly individual practice.'

As the British sociologist Roy C. Wood has remarked, even by sociologists' standards, this was a breathtaking generalisation, and Fischler's claims led to a flurry of academic research on the family meal which has largely concluded that, despite an increase in the consumption of snack foods, the family meal is still alive and well. Meals remain the most common and most important form of food consumption.

But that is not to say they haven't changed. The methods of food preservation and preparation and the content of the family meal have undergone considerable change since the end of the Second World War. Although detailed sociological evidence of this is lacking, it is clear that domestic technologies – the fridge, the freezer, the microwave oven – the improved quality, increased quantities and wider availability of foods, the promotion of pre-cooked and packaged convenience foods have all altered what we eat and how we cook it.

There has also been a growth in eating out – meals eaten outside the home are a significant part of life for a large segment (though probably still a minority) of the British population today. There is no doubt that, as with snacks, there has been an increase in the consumption of processed foods and this has generally made food preparation easier. Although again there is little reliable research evidence, this trend seems likely to result in more family members being able to take on some of the burden of meal-making. This may lead to increased individualisation in cooking and eating, with people able to take greater responsibility for their own food choices and meal preferences because they are less reliant on the cooking skills of a (most often) wife or mother for their meals. One result might be that the communal dish begins to decline as individuals produce their own meals. Another possibility, suggested by some research, is that variations are created around the main theme – substituting pasta for rice, for example, or oven chips for microwaved jacket potatoes – so that individuals making changes can still eat together with the rest of the family.

In one aspect of his analysis, then, Roger Scruton may be correct. Individualised eating – eating according to individual tastes and preferences – may be on the increase. But how important is this in terms of the continued existence of a family meal? Is it the sharing of the particular components of a meal that is important or is it the sharing of space and time? Most of us do not feel the urge to choose the same menu items as our fellow diners when we eat out; the meal is fundamentally a social occasion. And although eating out may be more and more popular, does this necessarily mean that the meal out is not taken as a family? All those visits to McDonald's, the packed 'family' rooms in the pub at Sunday lunch time? These are surely more often than not family events.

Significant changes in content and methods of preparation should not be taken to be an indication of a corresponding change in the meal as an event. The meal today may not conform to the image frequently conjured up in popular commentary, but it does still exist and it still has social meaning and significance for those who take part in it. Several studies confirm this. Nickie Charles and Marion Kerr's survey of two hundred families in the north of England in the mid-1980s, for example, showed that, regardless of social-class variations, most people ate three meals a day and at least one of those was a family meal. Interviews with women from these families showed further how a 'proper meal' at home contributed to their sense of being members of, and responsible for the maintenance of a 'proper family'.

We shouldn't forget, of course, that for a large number of families, income, or lack of it, is a powerful structuring force on family organisation. This is especially so in the case of food and eating. The opportunities for individuality in food content and food preparation are still only open to the relatively well off. Research carried out in the East Midlands and published in 1994 by Barbara Dobson and her colleagues found evidence that many low-income households eat together simply because it is more economical to do so.

Perhaps the most significant post-war change from the point of view of the family has been in the role of women. In several respects women's changing roles have had a profound impact on the social organisation of the household. Sociologists' interest in these changing roles has led to research on the division of labour in the home, which shows that the major roles that continue to be associated with women rather than men are shopping for food and cooking. This fact tells us a great deal about the state of the contemporary meal and its status in the home. Several studies have shown that the home is both the site of social and physical renewal and the site of relations of power and control. Although meals obviously have a nutritional dimension (those involved in hard physical work or who work long hours, infants and young children are all perceived to have particular nutritional needs which must be met), they also have a social dimension.

The tasks of shopping for food and preparing meals generally follow the divisions of gender. In a seminal study carried out in the early 1980s, Anne Murcott's research on young mothers in South Wales showed how the 'cooked dinner' exerts a form of control in the home and, because men generally determine the contents of the meal (through the expression of tastes and preferences), the cooked dinner is symbolic of unequal gender roles. 'The cooked dinner', argues Murcott, 'symbolises the home, a husband's relation to it, his wife's place in it and their relationship to one another.'

This idea was echoed in later research carried out in Chicago by the American sociologist Marjorie DeVault and published in 1991. She found that in some circumstances food consumption in the form of the family meal serves to 'socially construct' – that is, in a sense, to produce – the family and cement the relationships within it. Families come to maintain their identity as families by eating together. Again, in DeVault's study, the burden of meal-making fell mostly to women. For them, 'feeding the family' meant two things: not only providing nourishment and satisfying their partner's and children's tastes, but also maintaining the family unit – keeping the family together.

Sociological research on family eating patterns shows, then, that one reason for the resilience of the 'cooked dinner' for the family is its symbolic value. Despite the developments in domestic technologies and convenience foods, the family meal persists because it is an event which brings the family together. This is also evident from the research we carried out recently among children and families in Leicester. Our data reveals a pattern of differing family arrangements, influenced very much by the age of the children in the household. Families with older children, as well as families with mothers in paid work, were less likely to eat together as a family every day than those containing younger children and a single breadwinner. For the older families, evening meals on weekdays would involve, perhaps, only one parent with the children, or the out-of-school activities of different children would mean staggered meal times. For younger families, eating together was the favoured option simply because it was the most practical. In some households, evening meals might be eaten in front of the television, or at least with the television within earshot (not always eyeshot). But eating together was evidently important in all cases and the family meal was revered as an essential component in family life, to be enjoyed whenever circumstances would allow.

In our survey of 223 children aged between 11 and 18 we found that 52 per cent shared meals with the whole family every day; only 15 per cent said they ate alone. Some 55 per cent said their family usually eat round the table together at evening mealtimes. Our follow-up interviews with families bore this out. Asked if eating together as a family was important to them, one man said: 'Very important, yes, it's fundamental . . .' His wife added, 'We can't [always] do that during school time, but we do eat, say, on Fridays and Saturdays and Sundays and any time when it's holidays or anything, we always eat together.' Another mother said, 'Yes, we've always had family meals, right from babies they've had sort of meals with us and they've mostly ate what we eat. We've always encouraged them to have what I would class as proper dinners, meat and two veg type dinners . . .'

The social aspect of the occasion was stressed more often than not in these interviews. For one couple, the content of the meal was the least important factor in eating together. The father said, 'I think you can have a good meal with bad food, but you can't have a good meal without good company . . . so I think the meal aspect is very important and the food is usually, that's irrelevant to the event.' His wife agreed: 'Yes, I think it's a time when you gather together to talk about things.' One father, whose job meant that he was often home too late to join in with the family meal during the week, told

us how he frequently brought take-away meals home with him instead, but would always buy a little more than he could eat so that
he could share his meal with his children. 'I like to get something a
little extra, you know, that they'll like, so that they can join in.'

As we have seen, the supposed decline of the family meal is commonly linked in the minds of pundits with what they perceive in the
great mass of the public as an unhealthy fondness for television.
Television-viewing – often characterised as the quintessential un-
sociable (if not anti-social) pastime, the destroyer of conversation –
has contributed significantly, it is claimed, not only to the decline of
the family meal, but also, it is implied, to the break-up of communal
living and the loosening of family ties. One of our research aims was
to see how far television played a part in shaping people's food
choices and eating habits. Were they linked in any way? Were young
people being subjected to powerful messages of unhealthy and un-
sociable eating practices, and, more importantly, were they succumbing to them? To explore this we analysed a two-week sample of
peak-time television. Our sample included programmes as well as
adverts. Previous research on food on British television has concentrated on advertising only, ignoring the fact that food and eating
are featured in programmes as well – in news and current affairs
programmes, consumer/advice programmes, as well as in drama, comedy and soap opera and, of course, in cookery programmes (which
currently account for fifteen hours of British television's total weekly
output).

Our analysis showed that television creates a strong impression
that eating is something most people do alone. In fact more than 60
per cent of all the eating scenes we analysed in programmes and
advertisements contained a lone eater, and in more than 50 per cent
of cases the food being eaten could be categorised as a snack rather
than a meal. On television the family meal seems to be in decline, but,
as we have shown, our findings from our interviews with families
indicate that the reality – at least for those households containing
children aged between 11 and 18 – is rather different. Eating is a
shared social activity which parents and children value highly. Our
research leads us to conclude that what people see on television has
no simple connection with the pattern of family activity.

The current and probable long-term impact of the trend towards
individualised eating on household eating patterns is likely to be the
focus of several research studies in the future, as sociologists turn
their attention to the minutiae of household food habits. But, given
the views of Matthew Fort et al., perhaps we also need research into
why it is that journalists and commentators perceive a decline in
family eating. Are they affected by what they see on television in a

way that the people in our study seem not to have been, or could it simply be that they are generalising from their own experience? If they are, then, given the contrast with the experiences documented in our and other sociological studies of household eating patterns, the case for a sociology of the eating habits and domestic organisation of the metropolitan middle class, with special reference to that most important segment of it – those in the world of media punditry – seems to be a strong one.

Further reading

Beardsworth, Alan and Keil, Teresa, *Sociology on the Menu. An Invitation to the Study of Food and Society*, Routledge, London, 1997.

Mennell, Steven, Murcott, Anne and Van Otterloo, Anneke H., *The Sociology of Food. Eating, Diet and Culture*, Sage Publications, London, 1992.

Wood, Roy C., *The Sociology of the Meal*, Edinburgh University Press, Edinburgh, 1995.

Comfort food

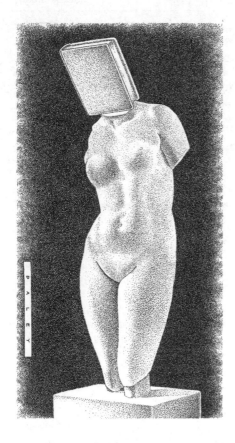

Interpreting starvation

Susie Orbach

Freud's psychoanalysis was a sumptuous affair. The cases that he first wrote about in *Studies on Hysteria* are stories in which mysterious physical paralyses with no explicable organic basis are unravelled and subsequently treated, restoring to the patient enigmatically lost aspects of themselves. It was Freud's great contribution to link an understanding of body and mind, psyche and soma and to insist, against the general current of nineteenth-century medicine, that hysteria was both a psychical and a physical event. For Freud this was not just a theoretical proposition. It is clear from his writing and from his reminiscences that his great empathy for his patients led him to try to enter into their symptomatology: to get the measure of it so that his interpretations, his understanding of the meaning of the symptom, the hysterical phenomenon, could come from an engagement with that hysteria.

By the post-Second World War period, psychoanalysis, cleaned up and sanitised in the United States and masquerading as ego psychology, and in Britain, in its Kleinian invocation, becoming much more a mentalist discourse, loses its sensual understanding. It becomes curiously dislocated from the body. To be sure, bodily distress, particularly sexual, is discussed, but this becomes in terms of symbols rather than through an active engagement with what bodily states feel like and engender. Although analysts who work with children, notably Winnicott, capture in their writing something tactile and sensual about the relationship between psyche and soma, this is rare, and British and North American analysis rushes forward at a fast mentalist clip, subsuming physical symptoms, physical practices, unusual or ritualised sexual practices into a schema where what is important to psychoanalysis are theories of the mind and the elevation of meaning and symbol at the expense of the body as the means of understanding and communicating with patients.

So how, then, has psychoanalysis dealt with a rush of symptoms which cluster around eating? Anorexia – the refusal to eat; bulimia – uncontrollable eating followed by purging; compulsive eating – eating without regard to physiological hunger? How has it addressed patients with eating problems? With notable exceptions and to the detriment of many who suffer with such distress, psychoanalysis has tended to see the eating problem as subsidiary to, rather than centrally expressive of, the psychological life of the individual. It has either trivialised the problem or expected it to go away with the right doses of interpretation, directed not so much at the eating *per se* as at the problem the eating is assumed to disguise. Until recently, for example, a psychoanalytic reading of compulsive eating would call for the interpretation of unresolved oedipal feelings or of anorexia nervosa as a refusal to accept female sexuality. Such interpretations lost much of their validity because they bypassed listening to the patient in favour of relying upon a construct: the woman is fat, therefore she wants the father's child. The woman is thin, she refuses a female rounded body, therefore she is pre-oedipally arrested. Absurd and crude as such interpretations sound, they encapsulate the kind of understandings that were previously available.

Part of the problem, of course, is that psychotherapists were unable to listen to their patients' despair about eating or not eating, or their obsession about food and about their body, without immediately translating the language of food and eating into something else, almost before it had been grappled with and discovered in its own terms. The vitality that informed Freud and the early psycho-analytic pioneers, and which gave birth to the practice of interpret-ing the unconscious, has become both reified and ossified. Instead of interpretation being part of a *process* of understanding and engage-ment with the lived experience of the patients, it now became a *thing*, a set of *a priori* formulations handed to the patient which could leave her or him painfully marooned with their pain.

This diversion of the patient's experience around food as though it were only valid as a metaphor has intrigued me. It is as though the actuality and the materiality of food, and by inference the materiality of the body, flesh, digestion, evacuation and its processes, are some-how disturbing and unseemly – an unfit subject for analysis. Perhaps thinking about such processes engenders discomfort in the therapist. Perhaps imagining oneself into the experience of an individual whose eating is disordered or chaotic is disturbing or incomprehensible. Perhaps entering into a dialogue about the eating practices of an indi-vidual is too private, more private than the revelation of a patient's sexual life.

But perhaps, above all such considerations, discourse about eating is often not engaged with by practitioners because of the pain it arouses both in the analysand and analyst. Perhaps what is exposed is so devastating, so excruciating, so pitiful that it becomes almost too much to bear. The eating or non-eating experiences of the patient and their manifold experiences of their bodies cannot be engaged with because, quite simply, it hurts too much. In place of engage-ment, then, interpretation – which is really nothing more than a particular kind of conjecture – is substituted. Patients and their symp-toms are 'read' as text; the body becomes an almost literary con-struction, as opposed to the problematic place in which the individual lives and breathes.

Paradoxically, this reading of the patient's body as text, or the reading of the symptoms of anorexia, bulimia or compulsive eating as symbol, were born out of work done in the 1970s on eating prob-lems by gender-conscious psychoanalytic clinicians engaging with patients with eating problems. The rapid explosion of such problems spawned the dissemination of the understandings gathered from patients whose eating was disordered, chaotic or disturbing to them-selves. The rich and graphic plethora of meanings were so arresting and evocative that they soon entered the cultural landscape through books such as my own *Fat is a Feminist Issue*, published in 1978. Such meanings then found their way into the Academy, where those in cultural studies playing with themes coalescing around gender, the body, disguise and revelation seized on them as a new literary form. It wasn't long before this reading then fed back into psychoanalysis itself, unwittingly, further devaluing thinking about the patient's actual experience and instead *reading* the action of eating or not eating as entirely symbolic and performative.

But, to backtrack, when I started work as a psychotherapist in the very early 1970s, it became both imperative and impossible to ignore the place of eating problems in the psychological life of many of the individuals, mainly women, that I was seeing. It was as though there was an unacknowledged or secret epidemic eating at the bodies, hearts and minds of women of all ages. Indeed, so unrecognised was this epidemic and yet so widespread that it was almost as though it were an aspect of being female, part of what initiates one into adult femininity. The women I was seeing took it for granted that they should be obsessed about their body size and distressed about their eating. It was simply a fact of life. Worse than that even, they felt help-less in the face of such preoccupations, making talking about them in any depth pointless. The only solution was to find a magical cure.

When, instead of concurring with such a stance, I paid attention to what they said about their eating and their bodies, it was as though I was listening to something between a code and a *patois*: a shortcut language used to explain something both intimate and social about how they conceived of their bodies, the meaning of food in their daily lives and a way to communicate about emotions. 'I'm fat' was not simply a statement about body size and the relationship between adipose tissue and muscle. Rather, I was to understand by it the myriad of culturally endowed meanings of the term 'fat'. I was not meant to question it, to ask the women (or myself) why or how they believed what they believed, I was not supposed to see the obsession with food as a way in which femininity is constructed in our culture and I was not to understand it, in the first instance, as anything but a negative judgement. Simultaneously I was supposed to know, without in any way drawing attention to it, that it stood for the expression of often profound emotional distress. 'I'm fat' could never be accompanied by 'I'm feeling good, content, well'. It might mean 'I'm full of self hate', it might mean 'I'm miserable', it might mean 'I'm needy', it might mean 'I'm in difficulty'.

As a psychotherapist, I had the distinct feeling that to ask what 'I'm fat' meant would be to breach something taken for granted, perhaps even to seem to expose an ignorance on my part that could engender distrust from the patient, indicating that I must indeed be very weird not to understand such a simple declaration. On the other hand, disconcerting as I recognised such a question might be, I also thought it would be ultimately useful and potentially liberating. It might allow for a different kind of language, one other than the repetitive refrain of fat and thin, eating and not eating. It might allow women to express through words rather than through concealed actions something more direct about their experience.

In posing the question and refusing to accede to the negative aspect of the statement 'I'm fat', or indeed to accede to the positive attribution that 'I've lost weight' was expected to evoke, I realised I was up against a formidable taboo. It was as though I was asking the individual to reorientate themselves in some profound way. But being located in psychoanalysis, a discipline so used to deconstructing what it hears, and being concerned that we needed to do more than simply accede, I did ask, and I did want to know what the individual meaning(s) of 'I'm fat' could be and why the idiom of food and body size was so ubiquitous, so unquestioned and so powerful in the lives of the women I was seeing. In order to comprehend that, not just at the level of symbol, I needed to enter into the experience of food and of eating for the women troubled by it. I needed to know, smell, feel, connect with the texture of their eating and non-eating episodes: the binges and the purges, the evacuation of what had been taken in but could not be held inside.

In her book *Female Desire: Women's Sexuality Today* (Paladin, 1984), Ros Coward made the point that pictures of beautifully prepared food are like pornography for women. They show the finished product over which we slave and then long for (because women are too conflicted to eat in a straightforward manner) without recourse to the labour process that has created it. I needed to go further than the details of the preparation into the emotional distress that made the preparing of food for others, and feeling content that they are fed, one kind of act, while preparing food for oneself and ingesting it quite another. I needed to look at that phenomenon in itself: how it was that eating was fused with guilt when performed by the woman herself, but could bring her and others pleasure when she prepared food for others. I needed, too, to understand why, what and how it felt for an individual to be gravitating towards food when not physically hungry or refusing it when starving. What's going on, physically and psychically when this is occurring?

Before interpretation could be of any value – beyond ensuring the cleverness of the therapist – it was imperative that the details of what an individual felt like before she started a binge, while she was eating compulsively, after she finished eating or, conversely, if she felt unable to eat, needed to emerge, to be held in front of us, not concealed, so that they could be, as it were, ruminated over and digested. In this way the physicality of the experience could be understood so that the divide between the psyche and the soma could be (temporarily) dissolved in the therapy. And, more significantly, the experience for the individual could become a *lived* rather than a split-off experience, one of which they could dare to be conscious rather than one of which, because of shame, self disgust and dissociation, they had little awareness.

One of the achievements of psychotherapy is to make available to the individual the incorporation (by which is meant the taking into oneself both psychically and physically) of that which is a trouble to one but is elusive. Through the recognition of something that has been dismembered, disregarded or split off, either because of repression, shame or extreme hurt, the individual has the possibility to occupy a new psychic space. That which has been discarded is accommodated to revitalising the individual and transforming their self-experience. Thus it is with eating problems. By not being afraid to enter into the details of an individual's eating or non-eating or binging and vomiting, by demonstrating that what may feel initially *verboten* for them – only possible of being enacted rather than held in mind and thought about – is not equally fearful to the therapist, the therapist is able to help the individual enter a conversation with herself about the eating, non-eating, bingeing, purging, a conversation which has the possibility of enabling the individual to connect up with her symptom and in the course of time to make creative links between that which has previously been rendered as somatic.

By endeavouring to enter into the experience with the individual, I am not so much trying to help them confront the actual ingestion of large quantities of food – that interests me little, certainly at the level of censure. The job is rather to help us both find a stance of curiosity and then acceptance towards the actions. With that established, even if it is hard for the individual to believe that she can develop an empathy towards what she regards as so shameful, we can then go on to recognise what the eating or not eating might be about. It is not that I am arguing that eating is devoid of the symbolic: how could it be? But a focus on the symbolic without recourse to actual engagement with the experience of food and eating, fullness and emptiness, for the individual cannot render the experience but symbolic. It can only lead an individual who suffers with an eating problem stranded in the symbolic or the prosaic – both positions are devoid of the texture of a lived experience, the very thing that is required to be restored to the individual if they are to have a life that is not defined by an eating problem.

I would want to argue that as long as analysts and therapists accede to the statements of an individual about body size, food ingestion or food refusal without exploring them, they are leaving the patient in the pre-symbolic, rather as though the arm of Freud's patient, Anna O, were to remain paralysed. The experience of the arm would not be engaged with and the reincorporation of the arm into the body of the person as an arm, rather than as a symbol, would not be effected.

I would also argue that as long as those enamoured by cultural studies valorise the body as the place in which we solely inscribe and fail to understand the human pain, suffering and struggle involved in eating problems, we will simply have modernised our interpretations to fit in with 1990s metaphors. More useful, I suggest, is to use our understandings and our vision and reading of eating problems and body preoccupations as a window into what is so deeply troublesome and problematic for women today, and to restore to psychoanalysis one of its more beautiful endeavours: the attempt to link our psychical and physical elements.

Further reading

Bloom, Carol, Gitter, Andrea, Gutwell, Susan, Kogel, Laura and Zaphiropolous, Lela, *Eating Problems: A Feminist Psychoanalytic Treatment*, Model Basic Books, Harlow, 1995.

Bruch, Hilde, *Eating Disorders: Obesity, Anorexia Nervosa and the Person Within*, Basic Books, New York, 1973.

Orbach, Susie, *Fat is a Feminist Issue*, Paddington Press, London, 1978.

Orbach, Susie, *Hunger Strike: The Anorectic Struggle as a Metaphor for Our Age*, Faber and Faber, London, 1986.

The kitchen revolution

Brian Harrison

King George V thought anyone who refused roast beef on a Sunday could not be an Englishman. In his conservatism about food, as in so much else, he spoke for his subjects. 'As a rule they will refuse even to sample a foreign dish', wrote George Orwell, discussing British working-class attitudes to food in 1944; 'they regard such things as garlic and olive oil with disgust, life is unliveable to them unless they have tea and puddings.' By then the food value of the British diet had been improving for a long time, while the age of physical maturity had been falling for decades. By the 1970s European men reached their maximum height at the age of 17 or 18, whereas fifty years earlier they did not attain it before the age of 26. The advance of birth control meant that there could be more food per person, and fewer wives now sacrificed their food to the male breadwinner. Twentieth-century welfare – school milk, school meals, meals on

wheels – advanced things still further, and in the Second World War national guidance on nutrition was improved and food shared out more equally.

Yet the war did nothing for the variety and quality of British food. The station buffet in the famous wartime film *Brief Encounter* was no cornucopia, and though the government-sponsored British Restaurants were cheap, they were Spartan. The war enhanced British insularity and lowered British expectations of food for long afterwards. 'I despair of English cooking', wrote Harold Nicolson in 1953 after consuming a low-grade meal at a Newbury inn. 'It is no good training the producer; it is the consumer who must be taught to notice when food is lazily cooked. They gave us what they call *Tartelettes de Fruit* – a crumbly piece of shortbread with two cherries and artificial cream.'

Only people now in their sixties can fully appreciate quite how much British food has changed. Our political system has been so successful in securing stability and continuity in government that we are in danger of underestimating the sheer scale of the non-political changes that have occurred in Britain since 1945. The history of food is important among these not just for its own sake, but because it indirectly illuminates a host of political, social and economic changes that straddle the conventional categories of historical study. Perhaps this is why food's history gets neglected: it is everybody's concern but nobody's speciality. Nor has it been helped much by the advance of women's history, given that feminist writers are keen to get women out of the kitchen. So, like the history of furniture or clothing, the history of food tends to be written up by connoisseurs, collectors and practitioners, with only an antiquarian outcome. Perhaps also there's a deeper difficulty. While historians enjoy eating as much as anyone else, food somehow seems a frivolous research topic that fails to enhance the serious and scholarly image they seek. 'There is still a decayed Puritan atmosphere in parts of Britain', wrote the Good Food Club's founder Raymond Postgate in his preface to the *Good Food Guide* for 1969/70. 'It is considered . . . ignoble to concern oneself passionately with the quality of food and wine.' The Good Food Club would, he thought, 'have received respect and consideration from the intelligentsia and the official world if it had called itself something like the Society for the Improvement of Popular Nutrition. But it would also never have got off the ground.' Yet the kitchen revolution that began in Britain in the 1950s, and saw a massive change in the variety of food and the nature of its preparation, is still in progress, and no historian of modern Britain should apologise for analysing what produced it. At least six of the influences upon this kitchen revolution – economic, educational, international, feminist, entrepreneurial and technological – deserve detailed consecutive discussion.

Without post-war affluence, the revolution could never have been launched. The outlook of earlier generations was shaped by scarcity, and the pursuit of the simple life was an important constituent of both Christian and early socialist values. But these austere values declined rapidly in the 1950s, with America setting the pace. Western industrial societies experienced abundance as never before, and each new possession whetted the appetite for more. Nicolson uttered his grumble at Newbury at a time when wartime rationing was already on the way out. Commercial television, that great impulse to consumption, was launched two years later. With the car conveniently waiting in the garage, eating out became more comfortable in the 1950s; in the owner-occupied home, stylish entertaining occurred. Factory-farming was beginning to convert poultry from Christmas luxury into regular standby, and for similar reasons fresh smoked salmon plunged in price in the 1980s, followed by venison in the 1990s. Food – together with houses, televisions and cars – could well have been in Harold Macmillan's mind when he famously claimed in 1957 that 'most of our people have never had it so good'. Television poured forth new ideas on what to eat, how to cook it, how to present it.

Philip Harben launched the first regular televised cookery programme on 1 September 1947. But it was the begowned Fanny Cradock, with her submissive dinner-jacketed husband 'Johnny', who brought 'kitchen magic' (the title of her programme) to the suburban home in the early 1950s, with flowers by Constance Spry. Food and its preparation were harnessed to Britain's class system in a decade that was especially alert to the intricate symbolism of social gradation. The middle classes pioneered the change, carrying their message beyond the relatively affluent south-east into the proletarian traditionalism of the north and west.

A society experiencing such abundant choice needed expert guidance. Since 1945 the impact of adult education has nowhere been more powerful than in food and diet. The paperback *Penguin Cookery Book* was published in 1952 by Bee Nilson, a journalist who had often spoken on BBC cookery programmes, and was an instant success. Its recipes owed much to her husband, a businessman who travelled widely in Europe. In 1957 the American idea of a consumers' association was imported, reinforced by its periodical *Which?*. But it was the English amateur who did most to improve British food standards. The Good Food Club (founded in 1950) consisted of people who enjoyed eating out enough to write down their experiences. Postgate pointed out in the Club's first *Good Food Guide* (1951) that the Club 'exists entirely through the voluntary work of its members, and its continued existence depends upon the thoughtful filling up of the forms to be found at the end of this book'. In its pocket-book-sized earliest versions, the *Guide* surveyed between 700 and 800 establishments and gradually refined the criteria for inclusion. Its direct impact was considerable, but more important was its message, which percolated far beyond its readers: that food and drink are important enhancements of life, and that a pride should be taken in how they are purchased, prepared and served. By the 1960s British pubs were beginning to lose their name for minimal and poor-quality food. The curiously British distinction between pub and restaurant, between drinking and eating, was at last fading away. Mergers between the big brewing, catering and leisure concerns were a natural consequence.

The gourmet's national impact should not be exaggerated. While new attitudes to food fuelled suburbia's social ambitions, conventional attitudes became the resort of populist politicians. On entering 10 Downing Street in 1964 the Wilson family was self-consciously ordinary, and its eating habits were satirised in *Private Eye* (apparently with some truth). R. H. S. Crossman's diary in 1968 records the Wilsons' suspicion that he had thought himself superior ever since spurning their offer of Nescafé instead of real coffee; he also notes the Wilsons' nervous speculation about his likely response to tinned salmon. Edward Heath, like Wilson lower-middle-class in origin, was not personally known for austerity at the table, but as Conservative Prime Minister he none the less wanted to distance his party from 'the unacceptable face of capitalism': from the expense-account 'fringe benefit' lunches that Labour's incomes policies had generated in British boardrooms. And although in the generous lunches provided at the Centre for Policy Studies the Thatcherites 'ate our way to victory' (in Alfred Sherman's phrase) during the late 1970s, Thatcherism grounded the party more overtly on the mass basis of support which it has always enjoyed. Populism at last reached the heart of the party in February 1991, with John Major's widely reported breakfast in a Happy Eater roadside restaurant on the way to a Young Conservative conference in Scarborough. The 19-year-old waiter Gavin Ward described the scene: 'a black Daimler rolled up and a man came in and said, "You might think I am off my trolley, but I've got the Prime Minister here. Is it all right if we come in?" With the bad weather we'd hardly anyone in. I was very surprised. I didn't speak to him, but he asked for some brown sauce.' In 1997 Major was ousted by a Labour leader whose election campaign flourished on his much-discussed appetite for chocolate bars.

If politicians' populism could slow down the transforming impact of affluence and expertise on food, it could not ward off a third important influence on Britain's post-war kitchen revolution: internationalism. In December 1940 Orwell saw the English working class as 'outstanding in their abhorrence of foreign habits'; even when obliged to live abroad for years, he said, 'they refuse either to accustom themselves to foreign food or to learn foreign languages'. Bacon-and-eggs and fish-and-chips were still being widely consumed by British holidaymakers on the Costa Brava in the 1960s, but by then the middle classes had already begun to move on. Hungarian and Polish restaurants had been catering for the small enclaves of Central European immigrants in Britain's big cities since the 1930s, but in the 1950s it was French cookery that took the middle classes by storm. Elizabeth David brought a new cosmopolitan seriousness and even scholarship to cookery with her *Book of Mediterranean Food* in 1950, following up with many more such publications. In the *Good Food Guide's* first edition Postgate saw no reason why British food should be worse than French; herbs, garlic and spices thenceforth enlivened middle-class soups and stews. Vegetables, no longer boiled flavourless, acquired a new glamour, and in the 1980s even became central to the visual impact made by 'nouvelle cuisine'. Sophisticated kitchen shops sprang up, and from this Frenchified, design-conscious world the young Terence Conran launched himself as restaurateur.

The British people were cultivating their Eurostomach long before they joined the Common Market in 1973, and by the 1980s French bakers at last showed signs of toppling the Eccles cake and the bath bun from their pedestals.

These international influences were not exclusively European. Political internationalism through the United Nations disappointed many post-war hopes, but culinary internationalism triumphed after the late 1950s. Central to the process were the many immigrants to Britain: Italian, Spanish, Greek and Cypriot. Their coffee-bars and restaurants opened on to British streets humming with Italian Lambrettas. In the 1950s they provided the sort of unsupervised meeting-place for young people that the Edwardian teashop had earlier provided for emancipated women. And whereas in 1957 there were only 50 Chinese restaurants in the whole of Britain, six years later there were more than 1,400 in England alone, catering for nearly a third of Britain's diners-out. Rice, hitherto used mainly in its short-grained variant for puddings, was revealed to Englishmen in all its savoury dimensions – Patna, long-grain, arborio and fragrant – and during the 1970s Britain's rice imports doubled. Thereafter, tastes from locations ever more exotic made themselves manifest in new restaurants – from Japan to Mexico, from Indo-China to Africa – all backed up by specialist food shops.

Reinforcing internationalism in its transforming impact on British cuisine was feminism. Together with child-rearing, home decoration and beauty care, cookery was incorporated into the very weak inter-war variant of feminism that emphasised the complexity and importance of the housewife's domestic tasks. The unpaid female pseudo-professionalism peddled in inter-war women's magazines encouraged trapped suburban housewives to embrace their kitchen aids as symbols of sophisticated femininity. 'Home cooking can and does enable a woman to express her creative instincts', Crawford and Broadley pronounced in their comprehensive study of *The People's Food* (1938), 'and so achieve a degree of mental satisfaction which other household duties ... do not provide.' Such attitudes, interrupted only temporarily by women's war work, did not give way to the new feminism until after the 1960s. Thereafter, the career woman needed to approach cookery in a new way. Pioneer feminists like Annie Besant, Charlotte Gilman and Sylvia Pankhurst had predicted that women would be liberated through communal cooking and professionalised housework. 'The selection and preparation of food should be in the hands of trained experts', wrote Gilman, 'and woman should stand beside man as the comrade of his soul, not the servant of his body.' She thought women's emancipation would strengthen the demand for public buildings: 'great common libraries and parlors, baths and gymnasia, work-rooms and play rooms, to which both sexes have the same access for the same needs'. Yet the vote was what most Edwardian feminists wanted; few wanted to move on towards challenging the separation of spheres between the sexes. So Gilman's predictions have not been realised. People have chosen to live in owner-occupied, individuated homes, and households are growing steadily smaller.

It is from capitalism, not from socialism, that the pre-packed convenience foods have come. It is the mass retailer, not the domesticated male, who has done most to mitigate what might otherwise have been the disastrous impact of the women-at-work on home cooking. It is not communal living but the individually owned electric cooker that enables the career woman to dish up the meal. The convenience food is nothing new. Pies, tripe, cold cooked meats and bacon and eggs had been the Victorian millgirl's standbys, and it is to the textile districts of the north that we owe fish and chips. What the twentieth century witnessed was simply a broadening out of the market for convenience foods as married woman moved fully into paid work. Between the wars almost every kind of meat, fish, soup and fruit became available in tins, and by 1928 more than a million packets of potato crisps were being sold.

So professionalised preparation of food emerged, not from the socialist utopia's specialisation of function, but from mass retailers whose products the freezer and microwave oven could preserve and prepare at home, as well as from the restaurateurs whom double-income families could increasingly afford to patronise. Americanised ready-to-eat cereals made great strides in Britain during the late 1930s. By the 1960s cereals were ousting porridge, and from 1972 muesli, a European intrusion, made its appearance and the traditional English breakfast was banished to the weekend. Nor had the married woman in paid work much time for the household skills once so prized in a housewife. Bottling fruit and making jam went the way of polished surfaces and open fires. Fewer and fewer men could imitate the Yorkshire miners who still threw any meal not prepared by the wife 'to t' back o' t' fire'. More and more men were taking up cooking themselves. All this undermined the concept of a single synchronised family meal with parents presiding. Kitchen technology freed husband, wife and children to pursue divergent timetables and tastes. By the 1970s Chinese take-aways complemented fish and chips, and the formal dining-room gave way to the cafeteria kitchen. The microwave oven, like the video recorder and the answerphone, brought a new flexibility to life. The main meals now took place at the start and end of the day, whereas morning coffee, lunch and tea went into decline. Breakfast was now more likely to offer fruit juice, cereal and yoghurt than bacon and eggs. As for dinner, it shed the dishes that required suet and dripping, and substituted poultry and fresh vegetables, with London setting the pace for the rest of the United Kingdom.

Behind all this lies a revolution in food retailing pioneered in America, and pushed further in Britain than anywhere else in Europe. The Victorians would have felt quite at home in the food shops of Britain in the 1950s: small concerns managed by the proprietor, who employed assistants well informed about his stock and his customers. Housewives then wanted items weighed out, wrapped, and even delivered to the home. But already the supermarket's pre-packed goods were on the march, filling family dustbins with wrappings and plastic. Shopping slowly ceased to be a personal and almost daily relationship between housewife and shopkeeper. With the advent of Americanised hypermarkets in the 1980s shopping became a car-borne, family-based adventure. Extended shop opening hours packed the aisles of Saturday's food cathedrals with customers, but emptied the aisles of Sunday religion. The family that shopped together stopped together. Sainsbury's tandoori chicken and Marks and Spencer's avocado pears from Israel and plums from Chile promoted new tastes and defied the tyranny of the seasons. Strawberries, once only a summer delicacy, became available all the year round. These hypermarkets were triumphs of co-ordination, pavilions of adult education.

There was still room for the relatively pricey specialist shop and the neighbourhood general store. But the overall outcome was a massive overall concentration of ownership. Between 1960 and 1990 the number of grocery outlets in the United Kingdom fell by two-thirds. The separation of spheres between the sexes persisted, but in a new form. Women, playing a diminishing unpaid role in the kitchen, found a growing role from the 1970s as paid part-time employees in food retailing and catering. Shop interiors, display, health and hygiene kept up with society's rising standards of comfort. Hard floorboards gave way to carpets, and goods moved out from behind the counter towards the customer. The sights and smells of the family grocer's weighings up and the personal service had now long gone, but for many customers (including the shoplifter and the saboteur) the retreat of the shop assistant was a liberation. Besides, the hypermarket could offer what was in effect an enclosed all-sufficing world where almost everything was on offer: recreation for the children, fuel for the car, restaurants for the family and cashpoints for the wherewithal.

New foods required new technologies. Though in absolute terms more was being spent on food, it took up a dwindling proportion of the household income: nearly a third of it between the wars but only a sixth by the 1970s, and its role in the Retail Price Index dwindled after 1962. By contrast, consumer goods (including cookers, freezers and food mixers) took up an ever-rising proportion of household income. The shrewd purchase of food and prevention of its decay had been among the nineteenth-century housewife's leading skills. Norman Tebbit recalled in his memoirs the eagerness of Edmonton's fridge-free stallholders in the 1930s to clear their stocks on a Saturday night, and how 'the bargaining between hard-up customers and stallholders rose in a crescendo as the evening drew on'. But the refrigerator brought all this to an end. With its freezing compartment it made shopping less demanding and less frequent because food was more easily kept fresh.

By 1970 peas in the pod had grown scarce in the shops because four-fifths had already been bought up for freezing or canning. But canned food was now giving way to frozen, and in 1968 John Apthorp founded Bejam to sell food for freezers. Ten years later he had 151 stores, but by then multiple grocery retailers had moved in, and the freezer centre's specialist role became redundant. Households owning refrigerators rose from 60 per cent of the total in 1969 to more than 90 per cent in 1978. By then, the deep-freeze was becoming a necessity, and three years later almost half the nation's households possessed either a deep-freeze or a fridge-freezer. Its impact was less to encourage people to consume new foods than to buy more of the same foods less often. Responsibility for storing food was increasingly transferred from the shop to an enlarged home which could store food bought in bulk. Freezers also fuelled the middle-class fashion of the 1970s for allotments, and by 1979 the urban invasion of the countryside to 'pick your own' accounted for about half Britain's raspberry crop and a quarter of its strawberry crop.

Here again, one consumer good led on to the next, for the freezer fostered new types of cooker. Whereas only 6 per cent of British families owned an electric cooker in 1936, nearly a third owned one by 1961 and nearly a half by 1980. By then the microwave oven was transforming home cooking because it was so good at heating up convenience foods. Launched in the mid-1970s, it took off in the mid-1980s; in 1984 the number purchased doubled within a single year. The British market for microwaves was now the third largest in the world, surpassed only by the United States and Japan. By 1991 more than half the nation's households owned one.

The affluent consumerism so far celebrated in this discussion was not trouble-free, and doctors, humanitarians and environmentalists sounded warning notes. This was not the first time since the industrial revolution that bewilderment resulted from diversity of choice, and by the 1960s people found themselves getting fat and dying from heart attacks. A survey in 1984 revealed that two-fifths of British men and a third of British women were overweight, and politicians were beginning to preach preventive medicine in its dietary dimension. Not for the first time. The Conservative MP Florence Horsbrugh made herself profoundly unpopular with the labour movement in 1936 by urging the nutritional value of carrots and water. Hunger, she said, 'is not widespread in this country . . . What is widespread is the total ignorance of real food values.' Half a century later Edwina Currie ventured on to equally dangerous territory by pointing out that ill-health in the north of England did not stem directly from poverty, unemployment or Conservative policy: people were spending too much on cigarettes, drink, and fish-and-chips.

Controversy raged among nutritionists and doctors on which diet was most healthy. Well-known advertisements of the 1950s were 'drinka pinta milka day' and 'go to work on an egg', but the bugbear of the forthright and influential nutritionist John Yudkin thereafter was sugar, which he pronounced 'pure, white and deadly' (the title of his most famous book). Others turned their fire against fat and alcoholic drink. Fibre and garlic became the rage in the 1980s, and by the 1990s cholesterol was the demon to be fought. By then, the rather English compromise of the 'balanced diet' and the 'healthy lifestyle' was being embraced, and the health-giving virtues of wine were being rediscovered. Perhaps more powerful than medical advice as an influence on diet was the growing preoccupation among women for a lissom figure and among men for a sporting physique. By the mid-1980s health clubs were losing their cranky image and self-help in health was becoming big business. Within high-tech gymnasia 'washboard stomachs' sprang forth miraculously from 'beer bellies'. Whereas the pop stars of the 1960s did little to advance a healthy lifestyle, the sporting heroes of the 1980s were widely emulated. The consumption of fats, milk and eggs went into decline during the 1980s, whereas fish, poultry, salad and fresh fruit flourished and the consumption of fruit juice trebled within a decade. White bread at last gave way substantially to brown, and sausage sales plunged.

The new puritanism was reinforced by humanitarians concerned about the exploitation of the workforce or of animals or of both. In the campaign for 'organic' foods – well launched by the 1960s with carcinogenic chemicals and food additives in its sights – medical, humanitarian and environmental motives intertwined. In 1977 Oxfam claimed that Britain must shed the 'steak house mentality' and solve the world's food problem by shifting from meat to cereals and vegetables. By the 1980s moral pressures had become increasingly a fact of business life, and young people were turning vegetarian from a combination of humane and environmental motives. By the 1990s butchers had begun to experience something of the odium incurred by furriers a decade or so earlier, and in 1994 the RSPCA launched its 'freedom food' label in conjunction with two hundred large food producers, hoping to encourage farmers to improve their standards of animal welfare. By 1997 there were three million vegetarians in Britain, of whom a quarter of a million were vegans. Yet, in so far as they lent new dignity to the vegetable, even the vegetarians were making their contribution towards a kitchen revolution which at present shows no sign of ending.

Further reading

Historians have published surprisingly little on the history of food in Britain since 1945, and there is no historical study which links its history with wider social and economic developments during these years. However, Christopher Driver's *The British at Table 1940–1980*, Chatto and Windus, London, 1983, is a useful and pioneering book, and has a valuable historical section.

Savouring the antique

Emily Gowers

Among cuisines of the distant past, Roman food excites an almost morbid interest. Every few years a new book of Roman recipes comes out, and a handful of European restaurants specialise permanently in recreations of dishes like *patina* of fried anchovies or boiled goose *à la Apicius*, as if the hands-on experience of eating provided authentic contact with antiquity. Curiosity is usually mingled with a kind of titillating disgust. Modern eaters find themselves alienated but intrigued by the Romans' bizarre table manners and the less palatable ingredients of their menus: the stuffed Trojan pigs, the sows' wombs, the stuffed parcels of dormice, the feather down the throat.

These days, Roman food also attracts a more sophisticated kind of attention, thanks partly to a glut of foodie novels and films. Audiences who warmed to the quail *sarcophages* of the film *Babette's Feast* or the metamorphosis recipes of *Like Water For Chocolate* will relish the emperor Domitian's black dinner for his senators (funeral food as the theme, and an individual tombstone at each place-setting), or Apuleius' juicy serving-girl gyrating over the sausage in

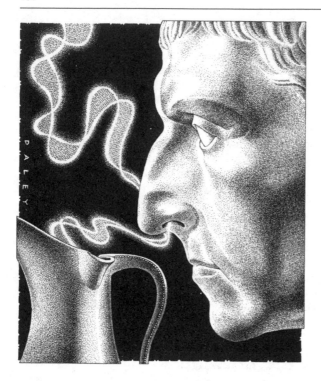

her cooking-pot. However, behind the media excitement lies solid intellectual interest, not just in the basic facts about food but also in food's fundamental cultural importance, its role throughout history as a focus for social, political, sexual and aesthetic manipulation. The Romans, with their highly ritualised meals, their sense of the power of food to influence people and their taste for the macabre, are ready for deeper scrutiny.

Where are the left-overs of Roman food to be found? Archaeology deals in tangible but enigmatic remains: bowls of broken eggs, charred walnuts and long-stale flatbreads fossilised in the fast-food shops of Pompeii; a rubbish-heap of oyster-shells from a military camp; a procession of dishes on a Tunisian mosaic; the outline of dining-couches on a villa floor. Much can be learned from teeth, bones and cooking-pots. But for the tang and bite of ancient food, its power of expression, we are inescapably thrown back on the written legacy.

As it survives, the literature of food is full of gaps and biases. First of all, it represents a minority, the literate elite. Second, most Roman writers had anti-materialist prejudices: not for them the ephemeral glory of being the first man to introduce peacocks or *foie gras* to Rome. Food was considered such a trivial subject that writers actually apologised before discussing topics such as vegetables or pig-farming. Nowhere in the sources – encyclopaedias, medical writing, comedy, satire, historiography, recipe books, table-talk – is there any full-length description of a typical meal or any straightforward description of the pleasures of Roman eating.

This is not only because the handbooks on etiquette and entertaining that did exist have been lost. The old Roman ethos was that food was just fuel for the rugged citizen's body, while the Greek philosophers believed that eating interrupted mental activity. The difference between the popular images of the two civilisations, the Greek symposium and the Roman dinner-party, is the food weighing down the Roman table. None the less, Roman writers did their best to erase that difference, summing up an ideal meal with vague oxymorons like 'the food was chaste but abundant' or 'elegant but simple', and passing on quickly to less material pleasures: recitals, conversation or convivial spirit; or aesthetic backgrounds for eating: picture-galleries, waterfalls, fruit-storerooms, treehouses, even wine-presses filled with the agreeable hum of squabbling workers. In this respect, the literary record reflects the cultural restraints that governed actual consumption: it seems that the Romans tried to compensate for the grosser aspects of eating through ritual purification, 'levitating' on couches, reading or listening to poetry recitals at the table, and forbidding anyone to pick up food that had been dropped on the floor.

On the other hand, descriptions of abnormal meals survive in abundance, split between rustic escapism (Cowper's 'A Roman meal . . . a radish and an egg') and hysterically exaggerated orgies, with not much in between. There is enough material to suggest that the Romans were extremely vocal about food, but vocal in a most selective way. Writers often boast of their own abstemiousness: Seneca breakfasted on bread and figs; Augustus fasted all day, or snacked on grapes and dates. Pleasure in consumption was always the preserve of other people, the kind who lacked control over their bodies. Gastroporn – reading recipe books in bed, or watching rainbow-coloured mullets die at the dinner-table – was for emperors or outrageous gourmets. Drooling cooks, slaves and parasites are confined to comedies set in Greece, though the food they eat is the juicy offal the Romans fetishised. One account of a toddler masticating a grape is uniquely indulgent.

What survives, then, is a strange looking-glass world of food yesterday, food tomorrow, but seldom food today. There are descriptions of floors drenched with sodden garlands and yesterday's wine; the rotting contents of misers' cupboards; an itemised bill for a meal

that was never eaten; overflowing doggy-bags (sows' udders, a pig's
ear, half a mullet, a pigeon dripping with sauce); mottoes for going-
home presents of food; blow-by-blow reminiscences of other
people's filthy dinners; or table-talk which distracts attention from
the real menu with learned discussions about food in Homer or cooks
in Athenian comedy. As for food in prospect, there is medical advice
about what to eat to build up the body or thin the blood; dinner
invitations which mention food with embarrassment; and show-off
recipes speaking of a closed gastronomic world where all the ingredients are on display, but all the quantities are missing.

There are two possible attitudes to the gaps and biases of literature. Among modern historians and archaeologists, the trend has been
to resist the biases and fill the gaps, to peel away the exaggerations
and uncover the eating habits of the average Roman family. A sober
picture has emerged: larks' tongues were a one-off gastronomic
hyperbole, and only the emperor Claudius is reported to have stuck
a feather down his throat. Most ordinary people experienced famine
and lived at subsistence level on a diet more continuous with the
rest of Mediterranean history. This usually involved a cereal base
with something piquant added, occasionally meat – dishes like beans
and bacon, sausage and porridge, bread and olives. This food may
not be central to the surviving literature, but the balance of staple
and relish remained a model of good eating from which dangerous
deviations could be measured.

However, to learn anything about the cultural significance of
ancient food, we are still dependent on the voices of the literate
and affluent. Recurring themes reveal shared cultural preoccupations.
Many meals described by moralists or historians are meals of the
imagination, not meals of documentation; that we have to accept. But
the deeper one probes into the Roman language of food, the more
one can see how the categories used bring in other worlds beyond
the stomach or the dining-room. Writers could not disregard the
power of food to impress, deceive, mark boundaries, set up barriers
or express allegiances. Food, in short, became a focus for Roman self-
definition, socially, and also in relation to the external environment,
other nations and the course of history.

Much of what the Romans wrote about food involves their feelings of discomfort with their own surplus: the vast wealth that poured
into an already fertile country as a result of imperial conquest. Originally that surplus was controlled by the patrician elite, who dis-
pensed bounty from their estates and cemented their social networks
with gestures of hospitality. Increasingly, however, this elite was
eroded and infiltrated by outsiders, who used new material resources
to win away the old dependants. Finally, the emperors emerged

at the top of the pyramid, undermining everyone with their public largesse and infinite powers of consumption. Augustus confused everyone by staging very formal dinners at which he himself turned up late, and by preferring to eat working-class bread and cheese when alone.

'The man with whom I do not dine is a barbarian in my eyes', reads a Pompeian graffito. Yet a dinner invitation did not guarantee equal treatment: often food was distributed according to social rank. It is not surprising, then, that Roman debates about food are bound up with matters of power, hierarchy and distinction, clung to by whose who were included, challenged by those 'barbarians' left at the dining-room door. This led to a degree of moral righteousness and interference in what people ate that is quite unimaginable to us: individuals were free with their criticism, and the state intervened with sumptuary laws designed to stem the conspicuous consumption of luxury foods and restore the proper boundaries between everyday and celebratory eating.

Many Roman writers stood on the margins socially: they were touchy interlopers, displaced aristocrats or quizzical foreigners. Their hostile commentary on social eating was a backlash against the seductions of competitive hospitality and display. The satirist Juvenal, a bona fide Roman displaced by foreign 'scum', uses a variety of tactics: outrage at social divisiveness (a dinner where the host and his friends eat princely fish and fruit, the poor hangers-on scabby apples); outrage at egalitarianism (a consul sharing snack-bar food with coffinmakers, muggers and eunuch priests); and proud defiance (serving his own meal of pure and high-quality country food in the heart of the corrupt city).

A close look at literary language also reveals a set of connections between the city of Rome, the Roman meal and the individual citizen's bodily capacity, all of which were thought to have expanded dangerously from their original compact form. The city was anthropomorphised as a giant maw (Cato called it 'a belly without ears'), with its gates as gullets engulfing the products of the world, vomitoria in its amphitheatres spewing out citizens, and sewers for bowels. Rome had so many steaming underground vents that one visitor compared it to a huge sacrificial animal puffing out its last breath.

Historians of the Roman meal worked on a similar model of continual expansion: the basic three-course meal – (primeval) vegetables, civilised (sacrificial) meat, over-civilised (unnecessary) dessert – became bloated with more courses, more choice and more fringe apparatus. The proverbial expression for the bounds of a meal, *ab ovo usque ad mala* ('from the eggs to the apples'), could now be translated (with a pun on *mala*, apples or bad things): 'from innocent origins to evil – or just desserts'. The old moderation was thought to survive only in the innocent countryside or among uncorrupted tribes, like the Germans, who, according to Tacitus, needed no trimmings or condiments to satisfy their hunger.

Finally, the Roman body seemed to have followed the same lines of progressive corruption and degeneration. One knight was too fat to sit on his horse, and a senator's son needed liposuction. In the past, hard work had created healthy appetites; now stale and under-exercised eaters needed spicy stimulants and sauces, which altered the proper balance between staple and relish. Indigestion, and emetics and vomiting (standard remedies for clearing impurity and excess, now perverted for gastronomic ends), were the enemies of correct bodily functioning. Medical writers recommended spending the day fasting before the main evening meal, with remedies like sweating in the bath or exercising the upper half of the body (with voice practice or military drill) to compensate for over-eating later, which might incidentally lead to violent dreams.

The vocabulary of gluttony, dyspepsia and overflow was also used to draw analogies between the badly functioning digestion and all kinds of social threat and disruption: political ambition, legacy-hunting, adultery ('like taking the food off another man's plate'), racial mixing and so on. Tyranny had strong connections with uncontrolled appetite: potential dynasts like Antony who vomited in public and dined first thing in the morning; and later the emperors, who were accused of all kinds of transgressive eating, from snatching tidbits from sacrificial altars to frequenting snack-bars to eating excrement. Fast-food shops and roadside inns were linked with dangerous egalitarian tendencies which undermined formal eating, and with dishonest marketing (landlords who mixed water with the wine or put eggs and bits of liver in bowls of magnifying water). Three disturbing notions – uncategorisable mixture, impatient appetite and unorganised eating – converged in a notorious mixed seafood dish which looked like pulp or vomit (fish, significantly, was an unpredictable haul which lay outside the categories of social control that applied to farmed cereal or sacrificial meat).

Moralists and satirists had an interest in exposing all the barbarities that polite table manners suppressed (butchery, funerals, decay, poison, inedibility, perverted sacrifice, snatching, brawling and social knifing), as well as the hollowness of display and gastronomic ambition. Here they played on the suspicions and hypochondria that clouded their readers' approach to all external substances. It was not just a reasonable fear of gritty bread or rancid meat. It was also the imaginative ability to see how the same food could be regarded as delicate and enticing in one context, corrupt and abominable in another. *Cena dubia*, a doubtful dinner – originally one that left you spoiled for choice – came to mean a far more suspect offering.

Gourmandise became food on the edge, associated with boundary-crossing and social anarchy: mushrooms with poison, fermented fish-sauce with putrefaction, sows' wombs (tastier after a miscarriage) with abortion, pastry confections with adulterous reshaping, animals containing spurious offspring with adoption and mixed marriage. The joke-shop marginal 'food' celebrated at the Saturnalia, the Roman carnival – painted or made of mud or excrement – might crop up at a sadistic emperor's table. Lechers ate brackish food – gherkins, anchovies – to conceal breath tainted by oral sex. Cannibalism, in a society in touch with famine, was a deep-seated fear: in remote country inns, human bones were reported floating in the pork soup; the Christians were rumoured to serve up human babies in pastry turnovers ('to deceive the incautious'). The ex-slave Trimalchio's dinner, satirised by Petronius, is exposed as a mixture of mutton dressed as lamb (in this case pork and pastry posing as rare delicacies) and gastronomic jokes touching on the margins of edibility.

All this, it is true, tells us more about Roman psychology than about Roman food. Hysterical rants were just one side of the coin. Food was still the instrument of display and honouring, a carefully pitched compliment to the prestige of the guests. You could not risk hearing them leave muttering, 'I didn't know we were such good friends', as the emperor Augustus once did after a rather inadequate meal. Martial can afford to serve a shabby chic dinner to his best friend, but has to compromise by adding sows' udders when entertaining his patron. Cicero repeats all the clichés about sturdy natural appetite, but lashes out at the caveman-like meals of the Epicurean philosopher Piso: shaggy rugs and half-rancid meat, with shop-bought bread as the final insult. The younger Pliny observes the exemplary country dinner of the veteran 'new man' Spurinna: discreet antique silver, just like a born aristocrat; dinner tastefully delayed for the sake of a recital; simple but elegant food. But could Spurinna have got away with serving such a dinner in town?

Perhaps it is bet-hedging and anxiety to please, as much as pretension and deceit, that characterise Roman cuisine. A famous recipe of Apicius for 'anchovy without anchovy – at table no one will know what he is eating' could just be a desperate face-saver, like 'mock cream'. Apician *patina*, made of sows' udders, fish, chicken, fig-peckers or thrushes, eggs, pine-nuts 'and anything else that is good', contained something for everyone – like paella or vincisgrassi, an image of fussy, all-inclusive hospitality.

Similarly, the iconography of the formal meal drew on other spheres of display and social control – the theatre, the circus and the triumphal procession – but these also provided the obvious images of festivity and celebration. The emperor Vitellius' 'Shield of Minerva', a preposterous dish of pikes' livers, pheasant and peacocks' brains, flamingoes' tongues and lampreys' roe, collected from the ends of the empire, sounds like blatant imperialism on a plate. So does a honey-cake in the shape of Carthage, which guests were invited to 'pillage'. But what about octopus dyed red like a triumphant Jupiter; food decorated with laurel leaves or garlands; 'castles' of melons and apples; eggs kicking off a meal like the egg-shaped bollards in the circus?

It would be difficult to write a history of Roman pleasure (as could be done for Greece), given the gaps in the sources and Roman inhibitions about consumption. But much more could be written about Roman taste, even if not in the same detail as has been done, for example, for seventeenth-century France. Were fashions in cuisine connected with other kinds of aesthetic decision-making, in rhetoric, architecture, dress? More of interest might be learned from the way in which different foods were categorised, or about how hierarchies of foods reflected social ranking: vegetables as country bumpkins, joints of meat as senatorial, snacks as plebeian, mixed and marginal food for the bottom of the heap.

Even so, the Roman dinner-party, unlike the Greek symposium, took place behind closed doors; all we are allowed to see is yesterday's scraps. Alexis Soyer, the flamboyant nineteenth-century chef and author of *The Pantropheon*, a history of ancient food, concluded: 'We can do little more than establish analogies, make deductions and reconstruct the entire edifice of an antique banquet by the help of a few data, valuable without doubt, but almost always incomplete.' That remains true today. We can follow our noses into the kitchen, as Roman foodies did, squawking like excited peacocks and craning over piles of meat, but there will always be meanings that we cannot fathom.

Further reading

D'Arms, J., The Roman convivium and the idea of equality', in O. Murray (ed.), *Sympotica*, Oxford University Press, Oxford, 1990.
Slater, W. J. (ed.), *Dining in a Classical Context*, University of Michigan Press, Ann Arbor, 1991.
Wilkins, J., Harvey, D. and Dobson, M. (eds), *Food in Antiquity*, University of Exeter Press, Exeter, 1995.

A recipe

Patina à la Apicius

Take pieces of cooked sow's udder, fillet of fish, chicken meat, fig-peckers or cooked thrushes' breasts and anything else that takes your fancy. Chop it all up carefully, except for the fig-peckers. Stir some raw eggs with oil. Season with pepper and lovage, pour over anchovy stock, wine and grape-juice, heat up in a saucepan, then bind with cornflour. Before that, add all the chopped meat, and bring to the boil. When it is done, transfer with the juices and ladle into a pan with whole peppercorns and pine-nuts in layers, placing an oil pancake under each layer of meat-sauce, like a lasagne. Finally, skewer one pancake with a reed and secure on top. Season with pepper. In fact you should have bound the meat-mixture with eggs before putting it in the saucepan.

This rather ad hoc concoction is named after the extravagant gourmet Apicius (first century AD), but in this form probably dates from the fourth or fifth century AD.

Cooking the cannibals

William Arens

While travelling through Scandinavia in the summer of 1795, seeking some relief from a suicidal depression over a love affair gone sour, Mary Wollstonecraft happened to come across a public execution in Copenhagen. As a liberal reformer on many issues, she remonstrated against the effect of capital punishment, which she thought 'hardened rather then terrified' those potentially in need of a lesson in comportment. Shortly thereafter, Wollstonecraft jolts the reader of her published letters to her former lover with a casual 'there was something I forgot to mention to you'. What apparently slipped her mind was the fact, relayed to her by a 'man of veracity', that after the deed was done two men stepped forward from the onlookers and proceeded to drink a glass of the deceased's blood as a presumed folk remedy for apoplexy. When she took issue with this custom, the author was reproved by a native with the question: 'How do you know it is not a cure for the disease?' Presumably experiencing the usual logical problem in proving a negative case, Wollstonecraft merely declared her interrogator ignorant and the custom 'a horrible violation of nature'. She then dismisses the subject as quickly as she raised it, as if it were a minor problem of native morals and manners.

In fact, Wollstonecraft should not have been so exercised and perplexed for, back in her native England, as well as across Europe at the time, and up until the early twentieth century, dessicated human body parts and fluids were regularly sold in apothecary shops as remedies for a whole host of maladies – apoplexy no doubt among them. Indeed, the medical profession still relies on related proced-ures today, such as injections of human pituitary extracts to encourage growth in stunted children, often with about as much demonst-rated benefit to its recipients. Perhaps this is a different matter; or is it? I can only say that in those parts of the world with which I, as an anthropologist, am familar, such behaviour is looked upon by the natives as bordering on, if not, cannibalism itself. We, of course, would dismiss such a garbled perspective as gross ignorance, for how would these 'natives' know that such protocols are not a cure for certain diseases? Negative cases are very perplexing.

This scenario raises some interesting questions about human ingestion habits and their interpretation. Are or were the British cannibals? Obviously, this is an issue of perspective shaped by our position in time and space. Why do we see cannibalism – however defined – so often and clearly through the mists of time and distance, while failing to appreciate what is happening here and now? What may be obscuring the issue for those so desperately trying to make sense of it, like Wollstonecraft and so many after her, is this temporal and cultural intimacy. We don't expect cannibalism in twentieth-century Britain, and so specific practices, even though they include suspicious characteristics, are not identified as cannibalistic. Perhaps more importantly, the substances involved when human pituitary extracts are injected into children are not deemed food and the consumption not 'eating'. Thus, this admittedly bizarre feature of Western society is interpreted as a rational medical treatment rather than as a superstitous ritual. When the potential interpretation of cannibalism enters the equation, our minds dredge up established and explicit images, and the context changes radically. People as food is another matter entirely.

The earliest literature from 'our' side of the equation about contact with 'other' cultures often suggests we are entering into the past. These authors treated the mysterious cultures they encountered as relics of human history rather than as contemporaneous with themselves. These same reports indicate that, for their part, the 'natives' also saw our representatives as coming from the ghostly past – as another sort of mythical ancestor returned to earth. From this perspective anything is possible, as each side struggles to make sense of the occasion and the other. The difference is that usually only one side records the encounter, in print at least, and in the process mythical thought enters the historical record. Indeed, where are the man-eating Caribs or Aztecs today except in the history books of their conquerors?

In contemporary parlance, the cannibal is 'invented', as we deny the stranger in space our time and its prevailing sensibilities. In effect, 'they', these strangers of other cultures, become our past – Neanderthals, cavemen, or primitives – what we once were at a distant point of human history. This intellectual process of course demands that we also create our rather obscure past as one characterised by cannibalism.

The result of this culture contact and its interpretation over the centuries can be characterised as myth-making on the part of explorers, conquistadores, missionaries, travellers, colonial officals and last, but definitely not least, academics, including anthropologists. Indeed, what is a myth if not an eternal truth subscribed to by all, irrespective of other apparent differences? This was what I argued in more elaborate form in my 1979 book *The Man-Eating Myth*. The results were not as persuasive as I had hoped or would have liked. Many anthropological colleagues, as I set a minor cottage industry into motion, took vehement exception to my conclusion that the apparently widespread existence of the practice of cannibalism was little more than an exercise in myth-making.

Seemingly, I had not only set upon a cherished cultural notion, but also a privileged group which included (and implicated) those in our society charged with interpreting other times and places in what was assumed to be an objective fashion. I soon learned that there is nothing like an academic discipline scorned, and that my chances of convincing my colleagues to accept that there might be no cannibals yonder were akin to trying to persuade a convention of UFO buffs that there are no aliens visiting us from the future. Everyone was having too much fun with the possibility to allow rationality to ruin the party. Indeed, at a convention of anthropologists a special panel was convened to look into the issue. It soon pronounced my argument unacceptable. Some of the convention's members even went on to allege that I was engaged in a cover-up of the evidence for the existence of cannibalism. One Oxford don was more succinct, and, I believe, inadvertently correct, when he snorted in a review that the idea there are no cannibals was 'dangerous'.

The overall response in print to my argument was interesting. Starting with cultural anthropologists, many confirmed, in politically correct fashion, that the general message about over-exoticizing the generic 'other' was a reasonable one. Collectively, they opined that we could not be too careful about this responsibility to members of our external constituency; who were, after all, the source of our academic careers. It was admitted that many of those who have come down to us in history and anthropology books as cannibals may, in fact, not have been, and that such errors were the result of our uncritical reliance on unsophisticated predecessors. Because of the often close resemblance on the ground between missionaries, colonial officers and anthropologists, some of those who responded to my argument agreed that it seemed a good idea to establish the differences between the conclusions of the academics and those of the other fieldworkers.

Less sophisticated brethren did not entirely grasp the subtle complexity of the situation, however, and rushed into print in defence of these early visitors to an often fantastic New World. The most amusing was a colleague who penned the catchy academic slogan: 'Three Cheers for Hans Staden', Staden being an illiterate sixteenth-century Dutch seaman who fell in among some South American cannibals, or at least thought he had. The hero of the piece not only somehow survived his encounter with man-eaters, but later also managed to produce an 'as told to' book about his harrowing experiences upon return to Europe. At least one contemporary anthropologist thought it a rather good read.

Apart from a few such exceptions, it was generally concluded that the image of cannibals here, there, and everywhere might well be a regrettable overstatement. However, there were also anthropologists who would then go on to say that they had it on good authority that the subjects of their own research were truly cannibals and had, indeed, been so until fairly recently. 'Recently' however, did not include the period during which the anthropologists in question were conducting fieldwork, so the custom had not been personally observed. (This argument is reminiscent, in an admittedly convoluted way, of a local informant who confided to a colleague that the reports of cannibalism among his people were greatly exaggerated because the only one he knew was his brother-in-law.)

In sum, the overall response to *The Man-Eating Myth* was the admission by anthropology that although the general image of rampant anthropophagy by the 'natives' might be flawed, this conclusion did not hold true for native South or North America, New Guinea, the other islands of the Pacific, Africa, or the Arctic. Of course 'they' (the 'natives') – wherever located in any given instance – were no longer cannibals. Thus, the conclusion was difficult to contradict. Anthropologists could have their cannibals and eat them too. There was a particularly notable agreement that cannibals did exist, until practically yesterday, in the Highlands of New Guinea, the 'final frontier' of Western cultural contact. In this instance many smugly noted that the evidence for cannibalism in New Guinea emerged from medical research rather than from the usual less reliable forms of documentation. In the light of the exalted position of science, how could any rational person doubt this research? I discovered, with perhaps even more smugness, that one could.

The story began in 1957, with the arrival in New Guinea of Dr. D. Carleton Gajdusek, a peripatetic American research paediatrician on his way home from a fellowship year in Australia. Why he decided to visit this particular part of the world did not become clear until recently. However, the eventual results of the sojourn proved to be of monumental importance for both modern medical science and for Gajdusek himself. Eventually, he would receive the Nobel Prize for medicine in Sweden and then, later on, be arrested and plead guilty to the sexual abuse of minors in the United States. He adopted and brought to his home a number of boys from part of New Guinea well known for institutionalised male homosexuality between youngsters and adults. Laudatory reports of Gajdusek's charity, including references to his bringing a number of the lads to the Nobel ceremonies, were recounted in the media.

The intervening stages in the process from public acclaim to disgrace were less dramatic. Having arrived in New Guinea, Gajdusek quickly learned of an epidemic disease called kuru raging among a Highland population called the Fore. He made his way to the locale and initiated a research project with neither funds nor permission from his superiors at the National Institutes of Health in Washington, DC, nor the Australian authorities, who had their own plans. (These were delayed by bureaucrats wrangling over who would pay for the airfare and medical insurance for their Australian candidate.) Admirably undeterred by such mundane concerns or niceties, Gajdusek, relying literally on shoe leather, flashlight, kitchen table, and penknife, carried out the basic work which was to garner him the Nobel Prize twenty years later.

Although many have justly commented on the brilliant and heroic nature of Gajdusek's work under such circumstances, as his published diaries intimate, he was at peace with himself and the local cultural environment for perhaps the only time in his life. Under these peculiar conditions, Gajdusek was able to demonstrate that kuru (related to many medical problems, including the degenerative illness Creutzfeldt–Jakob disease) was a 'slow virus' rather than a genetic occurrence. As such, it is capable of transmission via personal contact. The problem then was to identify how the natives were passing on the malady to each other in epidemic proportions.

Gajdusek eventually intimated over time, with the intellectual encouragement of cultural anthropologists included in the expanded research team, that perhaps the illness was spread by local 'ritual' cannibalism: the kin ate the remains of those who had died from kuru. He admitted that cannibalism itself was not the agent of transmission since ingestion (as opposed to other forms of contact with infected tissue) was not the culprit, but it soon became popular, scientific and anthropological lore that man-eating spread the disease. The distinction Gajdusek referred to between eating and touching corpses (common in mortuary activity) was subtle at best, and subsequently obscured by publishing 'pictures' of the ritual cannibalism alluded to in his Nobel Prize lecture. Thus, most thought, and still believe, that Gajdusek had provided modern photographic documentation for cannibalism. But this was not the case, for Gajdusek candidly admitted to me in correspondence on the subject that what the natives were eating in the 'cannibalism' photographs was actually pork! He went on to say, by way of explanation, that this is what the scene would have looked like if he had actually seen it. Apparently he had not observed cannibalism 'in the flesh', but the anthropologists involved assured him that the natives were cannibals until recently.

The issue might have faded into academic history if not for the recent concern over the eating habits and maladies of contemporary Britons and the outbreak in the United Kingdom of BSE. A reasonable reflection on the Britons' mad cow disease might suggest that perhaps the poor Fore of New Guinea suffered from 'mad pig' rather than 'mad people' disease. Mad cow disease is a variety of Creutzfeldt–Jakob disease (suspected to be caused in North Africa by eating infected sheep) which in turn is a variant of the New Guinea kuru. Initial suggestions in the United Kingdom that the virus might be the result of eating contaminated beef were rejected on the grounds that it was a well-known medical 'fact' that Gajdusek had 'proved' that this sort of disease could only be transmitted by ritualised people-eating, which obviously did not happen in the civilised United Kingdom. Now, however, it is generally accepted that mass-produced beef is the infectious agent. Thus, in Britain, people get the disease from eating what was once safe food, while those far away get the same result from engaging in ancient rituals involving eating each other. Not only is history a foreign country, but a foreign country is also history.

When I first reviewed the archaeological literature, every broken long bone and skull, and every mark on either, was apparently evidence that our ancestors were cannibals. Since a long-gone era was at issue here, it did not matter whether the evidence came from the remnants of Peking Man or Java Man in Asia, Zinjanthropus in Africa, or Cro-Magnon Man and Neanderthals in Europe. Our ancestors were cannibals all; the march of time had been a civilising process – for most. Although not an archaeologist, I intimated (as had Ashley Montagu before me) that perhaps not every broken bone or smashed skull was evidence for cannibalism. Perhaps, after thousands of years it would be reasonable for bones to be in a state of severe disrepair. Initially, this argument fell on sympathetic ears. On this score, the major difference between archaeologists and cultural anthropologists is the existence of physical evidence, and therefore what is generally recognised as scientific procedure. Moreover, as the bones, for the most part at least, had not disappeared, unlike the people and the cultural practices studied by anthropologists, the specimens could be re-examined. In some cases they were, in the light of my wary intimations on the subject, and the first results were encouraging. Some argued that it should be expected that bones found in caves might have been smashed by falling rocks over the millennia rather than deliberately broken by humans in a quest for succulent bone marrow or brain matter. Others suggested, on the basis of new procedures, that the suspicious condition of many remains was the result of trampling by the sharp hooves of animals.

Archaic mortuary ceremonies involving defleshing of bones were also considered as an explanation for some previously assumed cannibalistic remains. In one instance, presumed cannibal 'cut marks' on ancient bones were demonstrated to have been inflicted by an earlier archaeologist's sharp laboratory instruments. Thus, there was a hesitant and, in some instances, an unsettling general conclusion that perhaps not everyone in the undocumented past was a canni- bal. Although agreeing in principle with the need to be more cau- tious in reconstructing human man-eating prehistory, some inevitably argued that the era they themselves were studying was different. A typical strategy of the cannibal backlash literature involves review- ing the evidence for previous assumptions about prehistoric canni- balism and demonstrating the flawed nature of past procedures. The discussion then elucidates the careful and more precise nature of the research methods currently employed.

Rather than an occasional brief article, the new archaeology made man-eating the specific focus of a detailed, lengthy monograph. (According to one magazine, a multi-volumed 1,500 page text is now in the works.) No bone or stone is left untouched by scanning electron microscope, or statististical manipulation left unemployed by new forensic procedures, before the same old conclusions are reached – that those from the particular past in question were in- deed cannibals. Thus, on the basis of more careful scholarship, canni- bals have not only been relocated in pre-Columbian North and South America and the Pacific, but also in Spain, Italy and France. In sum, although previous commentators may have exaggerated the situ- ation, it still seems true that in the past everyone was a cannibal. It just takes longer to make the case.

This brief deconstruction of the situation does an obvious injustice to the careful nature of the research in question. Perhaps it is true that, at a particular prehistoric place and time, a given people under scrutiny did engage in the consumption of human flesh. This activity obviously has occurred, and will continue to occur, under dire condi- tions. The subsequent issue becomes one of interpretation. Was this a rare or sporadic incident involving group survival, a modern-day horror story, or everyday fare? In order to survive, people may have on one occasion eaten human flesh, but it is another matter entirely to label these people as cannibals.

The next step in the intellectual process is fraught with all the difficulties attending to cultural interpretation. As the evidence for the prehistoric motivation has disappeared, the commentary takes the form of personal and cultural projection. Was the past the good or bad old days? Despite my admiration for archaeology – for evid- ence does seem to matter to archaeologists – in this instance they seem no better than most other academics. Ritual, a most perplexing word in the lexicon of cultural anthropology, comes to the rescue of the interpretive archaeological mind with luxurious facility. Students of cultural behaviour may be prone to over-using the word to char- acterise those from afar, but they tend to restrict the concept to a particular part of the exotic experience. However, for archaeologists, almost everything coming to us from the past bespeaks of 'ritual'. In one sense ritual appears to be any former human activity that is now difficult to make sense of. The word ritual also conveys profound images of the supernatural or irrational. Eventually, the two concepts are conflated – our ancestors were 'ritual cannibals'. It may be true that archaeologists do not mean to convey this imagery of savagery. Each one attempts to deal with a specific time and place and rather technical matters, ideally in the context of exacting objective standards. However this is not the subjective message that seeps out to the general public, who are little interested in complicated procedures and the qualified judgements of scholars. For the public, if there is a clear and consistent signal from the murky past provided by academics, it is one of pervasive cannibalism.

This cannibalistic urge is understood as one we have apparently learned to overcome with time, even though it may still be extant at a distance among those who represent vestiges of an early savage era, such as the peoples of New Guinea. It is also true that neither archaeologists nor cultural anthropologists are responsible for how the public uses their research. However, it is naive to fail to entertain the inevitable consequences of the decision to focus on such issues as cannibalism, head-hunting, human sacrifice, infanticide, warfare and the like. In effect, many academic disciplines, including anthropology, choose to feed the popular imagination by reconfirming a prevailing imagery of a savage past.

Some time ago a colleague preparing a collection of essays for *The Anthropologist's Cookbook*, and aware of my unorthodox interest, asked for an entry from the cannibalism menu. She assumed, as I had at the time in light of the ubiquity of presumed creatures in the literature, that I would serve up numerous tempting recipes from around the world. I revisited the material for possibilities. The curious result was the inability to add to the cookbook with entries on cannibal cuisine. I learned from the usual cast of sources that among the savage races in Africa human flesh was popped into the pot for boiling. Some of the brave missionaries to Fiji and other islands of the South Pacific went into horrid detail about the unholy use of clay ovens normally reserved for pigs. In North and South America, the normal procedure, according to accidental explorers such as Hans Staden, was charcoal-broiling. Finally, more in our time, the New Guineans appear to favour steam-cooking in underground pits for their human repast. In other words, boiled, broiled, baked and steamed – but, no recipes. Apparently, human flesh was so tasty to these savages that nothing else was needed to improve the dish. No salt or pepper required – just the 'beef' or whatever we should call human meat. This lacuna suggests a rather odd state of affairs. Could it be that cannibals have no recipes? The inability to provide this minor but crucial bit of evidence on the presumed custom of man-eating is probably the best reason to conclude that cannibalism exists more in the limited culinary imagination of the observer than the native appetite. Perhaps the whole corpus must be taken with a large grain of salt on these grounds alone. There may be no need for erudite disputes over logic, epistemology, or ontology. No recipes, no man-eaters.

Further reading

Arens, William, *The Original Sin: Incest and Its Meaning*, Oxford University Press, London, 1986.
Peter Hulme (ed.), *Consuming Others*, Cambridge University Press, Cambridge, 1998.

The evolution of appetites
Geoffrey Ainsworth Harrison

The evolutionary lineages of humans and African apes diverged some 5–7 million years ago. The common ancestor was almost certainly a forest-living animal, which, rather like the present-day chimpanzee, fed predominantly on soft fruits. The distinctive features of the first humans – the *australopithecines* – arose as adaptations to a savannah environment. Tropical grasslands were becoming widespread in Africa at the time. They contain little in the way of soft fruit. There has been much speculation about what the *australopithecines* ate. It has been suggested that grass seed was an important ingredient of diet, but underground tubers, bulbs, corms and rhizomes are equally abundant and available throughout the year. An alternative hypothesis is that at least one group of *australopithecines* were scavengers, following and feeding off the herds of large herbivores which were also evolving at the same time in response to the abundance of grass. Without stone tools the relatively small *australopithecines* could hardly have hunted large game, but there must have been plenty of dead meat around, including carnivore kills and afterbirths.

Whatever the food-seeking of the *australopithecines*, there is good archaeological evidence that our own genus *Homo*, which first appeared about 2 million years ago, was involved in hunting. Many of the stone artefacts were suitable for a hunting economy, which not only required killing prey but also skinning and butchery. Animal bone associated with palaeolithic sites clearly support this conclusion. And hunting seems to have continued to be an important component of human economy until the beginnings of agriculture and domestication of animals, which is no older than about 10,000 years ago.

Notwithstanding the importance of hunting, and possibly scavenging, throughout our evolutionary history, it is possible to question the contribution that meat made to our ancestral diet. Certain peoples in the modern world, are, or were until very recently, without agriculture or animal husbandry. They are often grouped as 'hunter-gatherers', but whilst some, such as the Eskimo, are almost completely carnivores, most rely at least as much, and often more, on plant foods as animal ones. This is especially so of those with the simplest technologies such as Australian Aborigines and Kalahari Bushmen, among whom plants are of much greater nutritional importance than animals. It is customary for men to do the hunting and women the gathering. The former carries great social prestige, but it is the latter that provides most of the sustenance.

It therefore seems reasonable to conclude that humans have been omnivores throughout most of their evolution, and it is to a mixed diet of plant and animal foods that we have become adapted. However, diets in developed countries probably contain more meat and fewer vegetables than those of the past, and we certainly take in much more food overall than do traditional hunter-gatherers. For them, food shortage is a common experience often amounting to periods of acute starvation.

Another difference concerns some particular nutrients which are often rare in traditional diets but superabundant today. The three striking examples are saturated animal fat (which only occurs in small amounts in most wild game), refined carbohydrates and especially sucrose sugar (which only occurs naturally in large quantities in honey) and common salt (which is very limited naturally, except in marine or former marine environments). Foraging strategies for those substances must have been of great value in the past, since in small amounts they are important for nutritional health. Today, one only needs to go to the nearest fast-food take-away, which has well recognised their appeal.

Conversely, the comparative reduction in the intake of foods of plant origin has diminished the amount of cellulose fibre we consume. Previously, this was probably so abundant in diets that no special drive to seek it out was necessary. A number of people have pointed out, and particularly Stephen Boyden of the Australian National University, that if organisms are placed in environments that are very different from those which have produced their evolutionary history, we should expect to find symptoms of maladaptation. Boyden predicted, some thirty years ago, damaging consequences from an intake of too much fat, sugar and salt, and too little fibre. At the time there was little or no empirical evidence for this, but we now know that he was correct on all accounts. And obesity is one of the banes to health in modern societies.

While searching for certain kinds of food has in the past been advantageous, other potential foods have been avoided by, at least, some groups of people. Food taboos are extremely common. Many of these seem to be largely, if not totally, of cultural origin, but others may have a biological basis. Poorly cooked pork, for example, can be the cause of a variety of severe parasitic infections, and it seems likely that this has been recognised in those societies which place a taboo on eating pig products. Sometimes there appears to be a natural avoidance of some foods. A dislike of many green vegetables seems extremely widespread among children. The phenomenon has been poorly investigated, but could be due to the fact that some 'greens' and, specifically, brassicas, contain chemicals that can interfere with proper functioning of the thyroid gland. The thyroid is especially important during growth and development.

Variation in evolutionary nutritional experience is the most likely cause of many inherited physique differences between different human groups. Whilst obesity is prevalent in most developed and developing societies, it is especially common and often takes an extreme form in certain groups such as the Polynesian islanders of the Pacific region and various desert peoples like the Pima Indians of the southwest United States. During their history these people are likely to have experienced severe acute food shortages. In the colonisation of the Pacific islands, for example, boatloads of people would have been at sea for many weeks with little food. No doubt in some boats all would have perished, but in others there must have been survivors and these were likely to be the ones who could withstand starvation best. It is known from hunger-strikers that there is great variability in survival times and a major determinant of these is metabolic efficiency. Some people are just metabolically more efficient than others, and in Polynesian colonisation these are the ones who would have survived the sea journeys. This former advantage is now offset by the fact that it is the metabolically efficient who put on the most fat once food is unlimited. They are known as having a 'thrifty phenotype' and there is telling evidence that it derives from having certain genes which were of selective advantage in the past. Making up the 'thrifty genotype' are genes which predispose to non-insulin-dependent diabetes, and levels of such diabetes are extremely high among Polynesians and Pima Indians today.

Cases are also known where human biological evolution has quite specifically been influenced by voluntary changes in food practices. A well analysed example concerns the consumption of milk. The infants of all mammals feed exclusively for a time on their mothers' milk. To digest that milk fully they require an intestinal enzyme which digests milk sugar, lactose, breaking it down into glucose and galactose. The production of the enzyme which performs this digestion – lactase – ceases, however, when infants are fully weaned. In non-human mammals milk is never consumed again. In many human societies, however, pastoralism is a dominant economy and people of all ages rely heavily on fresh milk products for food. In these societies lactase production continues throughout life in most people. By contrast, in other societies which have either continued as hunter-gatherers, or long relied upon plant cultivation for their food, lactase production ceases in infancy. When such people as adults drink milk they are likely to be much troubled with flatulence and diarrhoea: caused by undigested lactose being decomposed by bacteria in the bowel. They are said to be lactose intolerant.

Tolerance/intolerance appears to be due to a single gene difference and it seems likely that the gene for tolerance has been favoured by natural selection in those situations where milk from other mammals was potentially available for exploitation. This would have been the case in those societies which had pursued animal domestication, but this only began to occur about ten thousand years ago. We thus not only have an example of nutritional opportunity producing human evolutionary change, but also of quite rapid change in evolutionary time.

Not all variation between populations in nutritional sensitivities, however, is genetic; cultural practice may produce situations apparently like the lactose tolerance one. Excessive reliance on a diet of maize can lead to a severe dermatitis and neurological morbidity. The condition is known as pellegra and used to be quite common among both poor whites and blacks in the corn-belt of the United States. Although maize is rich in many nutrients, it is somewhat deficient in a number of essential amino-acids and is particularly low in one of the B group of vitamins: niacin. It is this latter deficiency which is responsible for the main symptoms of pellegra. The disease, however, hardly ever occurs in the native Amerindian peoples of Central America and the south-west United States, who rely even more heavily than the corn-belt people on maize and its products. For some time it was thought that the difference in susceptibility to pellegra must be due to genetics, with the native peoples having people selected for resistance over the generations. The answer was much simpler. Traditionally, Amerindian societies boil their maize in limewater, and under such conditions of alkaline hydrolysis the amino-acid proportions are improved and much more niacin is made available for the human body.

Clearly, human beings have adapted to available food supplies both biologically and culturally and these processes permit an incredible range of diets, both between and within populations and for the same individual from one time to another. This has facilitated the spread of the human species over most of the land surface of the earth, with all its many and different environments. No other species matches *Homo sapiens* for dietary variety: we are the ultimate omnivores. But the range is not infinite. Some natural materials, like wood and grass, have no nutritional value for human beings, and a number are actually poisonous though they are important foods for other animals, as, for example, various wild berries.

Equally, though more subtly important, is the issue of balance. Qualitative nutrient requirements for humans are well enough known, but absolute and relative quantities are still poorly understood. Nutritional requirement tables tend to treat all people as being the same, except for the effects of size and, sometimes, sex. Quite clearly they are not: we still know far too little about the specific requirements of children and the aged, and many groups of people seem to survive on a diet well below the published figures of minimal nutritional requirements. Then, again, individual differences are ubiquitous: everyone knows cases where on much the same diet and lifestyle one individual becomes obese while the other is 'skinny'. These issues of variability are of crucial importance to our health and need substantial research. One can, however, be sure that an understanding of our evolutionary history will play an important part in finding the right answers.

Further reading

Boyden, S., *Western Civilization in Biological Perpsective*, Clarendon Press, Oxford, 1987.

Harrison, G. A. (ed.), *Human Adaptation*, Oxford University Press, London, 1993.

Katz, S. H., Hediger, M. L. and Valleroy, L. A., Traditional maize processing techniques in the New World, *Science* 184, 1974, 765–73.

Kretchmer, N. O., Lactose and lactase, *Scientific American*, 227, 1972, 70–8.

Rivers, J. P. W., The nutritional biology of famine, in Harrison, G. A. (ed.), *Famine*, Oxford University Press, London, 1988; 57–106.

Consuming nations

Shannan Peckham

'The destiny of nations', wrote the philosopher of gastronomy Brillat-Savarin, 'depends upon the manner in which they feed themselves.' At the close of the twentieth century there are many who might concur with such an assertion. Diet remains an issue both of national government and of popular concern; construed as nothing less, in fact, than an index of the nation's health. If, as Marx would have it, individuals are defined by the objects they hunger after, so by extension might collective identities be shaped by communal appetites and the foods that are consumed. 'Tell me what you eat', Brillat-Savarin said, 'and I'll tell you who you are.' Stereotypes of national characters are often evoked in relation to national cuisines. To the Greeks, the Italians are *Makaronades*, to the French, the British are

Rosbif, to the British, the French are Frogs and the Germans *Krauts*. Food can become a powerful metonym for national cultures; Coca Cola has become inseparable from the Stars and Stripes since the Second World War.

In travel guides foreign cultures are likely to be identified first and foremost with the foods to be tried and avoided; to travel involves the risk of becoming sick. Conversely, international cuisine is promoted and consumed as a touristic experience, so that a meal at an Indian, Italian, Greek or Chinese restaurant becomes a substitute for travel. Such displays of national foods underline the extent to which foreignness, or the exotic, is constructed from within and is an important part of self-definition, just as that quintessential Mexican dish of chilli con carne is, in fact, a Texan invention.

Eating (and the etiquette that surrounds it) is a cultural practice that marks off insiders from outsiders. Similarly, definitions of whether something is edible or inedible are culturally contingent. Claude Lévi-Strauss relates how, during the Allied landings in 1944, American troops destroyed a number of Normandy cheese dairies because they reeked of corpses. To this extent, food and eating are inextricably bound up in the process through which a collective consciousness is maintained in an imagined community of like-minded consumers.

Pondering what he called 'the question of nutrients' in *Ecce Homo* (1908) Nietzsche upbraided the German spirit as 'an indigestion', noting that the nation's cooking was characterised by:

> overcooked meats, vegetables cooked with fat and flour; the degeneration of pastries and puddings into paperweights! Add to this the virtually bestial prandial drinking habits of the ancient, and by no means only the ancient Germans, and you will understand the origin of the German spirit – from distressed intestines.

For Nietzsche, nations were the product of the foods they ingested. The dishes a nation craved were a poignant measure of that culture's relative infirmity or well-being. This was a view that became prevalent at the end of the nineteenth century when national economic performance was explicitly linked to nourishment; the quantity and quality of foods consumed were deemed inseparable from the measure of the nation's industrial output. As one American contributor to *The Century Magazine* remarked in 1888, in a comparative article on European and American dietary habits entitled 'What we should eat':

> We live more intensely, work harder, need more food and have more money to buy it. The better ways of the American working-man as compared with the European, the larger amount of work he

turns off in a day or a year, and his more nutritious food are, I believe, inseparably connected.

A distinctive cuisine and a shared food vocabulary function as central elements in the definition of a national culture. Cookery books can be put to ideological uses by demonstrating the homogeneity and antiquity of a nation. Kuwaiti, Algerian and Saudi cookbooks, for example, argue on historic grounds for distinctive cuisines to be differentiated from other Arab cuisines. Similarly, books on Persian food trace its origin from the third-century Sassanian empire. Sometimes such books are written in exile and project a nostalgic, idealised view of the homeland.

In nationalist projects, food is construed as a cultural artefact and emphasis is placed on the nation's historical claims to it, even though these foods might be shared by many other nations. Hungarian and Greek cookbooks, for example, play down Ottoman influences. After the 1974 Turkish invasion of Cyprus it became *de rigueur* to call 'Turkish' coffee 'Greek', or even 'Byzantine'. A food conference held at Thessaloniki in 1991 focused exclusively on the rich culinary traditions of provincial Greece, Ancient Greece, and Byzantium. In Greece at the end of the nineteenth century, an organic national cuisine was increasingly celebrated. Nikolaos Politis, Professor of Mythology at the University of Athens, and the man who coined the Greek word for folklore in 1884, listed food ('common and special victuals of the Greeks') as an important area of study for scholars concerned with preserving and codifying national traditions which were in danger of being swept away by the onslaught of a cosmopolitan modernity. At the same time, Greek rural fiction celebrated the folkloric customs of Greece, of which culinary lore was an important dimension, even while writers such as Alexandros Papadiamantis bemoaned the consumption of 'pickled foods and European tinned food'.

It was not until the twentieth century that a Greek cuisine was standardised. The man largely responsible for this was the cook Nikolaos Tselemendes, who was born on the island of Siphnos, but spent his childhood in Constantinople, and whose name became synonymous with 'cookbook' in Greece. Tselemendes' manual, which was published in the 1920s, set out to place Greek cooking on a level with other Western cuisines, even while the author argued for the ancient Greek origins of French cooking. In particular, Tselemendes sought to wean Greeks off their excessive attachment to spices, which he considered a pernicious legacy of Ottoman rule. However, the massive influx of Greek immigrants from Asia Minor after 1922, following Greece's crushing defeat by Atatürk and the ensuing exchange of populations, severely undermined the notion of a unified, homogeneous, national cuisine along the lines laid out by Tselemendes. These refugees from Turkey brought with them spicy Anatolian dishes and other 'foreign' cooking practices, and they were nicknamed in Greece *yiaourtovaptismeni*, meaning 'those baptised in yoghurt', a reference to the liberal use of yoghurt in their food.

In France, where, as Roland Barthes observed, food enables a Frenchman 'to enter daily into his own past, and to believe in a certain culinary "being" of France', a similar concern was demonstrated after the First World War when local food traditions were recorded as part of a drive to preserve the nation's distinctive character; a character which was construed as being enshrined in regional folklores. As Elizabeth David remarked in the introduction to her *French Provincial Cooking* (1960):

> After the 1914 war patriotic Frenchmen began to feel that the unprecedented influx of foreign tourists ... was threatening the character of their cookery far more than had the shortages and privations of war ... It was at this time that a number of gourmet and gastronomically-minded men of letters set about collecting and publicising the local recipes of each province in France.

The collection of such regional lore was bound up with what Arjun Appadurai has called the 'textualization of the culinary realm', while the drive to preserve regional cookery was fraught with the same contradictions that haunted folklore, a discipline predicated on the preservation and celebration of local, oral customs, which it ultimately aimed to subsume within a written, national cuisine. Eugen Weber has shown how the modernisation of rural France from the 1870s, and the concomitant drive to turn 'peasants into Frenchmen', involved the transformation of dietary habits, as the regions were brought into the market economy and rural communities gained access to hitherto restricted provisions.

Claims for a national food are inseparable from claims to a national identity. To speak of a national identity in the first place is immediately to assume an analogy between the nation and the individual. Eating, it could be argued, is one of the ways in which the relations between nation and individual are embodied. From this perspective the infant's bond with the mother provides a symbolic equivalent of the subject's affiliations with the nation. If eating is essential to assimilation of the self, so might it also be true for national communities. It was Freud in his *Three Essays on the Theory of Sexuality* (1905) who explored 'the reasons why a child sucking at his mother's breast has become the prototype of every relation of love' – love for the motherland, for example. While Freud was penning his thesis, the association of motherhood with the nation (or motherland) was given emphasis in Britain in debates over the defective quality of women's milk and its substitution by cheap sweetened condensed milk. As reproducers of the nation through whom the nation's young imbibed their values, the poor health of women was a matter of national concern and was closely connected to fears about malnourishment and the deterioration of the national physique.

The defective quality of mothers' milk endangered the country. Sickly mothers were producing invalid and mentally feeble children. It was in response to this anxiety, for example, that the National Milk Publicity Council was active in promoting the consumption of milk in schools from the late 1920s, and in 1934 a Milk Act was passed, providing milk at a heavily subsidised price. 'Natural' national identities needed to be supplemented with substituted milk. During the Second World War the National Milk Scheme was introduced (1940) which supplied milk to all expectant mothers and to young children, while milk became free of charge in schools in 1946; a provision which came to an end with Margaret Thatcher who, as Secretary of State for Education and Science (1970–4), censured the meddling 'nanny' state.

In most secular societies the state was the regulator of dietary regimes, in a sense inheriting a canon of culinary prohibitions and prescriptions from the sacral institutions it displaced. In Britain the austerity of an enforced patriotic diet during the Second World War (rationing came to an end officially in 1954), prefigured the state's increasingly interventionist role as the arbitrator of the nation's dietary welfare. The National Food Survey was founded in 1940 and a Ministry of Food created. Lord Woolton, the Minister, spoke of the 'kitchen front'. Citizens were encouraged through a campaign of 'Digging for Victory' to produce food at home and to cultivate vegetable plots. In this way the discipline of the household economy was maintained in a composite act of solidarity, self-reliance and defence, which was celebrated in a 1990s BBC2 documentary and in an exhibition held at the Imperial War Museum in London.

Of the many apprehensions which the BSE scandal has raised in the 1990s in Britain, perhaps the most central has focused on the health of the state in its role as dietary arbitrator. Among the general public the Conservative government's failure in handling the crisis in an effective manner made visible a construed rottenness within the system. It was as if the contamination of British livestock stood as a symbol for the corrupted body politic, driven by internal dissent after eighteen years of in-breeding. Not even the diplomatic affirmation of the German Chancellor Kohl, a self-confessed gourmand, on a visit to John Major at Downing Street, that he would eat British beef with the then British Prime Minister could restore confidence.

Now, more so than ever, national politics is about conspicuous consumption. The President of the United States can be chosen on his knowledge of the price of a pound of butter and cheese. Deals may be sealed over banquets, but politicians are required to display their intimacy with popular food in a symbolic gesture of their electability. Unfortunate examples of culinary insensitivity on the part of politicians are increasingly highlighted in the media as political *faux pas*. Thus, Peter Mandelson, in the 1992 election, mistook mushy peas for avocado purée, while Alain Juppé recently outraged an electorate in France by indulging in a feast of ortolans, cruelly exposing the gap between delectability and electability. As the gastronome President of the United States Thomas Jefferson remarked in a letter to the Marquis de Lafayette, really to know his constituency it was no longer enough to have the good intention of distributing cake; a politician had to survey the citizens' kitchens and sample their food at first hand.

Today it is no exaggeration to say that politicians and their entourage vie for the title of the nation's ideal master consumer *and* cook, acknowledging the fact that food remains the quickest way to the heart of the nation. Cue to John Major tucking into a full English breakfast of beans and sausages at a roadside Happy Eater, while journalists dissect the menu of the dinner hosted by the Blairs for the Clintons at the London restaurant *Le Pont de la Tour*. Meanwhile, Denis Healey advertises the dietary riches of Sainsbury's on television and Nigel Lawson, the messiah of the profligate 1980s, promotes the benefits of a frugal dietary regime in his recent cookbook. Hillary Clinton assures an American public that there is nothing she likes better than baking cookies, while Norma Major and Cherie Blair confide their favourite recipes in women's magazines, outbidding each other in their claims to be the first lady of the nation's first kitchen.

Such public demonstrations of cooking and eating project powerful messages of integrity and reinforce stereotypical models of domesticity. They suggest that the politician in question eats from the same plate as the public, is subject to the same consuming passions. Here, the harmonious intimacies of a domestic space are blown open to the world; homeliness finds its equivalence in nation-ness, the kitchen chopping-board in the stately veneer of the Cabinet table.

Arguments about a nation's decline and rejuvenation are often reflected in anxieties about the dynamism or health of its culinary culture. In the run-up to the 1997 general election two reports prepared by independent British charities, the National Food Alliance and Save the Children, suggested that malnutrition was prevalent and on the increase among low-income families in Britain. By the same token, concerns about the McDonaldisation of national culture and the slide into what E. M. Forster called 'the spirit of gastronomic joylessness' are frequently articulated. The adulteration and impoverishment of the national diet stand as an allegory for a host of other cultural and economic invasions that threaten the community's integrity, overwhelming indigenous values. The proliferation of fast-food franchises and consumerism calls for local resistance.

There is, of course, nothing new in the fear of such invasions, nor in the projection of a homogenous national culinary culture that flourished in some resplendent, but unspecified, golden age. That other *fin de siècle* in the nineteenth century, for example, was dominated by similar concerns about the homogenisation, degeneration and impending collapse of the nation; concerns which found their expression in anxieties about the corruption of the nation's culinary culture. As one writer noted in the pages of *Macmillan's Magazine* in 1886:

> In the years to come it will be debated whether the great minds of the later Victorian era were more concerned with their souls or with their stomachs . . . the soul and the stomach, irreligion and indigestion, doubt and dyspepsia – call them what you will – these are the cardinal notes of our great enquiring age.

In part, the anxieties stemmed from an appreciation of the fact that the population was no longer producing the food it consumed. Massive imperial expansion had opened up new tastes and brought new foreign foods home, while technologies of conservation, storage and transport facilitated and encouraged this flow. Canning, in a basic form, had been developed at the beginning of the nineteenth century, but it was not until the 1860s that cheap tinned beef and mutton were imported in any bulk from Australia, and later from Chicago and Cincinnati in the United States, as well as Argentina. In the last two decades of the century vegetables and fruit were also being imported from the United States.

The commodification of food divorced edibles from any concrete social relations, so that consumers no longer knew what they were consuming nor where it came from. Apprehensions about this ghostly consumption may be related to late nineteenth-century literary preoccupations with demons, vampires, ghosts and invisible maladies. Foods were figuratively disembodying the nation. The metaphoric connections between canned food and disembodiment were, in fact, drawn out in the gruesome name 'Sweet Fanny Adams', first bestowed by sailors in the Navy to the meat produced at a canning factory in Deptford in the 1860s, but still in usage in the twentieth century. Fanny Adams, the victim of a brutal murder, was discovered hacked into small pieces that recalled the coarse and unappetising meat in the cans. Two decades later in the autumn of 1888 the Whitechapel murders took place and, in the midst of the debates on degeneracy, the privacy of the stomach was shockingly opened up for the nation to contemplate.

Food was not only consumed, it was consuming. At the turn of the century a connection was being drawn between the nation's unsavoury diet and the deterioration of the national physique. During the Boer War, for example, the army was hard put to recruit soldiers of a suitable physique, and the minimum height for the infantry was consequently reduced to five feet. It was no longer a case of defending the nation from outside. Steps were required to safeguard the nation from those degenerative influences that had accumulated within. It was in this light that the Inter-Departmental Committee on Physical Deterioration (1904) was convened, and argued, among other things, for the need to reduce alcohol consumption and to improve the poor quality of foods being consumed.

Like the new literature which was circulated in popular newspapers and was now accessible to increasingly large sections of the population through the spread of literacy, many contemporaries argued that tinned food was detrimental to the nation; indeed, that as things were going it might even destroy the nation. Thus as late as 1937, in *The Road to Wigan Pier*, George Orwell declared that 'the really important thing about the unemployed, the really basic thing if you look to the future, is the diet that they are living on'. Everywhere he looked, Orwell noted ominous signs of 'physical degeneracy' and he concluded:

> [T]he English palate, especially the working-class palate, now rejects good food almost automatically. The number of people who prefer tinned peas and tinned fish to real peas and real fish must be increasing every year, and plenty of people who could afford real milk in their tea would much sooner have tinned milk – even that dreadful tinned milk which is made of sugar and cornflour and has UNFIT FOR BABIES on the tin in huge letters. In some districts efforts are now being made to teach the unemployed more about food-values and more about the intelligent spending of money.

Poverty could only be spoken of in terms of unsatisfactory consuming habits or perverse consumption. The frail physical constitution of the nation's poor was clearly connected to their deficient diet, yet as the eponymous hero of George Gissing's novel *The Private Papers of Henry Ryecroft* (1903) remarks, the nation's eclipse was also linked to the contamination of local foods by foreign imports of inferior quality. He is exasperated by the sight of foreign butter in a shop window and admonishes: 'This is the kind of thing that makes one gloomy over the prospect of England. The deterioration of English butter is one of the worst signs of the moral state of our nation.' As Ryecroft's assertions suggest, the novel as a genre provided an important space in which the nation saw itself consume. The novelist's task was both to record the nation's current consuming habits and to evoke them as they ought to be, with contented protagonists sitting down to well-cooked and wholesome national repasts.

It was, perhaps, in part the threats posed to a unified national culinary culture that called for the order of cookery books such as Isabella Beeton's bible of household management which was published in 1861 and sold 60,000 copies in the first year. In her smart new home in the suburb of Pinner, which was installed with the latest commodity of a bathroom and an innovative hot-water system, Beeton represented a new class of consumer, commuting regularly to London. Indeed, her husband Sam Beeton was the publisher of such popular magazines as the *Englishwoman's Domestic Magazine*, *Boy's Own Magazine* and *The Queen*. For Beeton, cooking was embedded in an encompassing context of social relations that radiated out from the kitchen as the hub of the domestic and familial space. 'Badly-cooked dinners and untidy ways', she concluded in the preface to *Household Management*, were the chief sources of discontent.

Five years earlier the Crimean War had demonstrated the importance of cooking and the management of food to the successful outcome of military engagements, a relationship impressed upon the public by Alexis Soyer's *Culinary Campaign*, published in 1857. The author of best-selling cookery books and the chef at the Reform Club, Soyer had been in charge of supervising the victualling of the army hospitals in the Crimean War. Significantly, for Beeton, the mistress of the house resembled nothing as much as 'the commander of an army'. In the midst of potential chaos, Beeton the cook, like her contemporary Florence Nightingale, in the military camps of Constantinople and Scutari, promoted an ideal order, therein proving that the new consumerism was not an inevitable recipe for disaster. Beeton's cookery book was assembled by an army of women who sent in their recipes to be tried and tested in the staff headquarters of Mrs Beeton's suburban kitchen. No wonder, then, that her cookery book, with its ideas of home order, gave meaning to the patriotic sacrifice of the men on Scott's Antarctic expedition and subsequently in the prisoner-of-war camps in Singapore where prisoners read it, sustained only on canned food and wretched foreign gruel.

The drive to preserve the nation's food as a vital part of its heritage was not unrelated to the establishment of other national institutions at the end of the nineteenth century such as the Folklore Society, the Society for the Preservation of Ancient Buildings, the National Trust and the magazine *Country Living*. Cookery books, for the most part, promoted notions of a homogeneous and timeless national cooking, ideas that still remain powerful. One hundred years on, National Trust houses serve traditional tea and cakes for visitors who admire the authenticity of a Victorian pantry and may even purchase a glossy tome entitled *The Country House Kitchen*. Numerous food products, such as Hovis Bread, are similarly marketed through projections of an immemorial holistic view of English culture. Such an emphasis on food's placement in advertisements can be interpreted as a strategy to distinguish products within the global reach of an industry that effectively eradicates any singular attachment to place.

The place of food in a national culture is promoted, too, in political speeches that project Britain in terms of its essential middle-Englishness: a nation that rides bicycles, plays cricket and drinks tepid beer. In actual fact, many of the ostensibly traditional national dishes are of recent provenance: like the ploughman's lunch, which dates back only to the 1960s. Similarly, many of the ingredients that make up national cuisine, such as the potato, were introduced in the wake of colonisation. The English cup of tea is another such example. Condemned by one eighteenth-century commentator as a 'deleterious produce of China' which was wreaking the destruction of the nation, tea had nevertheless by the end of the century taken over from coffee and become the nation's drink, greatly increasing the consumption, too, of sugar. Other examples are the tomato and the chilli pepper which were introduced to Spain and the Mediterranean from the New World.

At the close of the twentieth century there are some commentators who maintain that with the proliferation of global networks national affiliations are dissolving. The explosion of scholarly and popular literature about the nation and nationalism in recent years may be one sign, as Eric Hobsbawm maintains, of the nation's demise. Evidence of such a dissolution, it could be argued, is further reflected in increasingly pluralistic culinary cultures. Foreign foods are now available everywhere. Comestibles as commodities are caught up in the dynamics of an economic system that compresses time and space, conflating hitherto discrete environments so that it is no longer meaningful to speak of national cuisines.

However, it may also be that the reverse is true: that in overriding national affiliations an increasingly global culture has incited even more virulent forms of nationalism. Similarly, it may be that the culinary multiculturalism that is construed today as evidence of the nation's obsolescence signifies precisely the obverse. The distinct categories of ethnic cuisine have not been dismantled, but remain firmly in place, suggesting that they are still potent. Today, it could be argued, commodified foreignness in the form of world cooking is served up by a mainstream culture and consumed in a feast that feeds the muscles of the ravenous nation, incorporating and finally annihilating all difference. Whatever the truth, it is manifestly the case that constellations of fears have gathered around the table, providing plentiful food for thought.

Further reading

Appadurai, A., How to make a national cuisine: cookbooks in contemporary India, *Comparative Studies in Society and History* 30, 1988; 3–24.

Burnett, John, *Plenty and Want: A Social History of Diet in England from 1815 to the Present Day*, Routledge, London, 1989 (1966).

Drummond, J. C. and Wilbraham, Anne, *The Englishman's Food: A History of Five Centuries of English Diet*, Pimlico, London, 1991 (1957).

Goody, Jack, *Cooking, Cuisine and Class: A Study in Comparative Sociology*, Cambridge University Press, Cambridge, 1982.

Mennell, Stephen, *All Manners of Food: Eating and Taste in England and France from the Middle Ages to the Present*, Blackwell, Oxford, 1985.

Zubaida, Sami and Tapper, Richard (eds), *Culinary Cultures of the Middle East*, I. B. Tauris, London, 1994.

A recipe

Macedoine

The Macedoine salad takes its name from the patchwork of states and ethnicities in the south-eastern Balkans. Alexander the Great ruled over the Kingdom of Macedonia in the fourth century BC. In the sixth century Macedonia was occupied by the Slavs and a century later the region was conquered by the Bulgars. After passing under Byzantine and Serbian control, Macedonia fell to the Ottomans in the fourteenth century. The struggle over Macedonia intensified with the disintegration of the Ottoman Empire, and following the Balkan Wars of 1912–13, the region was divided up between Serbia, Greece and Bulgaria. In the wake of the break-up of the Socialist Federal Republic of Yugoslavia in 1991, however, the so-called 'Macedonian Question' has once more emerged as a pressing issue and given the Macedoine salad an added topicality. First applied to a mixture of diced vegetables at the beginning of the nineteenth century, the name came to apply to a mixture of fruit, sometimes set in jelly. Mrs Beeton includes a recipe in her *Household Management*.

The recipe included here is simple to make with autumnal fruit and serves six people. The plum, which forms the centrepiece of the dessert, represents underlying continuities, while the surrounding fruit pieces evoke the ethnic and cultural diversity of the region.

3 apples
3 pears
6 red plums
1 punnet blackberries
1 punnet raspberries
Small bunch grapes (preferably Muscat)
1 tablespoon honey
2 cinnamon sticks
2 tablespoons sugar
Lemon rind and the juice 1 lemon
Bulgarian red wine
500 gms Greek yoghurt
Slivovitch (Balkan plum brandy)

First, peel and chop up the cooking apples and the pears. Place them in a saucepan with a little water. Add one full tablespoon of honey and one cinnamon stick. Put in the blackberries and allow to simmer on a low flame until the fruits are tender. Add the raspberries. Stir in and let stand until cool.

Meanwhile, place the plums in a saucepan, large enough for the fruit to sit comfortably, but not too loosely. Add enough water so as barely to cover the fruit, together with two generous tablespoons of sugar, and one cinnamon stick. Pour in one large cupful of the Bulgarian wine, and the lemon juice. Add the lemon rind and the Muscat grapes.

Bring to simmering point and cook gently until the fruit is soft (but retain shape). Let cool.

Now remove the cinnamon sticks. Take out the plums and place them in bowls. Pour the remaining juice with the grapes into the saucepan with the chopped apples and pears. Stir and add the contents to the plums.

To enhance the taste of the plums, pour the slivovitch into a soup ladle, or small saucepan, and warm over a flame. When the brandy is hot, light with a match and pour the flambé over the Macedoine. Serve with a helping of Greek yoghurt.

Feasting in the dark

Ian Christie

One of the earliest of all British fantasy films is entitled *A Big Swallow*. Made around 1901 by James Williamson, it shows a gentleman infuriated to find himself being photographed, who advances on the camera, opens his mouth as wide as the screen – and swallows both camera and operator whole. If cinema itself is a kind of consumption, hoovering up reality and feeding it to us in bite-sized chunks, then it seems strange that so little attention has been paid to the filming of the food process.

I have a very personal recollection of the close link between film-making and gastronomy. During the ten years that I knew the British film-making duo Michael Powell and Emeric Pressburger, I enjoyed some of the best meals of my life. Eating well was an article of faith for Powell and Pressburger, and even in their later years they remained true.

During World War II, they agreed deals with Arthur Rank over dinner at the White Tower restaurant in Percy Street, London, staying late and locking up after the owner had gone home. Powell even ran a hotel on the Riviera for some years, while Pressburger planned his travels with Michelin in mind and, famously, always carried emergency rations on a generous scale. Food, on and off screen, is inextricably woven through my memories of *The Archers*.

In the 1970s, the start of a tribute-screening of their newly restored *Life and Death of Colonel Blimp* (1943) – which includes a famous dinner-party scene set in 1918, in which the Blimpish Clive Candy hopes to persuade his German friend of Britain's goodwill towards the recent enemy – was delayed so that our dinner guests could finish their dessert at leisure. Years later, an escalating disagreement over a Powell – Pressburger joint appearance at the National Film Theatre was settled by a diplomatic lunch at their traditional restaurant, *L'Étoile* on Charlotte Street. Indeed, lunch with either of these gallant gourmets was often surprising: Powell sharing his delight in finally perfecting a cauliflower soup, or cracking open a *jambon en croûte* to reveal a welcome message spelled out in cloves; and Pressburger's reckless disregard for calorie-counting in preparing central European specialities, including a memorable potato cooked whole in a pound of butter.

There are younger film-makers today who keep alive the tradition that links cooking and cinema: Raúl Ruiz and Claude Chabrol spring to mind as serious gastronomes. Indeed, there is a line of speculation that claims the same skills are needed for both professions (e.g. planning, blending, improvisation, diplomacy). But to gauge the consumer's point of view, I carried out some modest fieldwork among family and friends to see what associations spring to mind at the mention of 'film and food'.

Not surprisingly, the young have one unanimous response – popcorn. Equally unsurprising is their amazement that popcorn is in fact a relatively recent staple of cinema-going in Britain. Twenty years ago, ice-cream still reigned supreme, sold by roving staff with trays, until a purposeful Americanisation of cinema-going brought in popcorn, along with new films starting on Fridays (instead of Sundays) and eventually the full panoply of multiplex theatres. It is hard to resist linking today's routinely massive buckets of popcorn and cola with a determined consumerism, which has certainly doubled attendance rates since 1986, but has also limited the range of films, especially non-American films, available in British cinemas.

Trendy teenagers and young adults, attuned to oblique or perverse associations, are likely to recall the opening riff from Quentin Tarantino's *Pulp Fiction* – in which John Travolta impresses his fellow hit-man by explaining that the French call a quarterpounder with cheese a *royale*. Video rental *aficionados* can point to recent hits like *Joe's Apartment* and *The Last Supper*. In the former, an innocent arrival in New York is befriended by the cockroaches in his slum tenement, who dance attendance – and sing, since it is a musical of sorts – before revealing their territorial imperative by wrecking an attempted dinner *à deux* with his girlfriend. *The Last Supper* is a rerun of a familiar theme: a group of West Coast sophisticates decide to better the world by passing judgement on their influential dinner guests. Say the wrong thing and you wind up as compost for the tomatoes. Food in these ironic post-modern movies, as in the British black comedy *Shallow Grave*, is more likely to be a trap or a nasty surprise than simple nourishment.

For older, more versatile film-goers, films with food at or near their centre unspool backwards from Ang Lee's *Eat Drink Man Woman* (1994), in which tense Taiwanese Sunday dinners focus the dilemma of which grown-up daughter will look after father – the meal as social ritual. *Like Water For Chocolate* (1991) is more a magic realist family saga in the screen version than in the novel, famous for its interpolated recipes. But above all, two mid-1980s films are still fondly remembered for their portrayal of lives devoted to the perfection of food as powerful metaphors. From Denmark came Gabriel Axel's adaptation of an Isak Dinesen story, *Babette's Feast* (1987), contrasting the sumptuous cuisine of Anna Karina's former Parisian chef with the simple asceticism of the nuns whom she serves. Here, potential excess and gluttony are sublimated into sacrifice and sacrament. Blessed are the frugal, Axel implies, for they shall be rewarded by an ultimate feast.

Juzo Itami's *Tampopo*, made in Japan a year earlier, also features a female chef. But Nobuko Miyamoto runs a noodle bar in downtown Tokyo, undistinguished until a passing stranger offers to initiate her into the secrets of irresistible noodlery. Like Itami's other satirical scrapbooks on contemporary Japanese life (one on funeral rites and the other on income tax), this is partly a disquisition on national character and customs, and partly a satire on movie styles. But it's also a funny, modern exploration of the familiar equation between sex and food, with dishes to seduce, to arouse, to satiate and to assuage. All human passion, Itami suggests, can be expressed through pork noodle recipes and rituals, thus amplifying the message that delighted the repressed British viewers of Tony Richardson's lip-smacking *Tom Jones* back in 1963.

But, after the life-affirming qualities of *Babette's Feast* and *Tampopo*, true cinephiles will turn to the dark side of food on film, eating as life-denial or a form of aggression, in two garish, brilliant films that have both given viewers (and censors) serious qualms. The more recent is Peter Greenaway's *The Cook, The Thief, His Wife and Her Lover* (1989), in which a brutal psychopath uses the restaurant he owns as a *grand guignol* theatre to humiliate and punish those in his power, especially his wife. Eventually she turns the tables on him, taking revenge for the killing of her lover by forcing her husband to eat the cooked corpse (although she shoots him at the last moment).

As in much of Greenaway's work, a clear set of antinomies underpins the violent action and lurid images: food and excrement; food and books; *haute cuisine* and decaying offal; and, of course, the raw and the cooked – life and death. The action of the film, unrolling in a series of melodramatic *tableaux*, springs from transgressive attempts to unite these opposites or substitute one for the other. Greenaway has given critics and audiences a hook on which to hang their unease, describing the film's model as 'classic Revenge Tragedy out of the "theatre of blood", with its obsession for human corporeality'. But another visual point of reference is Dutch seventeenth-century painting, which provides the background décor for this restaurant, where 'guests' can be, quite literally, attacked. Everything in this upmarket charnel-house of the late Thatcher period contradicts the visual and social order portrayed in the Dutch scenes of banqueting. Here, it is dog eat dog, and man eat man.

The other defining work of the dark cinema of food dates from 1973, and has rarely been revived in Britain (indeed has been largely obscured by its English title, *Blow-Out*, being taken by Brian De Palma's unrelated thriller). Marco Fererri's *La Grande Bouffe* is about four men who retreat to a castle to eat and debauch themselves to death. This neo-Sadean orgy – with its comic counterpart in Terry Jones's exploding fat diner in Monty Python's *The Meaning of Life* – marks the *ne plus ultra* of the cinema of disgust; a metaphysical rejection of the world translated into a relentless, nauseating spectacle of self-destruction.

Clearly, film, with its intensive visuality, is able to explore a range of extreme emotions and experiences by proxy. Cocooned in darkness, we watch what we desire, but cannot or would not want to experience in reality. In early mimetic theories of film (such as Siegfried Kracauer's *Nature of Film*), and in some recent forms of cognitivism, this might be described as 'kinaesthetic' stimulation; while in psychoanalytic theories (such as that of Christian Metz's *The Imaginary Signifier*) it is likely to be conceived as 'identification' with the screen phantasy. But whether this response is conceived in materialist or symbolic terms, it posits a special, intense interactive relationship between the screen world and the real world. Mostly this stops well short of spectators imitating what they see on screen, but there is a rich folklore of odd behaviour in cinemas which may deserve more attention than it normally gets in film scholarship – as a kind of psychopathology of spectatorship. Much of this, in fact, revolves around food – since cinemas are the last remaining examples of indoor entertainment venues where eating and drinking are not only allowed but actively encouraged.

When film shows started at the turn of the century, mainly in variety theatres, they followed the customs of the time, which included eating and drinking. As shops and even rooms were pressed into service to cater for the new craze, the habit continued. George Pearson, an English film pioneer, recalled his first visit to a 'penny gaff' which smelt of 'stale cabbage leaves and dry mud' because it had until recently been a greengrocer's. In Russia, as Yuri Tsivian has revealed, chewing seeds and eating nuts and apples were common, as was spitting the husks and cores at fellow members of the audience. When high-class luxury cinemas began to appear after 1910, seating was segregated to limit this skirmishing, and the foyer started to evolve as a café or bar, soon providing a social counterpart to the auditorium itself.

In Britain and America, with their strong temperance movements, foyers developed as tea-rooms, and there were even recurrent attempts to serve tea in the cinema. In the 1910s, this involved keeping the lights on, which proved unpopular; but Denis Norden recalled, from his days as a London cinema manager in the 1930s, how films would be stopped abruptly at 4.30 and the lights turned on so that afternoon tea trays could be passed around. Oranges were often handed out at children's shows, and the peel inevitably converted into missiles to throw at the screen.

Throwing things at other film-goers and at the screen has not been confined to unruly children's matinées, as is proved by the rich range of anecdotes collected in Ian Breakwell and Paul Hammond's *Seeing in the Dark*, an informal anthropology of auditorium behaviour. No doubt it owes much to the popular tradition of cinemagoing; and perhaps also to the peculiar kinaesthetics of watching vigorous, suggestive action from a fixed seat. But could it also be influenced by one of the earliest distinctive tropes of screen drama – the food fight, with its weapon of choice, the custard-pie? Like much else in film comedy, the mechanics of the custard-pie fight were apparently first worked out at Mack Sennett's Keystone studio around 1915. They were then taken up and developed by many popular screen comedians, with Laurel and Hardy's aptly titled *Battle of the Century* (1929) widely regarded by connoisseurs as the apotheosis of the genre.

Another theme that emerges from Breakwell and Hammond's book, which comes as little surprise, is the association between cinema-going and clandestine sexuality. A number of anecdotes recall memories of sexual initiation, and exciting or perplexing childhood observations of sexual activity. Significantly, many of these also feature food as an adjunct – nuts, ices, chocolates, all acquire erotic associations in this litany of surreptitious revolt. In the darkness of the cinema, freed from normal social constraints and stimulated by the eroticism of the filmic spectacle itself, there is scope for – well, let's say, some entertaining forms of semi-private satisfaction. As staunch latter-day surrealists, Breakwell and Hammond are well aware of the tradition that regards cinema-going itself as a surrealist activity. André Breton used to lead his followers in and out of cinemas at random, creating a kind of *collage vecu*, in which the dream-like condition of film-viewing was valued as an aid to liberating the unconscious. If scholarly film studies has largely disdained such matters, it has perhaps cut itself off from one of the key underlying attractions of film-going – and one reason why the cinema has so consistently attracted the attention of moral zealots and censors. A new public sphere, as Annette Kuhn defines it in her book on early censorship and sexuality, it is also the space of private fantasy and a measure of illicit behaviour.

Despite the crescendo of custard-pies and orange-peel, films and film-going in the 1920s were not all about the conspicuous waste of food. An important theme that links both American and Russian cinema in this decade is the exact opposite: hunger. As early as 1909, D. W. Griffith had pioneered the use of parallel editing in a terse moral parable, *A Corner in Wheat*, which shows a grain speculator who has driven up the cost of bread suffocated by his own wheat. After the Russian Revolution, the celebrated foundation of the Soviet montage school of film-making was a series of experiments in editing carried out by Lev Kuleshov in 1921; and what had first inspired Kuleshov was his earlier discovery that by intercutting the face of an actor with a close-up of a bowl of soup it was possible to trigger the audience's interpretation that the character was 'thinking about' food.

During the famine that followed the Civil War, many Russians would have occasion to think longingly about food – an early agitational film was starkly titled Hunger, *Hunger, Hunger* – and, in fact, the first great international success of the new Soviet propaganda cinema, Eisenstein's *The Battleship Potemkin*, starts with a truly dialectical food drama. The film's opening section is called 'Men and Maggots'; and it is the crew's complaint that their meat is crawling with maggots – rejected by an officer, despite the close-up evidence – which sparks a mutiny. Having treated the sailors like 'maggots', this same officer is thrown overboard to 'feed the worms', and the process of revolution, which will then spread to the city of Odessa, is started.

In the same year as *Potemkin*, the best-known of all early film-makers, Charles Chaplin, made one of his most enduringly popular films, *The Gold Rush*, also with food – or more precisely the lack of it – playing a vital role. Set in the frozen Yukon, Chaplin's masterpiece revolves around the Tramp's hunger and consequent obsession with food. Two sequences became immediate classics: one in which he cooks and apparently eats a boot, treating the laces as spaghetti; and another, when he tries to impress a girl by making two bread rolls dance, in a metaphor which elegantly and suggestively links food with sex.

Hunger and thirst have continued to resonate through self-consciously epic cinema, ever since Erich von Stroheim filmed the climax of his aborted masterpiece, *Greed* (1924), with harrowing realism in Death Valley. Apart from the distinctive American and Russian traditions of this theme, a striking example occurs in Theo Angelopoulos's first great international success, *The Travelling Players* (1975). Spanning fifteen years of Greek history, the film's core is the misery of World War II and its aftermath. One remarkable scene sums up the wartime experience of famine. The starving actors close in slowly on a solitary chicken seen on a snow-covered slope: as the *New York Times* critic wrote, Angelopoulos 'has filmed hunger'.

If scarcity marked the portrayal of food in the 1920s, then plenty was the keynote of the following decade. Alexander Korda set the trend with his rollicking *Private Life of Henry VIII* (1933), offering a shrewdly populist invocation of Merrie England in the celebrated image of Charles Laughton banqueting on chicken-legs. Jacques Feyder's *La Kermesse Héroique* (1935) continues in the same hearty vein, hinting strongly that the women of seventeenth-century Flanders charmed the invading Spaniards with more than a lavish banquet.

Russia, too, contributed to the panoply of groaning tables, laden with rich food and drink, in the series of late 1930s *kolkhoz* musicals by Ivan Pyriev – a Stalinist version of the 'Potemkin villages' originally created to disguise Russia's rural misery from Catherine the Great. Eisenstein would contribute an historical dimension to this bucolic image in his *Alexander Nevsky* (1938), with its bustling Novgorod market scenes, and in the formal wedding banquet sequence of *Ivan the Terrible* (1945), with its extraordinary procession of swan-neck dishes. After the war, with hunger and hardship still rife, the *kolkhoz* fantasy of abundance returned in such films as *Kuban Cossacks* (1950) and *The Cavalier of the Golden Star* (1951), which Khrushchev would single out for denunciation in his 1956 'secret speech'. Stalin, he claimed, had consistently used cinema for self-serving myth-making, and nowhere had this been more evident than in the spectacle of plentiful food that had occupied Soviet screens through the hungriest decades. An unusual instance of the politics of food imagery, which has more often related to scarcity and famine, but a reminder of how potent the theme remains, especially in Third World cinema and the social documentary tradition.

Surrealism, with its often anarchic call to revolt, has also provided a powerful inspiration for exploring the web of unconscious links between eating, sexuality and social order. Across the career of just one surrealist film-maker, Luis Buñuel, it is possible to trace a continuing assault on totem and taboo, much of it expressed through bizarre images of food and eating.

Buñuel's first film in his native Spain, in 1932, was a documentary on the barren region of *Las Hurdes*, known in English as *Land Without Bread*. From his subsequent Mexican exile after the Civil War, there are the extraordinary dream images of *Los Olvidados* (1950), in which a slum child imagines his mother thrusting raw offal towards him, and the atavistic parable of *The Exterminating Angel* (1962), with its dinner guests mysteriously trapped and only saved from turning on each other by the equally mysterious appearance of a flock of sheep. Back in Europe, Buñuel's last years yielded the parodic beggars' *Last Supper of Viridiana* (1961) and the disturbing comedy of *The Discreet Charm of the Bourgeoisie* (1972), in which a party of would-be diners are constantly frustrated in their search for food.

The rituals of food and drink, for Buñuel, conveniently signified the whole structure of 'civilisation', by which mankind seeks to create meaning and impose order on the absurdity of life. Challenge or remove them, and chaos threatens. The ultimate chaos is, of course, anthropophagy – cannibalism – a threat that hovers over more than one Buñuel film. And if surrealism's role is to challenge taboos, then the prevalence of cannibalistic fantasies is evidence of cinema's intrinsic surrealism. Probably the oldest such tradition in film is the vampire theme, which first appeared in early Bram Stoker adaptations, such as Murnau's *Nosferatu* (1922) and Browning's *Dracula* (1930), and has since – appropriately – refused to die. Yet for all the gore attending some vampire variations, this is metaphysical transgression: stealing the soul through drinking blood – a blasphemous satanic sacrament.

Cannibalism has a similarly magical basis, if it in fact ever existed on any widespread scale; but there is also what might be termed a pragmatic anthropophagy: eating the flesh of another *in extremis* to stay alive. Cinema is rich in examples of both – roughly, the 'zombie' and the 'survival' traditions – but it has also produced some remarkable and disturbing hybrids, in which challenging the taboo against human flesh-eating is in fact the subject of the film. From Curtiz's lurid medical thriller *Dr X* (1932), via such poignant and eccentric horror essays as Gary Sherman's *Death Line* (1972) – in which a cannibal-survivor preys on Underground passengers in Russell Square station – and Ruiz's *The Territory* (1981), this tradition has flourished in recent years, yielding both the guignol-chic of Jeunet and Caro's *Delicatessen* (1990) and no less than two versions of the same neo-Gothic police procedural story, in Michael Mann's *Manhunter* (1986) and Jonathan Demme's *The Silence of the Lambs* (1990).

To make a modern 'cannibal' comprehensible and compelling, as both Mann and Demme do, is to confront us with our worst fears – worse, to taunt us with the simultaneous desire to deny and indulge them. They may be far removed from any 'normal' attitudes to food and eating, but this is surely their symbolic, social function. These are extreme examples of cinema's ability to give therapeutic form to our deepest anxieties (just as, in related ways, Oshima's *Ai No Corrida* and Pasolini's *Salo* explore the erotics of death).

Deeply disturbing images of food are not, however, the only feature of contemporary cinema's cuisine: the context in which 'normal' food is prepared and eaten can also be highly significant. Meals, for instance, play an unusually dramatic part in many of Martin Scorsese's films. In *GoodFellas* (1990), a brutal mafia killing is followed by an alarmingly normal Italian-style meal, served by the director's own mother, Catherine Scorsese. And one of the most sensuous and simultaneously menacing of all food images in modern cinema occurs during a prison scene, as the mafiosi prepare their ritual pasta sauce. The boss, Paulie (Paul Sorvino), we learn in voice-over, while seeing a massive close-up of chubby fingers at work, 'had this wonderful system for doing the garlic. He used a razor and he used to slice it so thin that it used to liquefy in a pan.' Later, the central figure's drug-fuelled paranoia is signalled by his obsession with the meatballs and tomato sauce he's cooking as the FBI move in. 'Keep an eye on the sauce and watch out for helicopters', is almost his last order before the Feds arrive. Throughout *GoodFellas*, the exacting domesticity of Italian cuisine serves to highlight the terrifying normality of these mobsters.

For these Italian-American subjects, Scorsese can draw on his own memories and family tradition (*The Scorsese Family Cookbook* was published in 1996, shortly before his mother's death). *The Age of Innocence* (1993) however, with its nineteenth-century WASP setting, posed a new culinary challenge: how to recreate the elaborate dinners of Edith Wharton's high society and give these unfamiliar rituals dramatic meaning? Scorsese's solution was to go for the same total detail and authenticity as in his gangster movies. Every course and setting in every meal is meticulously researched, and its significance registered in the social dance that steers Newland Archer away from the exotic Countess Olenska and ensures he stays with demure, yet steely May Welland. Dining is no more innocent in this social jungle, where, to Scorsese's delight, the most violent thing that happens is a breach of etiquette.

Here, as so often at the movies, watching people eat – how they eat, what they eat and who eats – offers a profound insight into what makes them tick. Abstracted from the mundane reality of nourishment – yet with cinema's very own fantasy food to hand, in the unlikely shape of popcorn – we are encouraged to speculate on the symbolism and meaning of our daily bread.

Further reading

Breakwell, Ian and Hammond, Paul, *Seeing in the Dark: A Compendium of Cinemagoing*, Serpent's Tail, London, 1990.
Greenaway, Peter, *The Cook, the Thief, his Wife and her Lover*, Dis Voir, Paris, 1989.

Scorsese, Catherine with Downard, Georgia, *Italianamerican: The Scorsese Family Cookbook*, Random House, New York, 1996.

Tsivian, Yuri, *Early Cinema in Russia and its Cultural Reception*, Routledge, London, 1994.

Flesh sweeter than honey

Graham Ward

In recent years Christian theology has transformed itself. Not by feeding the poor, comforting the bereaved and tending the sick. Christian theology has always advocated practices such as those – and there is not a great deal of press coverage to be had from its advocacy. No, it has transformed its image by capitalising on its early investments in Platonic *eros* and becoming sexy. And the credit must go not to the physiques and talents of Whoopi Goldberg in the film *Sister Act* or those of Lineus Roach in *The Priest*, but to the feminists and queer theorists who have put the body back on the theological agenda. So seminar rooms now have grown accustomed to talk about penises, orgasms and vaginal lips, where once, out of undergraduate hearing, professors and lecturers muttered about 'pudenda'.

Possibly not since the medieval period has there been so much theological attention to *et incarnatus est*, to the representation of the genitals and trans-sexuality of Jesus Christ, to the engineering of bodies as souls in and through ecclesiastical practices, to scriptural and theological accounts of gender, to feeding on the body of Christ. Alongside this work, and supplementing it, has been research into physiology in late antiquity and the medieval period.

Ironically, the more talk is given over the body – talk that is dominating historical studies, ethics, philosophy, politics and ethics, as well as theology – the more complex embodiment becomes. The more we reach out to touch and hold, the more the fleshness of the flesh eludes us. Bodies are becoming ungraspable under this new intellectual examination. As Judith Butler tells us in her book *Bodies that Matter*, ' "materiality" has become a sign of the irreducible'. But one effect of that new interest is evident. No longer are bodies viewed as discrete, self-determining entities made up of these organs and those carbon molecules. They are being seen as malleable, permeable and frangible.

There was a time when, in talk concerning the physical body of Jesus, the social and political bodies which contextualised it, the

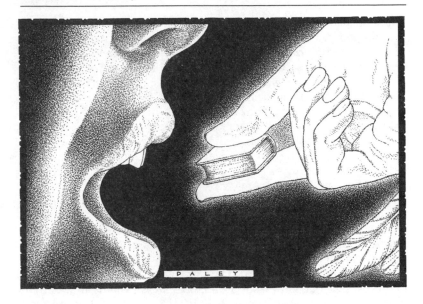

ecclesiastical body it gave rise to, the sacramental body which re-members it, the cosmic body of Christ which mythologises it – there was a time when all these uses of the word 'body' could be ordered by designating the physical body as the literal one and the other bodies as metaphorical. That time is no longer with us. We have returned to an albeit post-modern rereading of the medieval notion of the world as a text, where notions of 'sense' and 'reference' are part of the wider symbolic field of analogy, allegory and metaphor. These different bodies – physical, socio-political, ecclesiastical, sacra-mental and cosmic – are mapped one onto another in ways which make them inseparable, complex and mysterious.

Corporeality is again taking on the viscosity of ensoulment. Theo-logians who have listened to contemporary critical thinkers like Luce Irigaray and Hélène Cixous are wanting to talk again about the soul, the embodied soul, and without any of the usual Enlightenment embarrassment.

It is within this context – that has fostered a new interest in medi-eval art, music and mysticism – that Christianity today explores its con-cern with food or, more generally, with nurturing and nourishment. This concern has several interleaving dimensions. From its founding in New Testament scriptures, Christian theology takes account of ancient and contemporary interpretations of miracles such as the feeding of the five thousand on five loaves and two fishes, and the transformation of water into wine; the last supper and the institution of the eucharist; the love-feasts of the early church; the eschatological wedding banquet of Christ and His Church; and the changing nature of food prohibitions (eating fish and meats forbidden under Jewish law, not eating flesh dedicated to idols). These New Testament references issue from an Old Testament heritage: the orders of creation and the role of human beings with respect to those orders as they are depicted in the book of Genesis; the metaphors of paradisial fruitfulness and the land of milk and honey; the institution of the Passover in the book of Exodus; the cultic meal of mount Sinai which appears to seal the covenant between Yahweh, Moses and the elders of Israel; food sacrifices in the book of Numbers; the dietary laws of Leviticus and Deuteronomy; the feasts of Weeks (or first fruits), Tabernacles (or in-gathering of the harvest), Sabbath, Purim and Hanukkah; and the fasting of Yom Kippur.

The same New Testament references become inseparable from the tradition of feasts, fasting and festivals which gradually came to define the Church's liturgical year. Foremost of these are Advent (fasting), Christmas (feasting), Lent (fasting), Easter (feasting), and Pentecost (feasting with fasting on Ember Days). The rhythm of banqueting and abstinence does not follow, but nevertheless imitates, the natural cycle of plenty and dearth, harvest and famine. Onto this liturgical cycle other feasts were grafted – Candlemas (feast of the purification of the Blessed Virgin), Holy Week, Trinity Sunday, Corpus Christi and All Saints'. Along with these occasions, there were sessions of communal drinking on Rogation days, bonfires on Midsummer Eve, feasts on individual Saint's days and almost seventy days in the year when adults were required to fast. Special foods and recipes were appointed for some of these feasts – butter, cheese and eggs were brought for blessing at Easter, apples on St James's Day. Christmas mince pies were traditionally in the shape of the manger. On Good Friday the fast was broken after three in the afternoon (the time when Christ died) by the consumption of spiced buns decorated with a cross. In Naples, a special pastry (*pastiera*) was baked for Easter made of pumpkin, oranges, lemons and cinnamon. Throughout the year, fish was to be eaten on Fridays as a memorial to the crucifixion. Furthermore, where there was no concept of secular time, the social and political body was closely identified with the ecclesiastical body of Christ as deeds were signed and rents fell due on Lady Day, Lammas or Michaelmas.

Feasting becomes a social and political practice within a liturgically defined cosmos. Hence the interchange of ritual between Church and Holy Roman Empire such that the trappings and behaviour of one were reproduced or adopted by the other. Later, according to the French cultural critic Louis Martin and the English historian John

Adamson, in court ceremonial, the king's body took on the symbolism of the eucharistic host. The king would sit under a baldachin, be
venerated and withdrawn after the banquet in ways that paralleled
the handling of the eucharist by the priests. The social and liturgical
were indissociable, until, by the sixteenth century (according to the
French historian Michael de Certeau) the State's powers outstripped
the Church's and the age of the secular emerged.

In this fluidity between social and liturgical practices of feasting
(and fasting), it is not simply that you become what you eat – though,
as we will see, that is an axiom of eucharistic theology. Rather,
feasting (and fasting) structure the subject's living. They situate the
subject in a theological space which defines the nature and the
purpose of that living. The body is placed within what the American
anthropologist Tahal Asad, in his book *Genealogies of Religion*, calls
'an economy of truth', which aims at the 'formation/transformation
of moral dispositions [Christian virtues] . . . to construct and reorgan-
ise distinctive emotions'. As part of a larger set of ecclesiastical disciplines – pilgrimage, confession, prayer, the veneration of sacred
objects – the body is trained and coded. It is taught how to view its
own corporeality as contingent and, like the rest of creation, constantly in need of being nurtured and sustained by life-forces outside itself.

Because all that is created comes from nothing, comes from the
divine fiat which called that which is into being from absence, then
bodies come to be seen as gifted; the natural and the creaturely only
continue through their maintenance by grace. This continual sense
of living only in and through grace, this emphasis upon the natural
always being in need, always moving towards its completion in the
realm of the Godhead, announces a radical hunger at the heart
of things. Human beings are shaped by an eternal desire, a hunger
that nothing but grace can appease, a desire which means they
cannot rest until they find their rest in God. The need for food – and
the practices of fasting and feasting which activate, discipline and
satisfy that need – announces, corporeally, that infinite desire, the
unbridgeable distance (what Gregory of Nyssa termed the *diastema*
between the uncreated God and the dependency of creation). God
becomes mother, creation becomes Her child. The late fourteenth-
century English anchoress, Julian of Norwich, is by no means alone in
describing Christ, God's Word through whom creation came to be, as
our mother:

> [T]he second person of the Trinity is our Mother in nature in our
> substantial creation, in whom we are founded and rooted, and he is
> our Mother of mercy in taking our sensuality. And so our Mother is

working on us in various ways . . . for in our Mother Christ we profit
and increase, and in mercy he reforms and restores us.

Later in her book, *Showings*, she will develop this picture by explicitly relating the way a mother feeds her child milk to the manner in
which Christ offers His own body for our spiritual nourishment in the
eucharist.

The eucharist is the iconic focus for all the practices and symbolism
of feasting and fasting. Throughout the medieval period elaborate
rituals accompanied the manufacture of eucharistic hosts. There was
a recitation of psalms while the grains were collected, washed, fried,
milled, mixed with water and baked. As William of Blois, Bishop of Win-
chester in 1229 notes: 'The ministers of the church should be dressed
in surplices and sit in a proper place while they make the hosts. The
instrument in which the hosts are roasted should be coated with wax,
not with oil or fat.' The hosts were to be baked not fried, as Miri
Ruben, in her book *Corpus Christi: The Eucharist in Late Mediaeval
Culture* (Cambridge University Press, 1991, p. 42), points out.

The eucharist is the liturgical centrepiece – that which orders all
the other liturgical, ecclesiastical and social acts. The eucharist in-
forms all Christian understandings of feeding and food. Anthropological investigations into ritual, defilement and purity (the work
particularly of Mary Douglas and Victor Turner), enable us to assess
some of the human dynamics of the Mass. The thinking of both
these figures calls into question the division of the sacred from the
secular by drawing attention to the operation of the symbolic systems within which both spheres are situated.

In her classic book, *Purity and Danger* (Routledge and Kegan Paul,
1966, p. 4), Mary Douglas proposes that 'the processes of ingestion
portray political absorption' so that sometimes 'bodily orifices seem
to represent points of entry or exit to social units'. She examines the
ways the mystifying dietary laws of the Old Testament have been
interpreted since the nineteenth century, pointing up the way they
are either reduced to medical materialism (you do not eat pork
because pork can easily become infected in a hot country, etc.) or
ethical allegories (animals that creep and wriggle signify people given
over to their greedy desire and passions). She then situates these
dietary stipulations within the 'great liturgical act of recognition and
worship which culminated in the sacrifice in the Temple', so that
these laws, and the subsequent laws concerning washing and purification, are understood to negotiate the ambivalent and anomal-
ous in life. The Jewish food proscriptions create and patrol ancient
Israel's distinctive cultural boundaries, they establish and maintain a
certain order of creation against its potential contravention. Rituals

are, then, about the creation and control of experience. They per-
form a cultural identity and a cultural ideology; they are a means of
consolidating a community and articulating its value system.

Most importantly, with reference to Christianity, food and the
eucharistic feast, Mary Douglas's work enjoins us not simply to describe the contents of the action but to relate the action to the
symbolic systems which give it its significance. Food for Christianity
is not simply that which gives one energy to live. That reduces food
to medical materialism. The eucharist is neither simply the consuming of a wafer and the imbibing of a liquid nor a means of fostering
good group dynamics. Similarly, fasting is not simply about self-
discipline. This reduces fasting to an ethical allegory. Fasting was
concerned with enlarging one's spiritual capacity for God through
promoting the right kind of desire. Gluttony, since the time of John
Cassian and St Jerome, was understood as Adam's original sin, a sin
which provoked concupiscence. For Aquinas 'Gluttony denotes . . .
an inordinate desire' (*Summa Theologica*, IIa IIae q. 148). Fasting was
a metaphor for chaste desire. Aquinas writes: 'fasting is the guardian
of chastity' (ibid., IIa IIae q. 147).

The fourth-century Cappadocian Father, Gregory of Nyssa, points
the way to a Christian understanding of food (and, by implication,
abstention from food) in a manner paralleling Mary Douglas's. In his
treatise *De Opificio Hominis*, Gregory situates the meaning of food
within its far wider symbolic system, a Christian semiotics:

> I . . . do not understand only bodily meat, or the pleasure of the
> flesh; but I recognise another kind of food also, having a certain
> analogy to that of the body, the enjoyment of which extends to the
> soul alone. 'Eat of my bread' (Proverbs 9: 5), is the bidding of Wisdom
> to the hungry, and the Lord declares those blessed who hunger for
> such food as this, and says, 'If any man thirst, let him come unto Me,
> and drink' . . . 'famine' is not the lack of bread and water, but the
> failure of the Word – not a famine of bread, nor thirst for water,
> but a famine of hearing the Word of the Lord.

Similarly, the eucharistic feeding – and the mediaval mind could
become quite literal about this act of eating – is, ultimately, a
cosmological and Christological act. It announces a certain ordering
of creation in relation to Christ as the Word of God, He through
whom creation came to be. It announces a participation in that
ordering; a co-creative partnership with God (though not of equals)
in the ongoing maintenance of the right order. It is not simply a matter of belonging, of affirming a group identity and social-political
allegiances (though it is that also). Rather it is a participating in the
presence of God in creation. All the symbolism is oriented to and

facilitates this fundamental participation. Hence, coming to belong and continuing to belong are ringed by other rituals.

Before communion there has to be baptism and confirmation. Before mass the priest is meant to fast and, like the laity, practice confession. In the Mass there is preparation for receiving the elements through the hearing of the Word in the Scripture, the proclamation of the Word in the homiletic address and again, confession. The priest must wash his hands, and a strict ordering, placing and handling of the eucharistic elements is enjoined. This is enjoined sometimes in the text of the liturgy, but more frequently enjoined by tradition (in the guise of the priest who was taught while he or she was a deacon but now teaching his or her own deacon). The physical bodies being 'fed' in this scenario are also not reducible to medical materialism. In the way they are mapped on to a cosmological and theological structure, these bodies are freighted with timelessness. Past memorial and present performance rehearse a futural consummation.

Victor Turner, particularly in his early works, *The Forest of Symbols* (Cornell University Press, 1967) and *The Ritual Process* (Routledge and Kegan Paul, 1969), developed a four-stage model for the social process or drama. The stages move from an initial break with the social order, through crisis and adjustment to reintegration into the community (or a complete separation from it). Within this temporal and narrative movement Turner draws attention to the 'liminal period', the rites of passage which characterise certain sacred activities. His concern lies with the liminal *personae* – the subjects of these rites. To appreciate the distinctive structures within which these subjects are situated, he examines initiation rituals. Nevertheless, aspects of the liminal period which he exposes shed light on the participatory experience of a communicant, which culminates in eating the body of Christ and drinking His blood.

Liminal conditions are transformative. The subject is taken out of a familiar and stable state of affairs, the negotiation of the secular, and placed into a transitional space, a highly symbolic space in which they are fed. The subject is thus rendered 'naked' – stripped of the roles and offices normative to life outside – and vulnerable. As Turner notes, during the liminal period 'the nakedness and vulnerability of the ritual subject receive symbolic stress'. The body undergoes a ritualised disciplining. First of all it enters a spacing which makes its materiality dense with symbolic suggestion. This body sits, stands and kneels amidst the memorial tablets to other bodies, who, though dead, are nevertheless present in so far as the eucharist feasting joins with the heavenly feasting, the community of the sanctified and saintly. This body walks through a building built in accordance with the orders of the sacral: high, vaulted ceilings intimating transcendence, long narrowed approach, from the baptismal font, down the aisle to the sanctuary and the altar suggesting immanent procession, past walls of coloured light from stained-glass windows, past strong, magisterial pillars.

Besides the watermarks of the invisible within the visible, this body receives the impress of touch (the peace is exchanged), sound (of sanctuary bells, of singing, or orchestrated silences), smell (the incense and beeswax) and taste (the wafer and the wine). The liturgy is a banquet of the senses, like medieval feasting which was orientated towards the aesthetic more than the gastronomic. Bodies become sensoriums, open to the external. Bodies become what I have described elsewhere as transcorporated – conscious, that is, of possessing permeable boundaries and being traced on to other bodies, social, ecclesiastical and divine. This state 'enfranchises speculation', Turner notes. During the liminal period, subjects 'are alternately forced and encouraged to think about their society, their cosmos, and the powers that generate and sustain them. Liminality may be partly described as a stage of reflection.'

Unhinged for a time from the familiar, adrift within a highly organised temporality and spatiality which is cosmic in its suggestiveness, the subject is prepared first to observe the sacralising of the elements (bread and wine) and then to consume them and, thereby, identify with the sacral order itself. The feeding takes place within, and draws its significance from, the narrative process as a whole. The process itself centralises around what Turner calls the *sacra* – objects which embody the ultimate mysteries. It is in this way that the eucharistic feeding governs the nature and meaning of all other forms of feeding. The significance and purpose of food – in fact, the significance of our very need for food – is organised around both this liturgical cosmos and its *sacra*.

The body becomes a site for continual transformation. It is never stable. The symbolic system of the liturgy breaks down the notions of internal and external. In doing this the ambiguity of feeding (and reception by the senses generally) is amplified. For feeding (like the process of evacuating) crosses the body's thresholds where the outer becomes the inner (and the inner becomes the outer). The corporeal zones of ambiguity – which are frequently also erotic zones – are sites for the transformative process. So the moment of reception is a highly charged moment, saturated with significance and desire. The communicant kneels and, from the ninth century, receives the wafer directly into his or her mouth from the priest. From the eleventh century, only the priests could take God in their hands by holding the host. The moment of entry into the mouth is not without its *eros* and its ecstasy. Witness the thirteenth-century mystic and poet, Hadewijch:

he gave himself to me in the shape of the sacrament, in its outward form, as the custom is; and then he gave me to drink from the chalice ... After that he came himself to me, took me entirely in his arms, and pressed me to him; and all my members felt his in full felicity, in accordance with the desire of my heart and my humanity.

Taking the body of Christ into one's own body – Christ who, as head of the Church, is the Bridegroom before his Bride – entails becoming one flesh. Participation in the divine, through the eucharistic feeding, is true marriage. Again, the social and political is organised around the sacral and liturgical understanding of food.

The feeding facilitates a reciprocal exchange. This exchange is not simply that between the host and the guest, the one who prepares the food and the one who eats it. For in this exchange the food itself is the centre and substance. The food is not the token of a relation between host and guest, but that which grounds any relation and constitutes relationality itself. Christ gives Himself in the eucharist as the food. Both host and guest are drawn into this more fundamental giving. One exchange (between priest and communicant) crosses into a second exchange (between Christ and the communicant). The spiritual feeding comes in the second exchange as flesh is taken into flesh and God is eaten. As such, the feeding intensifies and affirms the physical nature of bodies.

According to the medieval physiology, blood, and therefore even the blood of Christ, is processed into both breast-milk and semen. In this way, spirituality is not structured dualistically. Similarly, it is not conceived that we leave our bodies behind and ascend to a spiritual plane. The spiritual feeding grounds our physicality in God. Throughout the liturgy our bodies have been engaged with a spiritual performance. At this point, we move out into the aisle and up towards the sanctuary and the altar in a procession towards the body. The feeding is the spiritual consummation of our embodiment. We, in our humanity, are identified with Christ, referred to earlier in the Creed as *et incarnatus est*. The communicant receives himself or herself as flesh ensouled in this moment.

Of course, this is a transubstantial reading of the eucharistic event. There are now Protestant traditions for whom there is no change in the elements and whose communicants receive a token of the body of Christ by faith or simply recall the institution of the last supper when they break the bread and share the cup. Nevertheless, the principle of liturgical feeding and God's descent into the communicant is the same. The Catholic tradition announces that principle more clearly and dramatically.

The liturgical feeding not only brings about the reintegration of the divided subject with itself by enabling that subject to become incarnate flesh. It brings about the reintegration also with that which unifies and sanctifies all things – the Word of God from whom creation proceeded. The feeding opens the body of the subject towards the body of the other. The feeding installs the primacy of being-in-relation-to, being as relationality. The subject becomes a member of a community of other bodies, the Church, and a member of Christ's own body – *the* body which regulates the meaning and nature of all other bodies. This coming-into-relation through feeding makes food the focus for a highly complex set of transferences or exchanges. It relates food to signification itself. Communion makes possible communication.

The bread and the wine signify more than they are as bread and wine, they effect an excess of signification. The source and sustainer of this excess (through whom, by whom and in whom, as the rite pronounces) is the Word. The result of this excess is a promulgation of the Word in the forms of preaching or prophesying, in the language of confession and witness: in doxology. The eucharistic sign, the incarnate food, becomes the measure for all true communication. From it proceeds the discourse of love which extends and further substantialises community relations. (In a vision of the heavenly realms, an angel holds a book wherein are written all the secret orders of the world. The book is handed to St John the Divine and, as the Book of Revelation describes it, 'I took the little book out of the angel's hand, and ate it up; and it was in my mouth sweet as honey; and as soon as my mouth had eaten it, my belly was bitter' (Rev. 10: 10).)

The eucharist does not conclude with the feeding. The moment of consummation/consumption cannot be held on to and idolised. The completion is not complete. The rite requires its non-identical repetition – once a day, once a week, once a month, once a year (dependent upon the ecclesiastical tradition). The feeding proceeds through fraction – the breaking of the bread, the pouring of the wine. But the breaking up that follows the moment of unification is not negative. Fracture promotes the expansion, through the dissemination of the body of Christ. At the end of the service, the communicants are sent out into the world to practice, through signifying actions, peace and love. The feeding remains central and eternally significant. The last pictures in the New Testament are of the celestial city, fed by a crystal river proceeding from the throne of God. The city consists of one street and in the middle of that street stands 'the tree of life, which bare twelve manner of fruits, and yielded her fruit every month; and the leaves of the tree were for the healing of the nations' (Rev. 22: 1). We return, via the eucharistic feast, to paradise and the God through whom, by whom and in whom all creation is nourished. All our feeding is figurative of this eternal providing. Even

our fasting is a form of feeding, as our deepening desire feeds on
the divine. And so all our feeding becomes in Christ a thanksgiving
(*eucharistia*).

Further reading

Asad, Tahal, *Genealogies of Religion*, Johns Hopkins University Press, Balti-
more, 1993.
Butler, Judith, *Bodies that Matter*, Routledge, New York, 1993.
Bynum, Caroline Walker, *Holy Feast and Holy Fast: The Religious Significance
of Food for Mediaeval Women*, University of California Press, Berkeley,
1987.
Duffy, Eamon, *Stripping the Altars*, Yale University Press, New Haven, 1992.
Fritzpatrick, P. J., *In Breaking of Bread: Eucharist and Ritual*, Cambridge Uni-
versity Press, Cambridge, 1993.
Marin, Louis, *Food for Thought*, tr. Mette Hjort, Johns Hopkins University
Press, Baltimore, 1989.

A recipe

Pastiera

Traditional Neapolitan Easter pastry. Each family has its own recipe.
It's offered to guests for a week around Easter.

5 oz whole wheat kernels
8 oz plain flour
4 oz butter
3 oz sugar
4 egg yolks
One and a third cups of milk
Grated rind of half an orange
3 oz caster sugar
1 tsp vanilla essence
8 oz ricotta
2 tbsp orange-flower water
1 tbsp chopped candied citrus peel
1 tbsp chopped candied orange peel
1 tbsp chopped candied pumpkin
Pinch ground cinnamon
2 egg whites

Soak the wheat kernels in cold water overnight. Combine the flour, butter, one-third cup of sugar and one egg yolk to make a dough. Form into a ball. Let it rest while preparing the filling.

Drain the wheat and combine with the milk, orange rind and one tablespoon of sugar. Cook over a low heat until porridge-like, remove from heat and stir in the vanilla. Combine the ricotta, three egg yolks, the remaining sugar, wheat, orange-flower water, candied fruit and cinnamon. Beat the egg whites until stiff and fold into mixture. Preheat oven to 350°F.

Roll out three-quarters of the dough and line a 9-inch pie pan. Fill with the ricotta mixture. Roll out the remaining dough and cut into three-eighths-inch strips. Arrange in a lattice over the pie. Bake the pastiera for about one hour. Let it rest before serving.

Edible écriture

Terry Eagleton

The link between eating and writing has a venerable pedigree. Francis Bacon famously observed in his essay 'Of Studies' that 'some books are to be tasted, others to be swallowed, and some few to be chewed and digested'. Literary language can be mouth-filling or subtly flavoured, meaty or hard-boiled, spicy or indigestible. Words can nourish or poison, and somewhere beneath this figurative equation lurks the eucharistic Word itself, a body which feeds other bodies, a sign which is also a meal. There are anorexic texts like Samuel Beckett's, in which discourse is in danger of dwindling to a mere skeleton of itself, and bulimic ones like Gerard Manley Hopkins's, muscle-bound and semiotically overstuffed. The language of Keats is as plump and well-packed as an apple, while less palatable poets like Swinburne are all froth and ooze. If Dylan Thomas binges on words, Harold Pinter approaches them with the wariness of a man on a diet. Bombast is a kind of verbal flatulence, a swelling which, like the bodies of the famished, conceals a hollowness.

Words issue from the lips as food enters them, though one can always take one's words back by eating them. And writing is a processing of raw speech just as cooking is a transformation of raw materials. One of Roland Barthes' structuralist models, bathetically enough, was a menu: just as a diner selects one item each from the 'paradigmatic axes' of starters, entrées and desserts, and then combines them along a 'syntagmatic axis' in the actual process of eating, so a literary work chooses items from various repertoires

(genres, formal devices, narrative forms) and then goes on to string them together. These are the kind of speculations which send most English critics scrambling for their Helen Gardner. The later, post-structuralist Barthes threw over this model for the delights of semantic indeterminacy, but nothing is more alimentary than the ambiguous. If there is one sure thing about food, it is that it is never just food. Like the post-structuralist text, food is endlessly interpretable, as gift, threat, poison, recompense, barter, seduction, solidarity, suffocation. The ultimate floating signifier for the English is the cup of tea, appropriate for the most diverse occasions.

Food is just as much materialised emotion as a love lyric, though both can also be a substitute for the genuine article. A sign expresses something but also stands in for its absence, so that a child may be unsure whether receiving nourishment from its mother's hands or breasts is a symbol of her affection or a replacement for it. Perhaps a child may rebuff its food because what it really wants is some impossibly immaterial gift of affection, rather as a symbolist poet wants to strip language of its drably functional character and express its very essence. Food looks like an object but is actually a relationship, and the same is true of literary works. If there is no literary text without an author, neither is there one without a reader. The doctrine of transubstantiation, which states that the bread and wine of the Mass become the body and blood of Christ, redescribes physical substances in terms of relationships. A chemist would still identify the consecrated elements as bread and wine, but this for Catholic theology would be as pointless as describing the proffering of a box of chocolates in physiological terms. There is a parallel mystery about writing: how come that these little black marks on the sheet are actually meanings? By what strange transfiguration do arbitrary physical inscriptions come to be the medium of spirit, a matter of human address in the way that random tracks in the sand are not?

Language is at once material fact and rhetorical communication, just as eating combines biological necessity with cultural significance. Hunger-striking is not just a matter of refusing food, as you might refuse a fourth helping of pudding, but a question of not taking food from a specific oppressor, and thus a dialogical affair. Starving here is a message rather than just a physical condition, semiotic as well as somatic. Food is cusped between nature and culture, and so too is language, which humans have as a dimension of their nature but which is also as culturally variable as cuisine. Nobody will perish without Mars bars, just as nobody ever died of not reading *Paradise Lost*, but food and language of some sort are essential to our survival.

Fast food is like cliché or computerese, an emotionless exchange or purely instrumental form of discourse; genuine eating combines pleasure, utility and sociality, and so differs from a take-away in much the same way that Proust differs from a bus ticket. Snatching a meal alone bears the same relation to eating in company as talking to yourself does to conversation. It is hardly surprising that a civilisation for which a dialogue of the mind with itself has provided a paradigm of human language should reach its apotheosis in the Big Mac.

Those starved words, gaunt bodies and sterile landscapes of Beckett's dramas may well carry with them a race memory of the Irish famine, a catastrophe which was the slow death of language as well as of one million people. The famine decimated the farm labourers and small tenants, who made up most of the Irish speakers, and using the language in post-famine Ireland rapidly became a symbol of ill-luck. It is possible to read Beckett's meticulously pared-down prose (for which French, he thought, was the most suitable medium) as a satirical smack at the blather and blarney of stage-Irish speech. Beckett hoards his meagre clutch of words like a tight-fisted peasant, ringing pedantic changes on the same few signs or stage properties like someone eking out a scanty diet. There is, perhaps, a

Protestant suspicion of superfluity here, in contrast to the extravagant expenditure of a Joyce, the linguistic opulence of J. M. Synge or
the verbal gluttony of Brendan Behan.

But all that reckless prodigality may itself have a bearing on food,
as a form of compensation in the mind for what is lacking in historical reality. In conditions of colonial backwardness, language is one
of the few things you have left; and though even that in Ireland had
been put down by the imperial power, words were still a good deal
more plentiful than hot dinners. Part of the point of language was
to bamboozle the colonialists; indeed the word 'blarney' derives
from the Earl of Blarney's doing just that in the reign of Elizabeth I.
The linguistic virtuosity of the Irish writers springs partly from the
fact that, like Joseph Conrad and many a modernist emigré, they are
inside and outside a language simultaneously. But it is also a form of
displacement, whereby you hope to discover in discourse a richness
denied to you in reality.

The most celebrated food-text of English literature is the work of
an Anglo-Irish patriot who bitterly recommended munching babies
as a solution to his country's economic ills. During the great famine,
this may well have happened; as Swift's fellow-Dubliner Oscar Wilde
observed, life has a remarkable knack of imitating art. Language in
Irish culture, however, is associated less with food, which was hardly
much in evidence, than with drink. As drink flows in, so words pour
out, each fuelling the other in a self-sustaining process. In fact, apart
from the notoriously bibulous trinity of Brendan Behan, Flann O'Brien
and Patrick Kavanagh, remarkably few Irish writers have been alco-
holics – far fewer than American authors, for whom alcohol seems as
much of a prerequisite as a typewriter. There is a fair amount of
eating in *Ulysses*, but the novel itself, at least in the view of the critic
John Bayley, is impossible to consume, 'sunk in its own richness like a
plumcake'. Bayley, with his English distaste for fancy foreign mod-
ernists, misses the point that Joyce's work is deliberately calculated
to induce dyspepsia. Modernist art was born at much the same time
as mass culture, and one reason for its obscurity is to resist being
sucked in as easily as tabloid print. By fragmenting its forms, thick-
ening its textures and garbling its narratives, the modernist text
hopes to escape the indignities of instant consumption.

It is significant that our word for the use of a commodity –
consumption – is drawn from the guts and the gullet. This modern metaphor has a rather more high-toned ancestor: taste. The
eighteenth-century idea of taste was partly a way of freeing artistic
evaluation from too rigid a consensus: taste was subjective, beyond
disputation, a *je ne sais quoi* which refused any total reduction to
rules. Just as there was no moral obligation to like rhubarb, so it

wasn't a capital offence to turn up your nose at Rembrandt, even if true gentlemen in fact turned out conveniently enough to relish much the same works of art. Similarly, what food you enjoyed was a private, arbitrary affair – until, that is, you tried ordering in your London club the kind of meal they ate in rural Cork. But this gustatory trope made room for individual freedom only at the risk of trivialising art to the status of a sausage, rather as the modern idea of consumption celebrates individual choice while threatening to drain it of value.

Food is what makes up our bodies, just as words are what constitute our minds; and if body and mind are hard to distinguish, it is no wonder that eating and speaking should continually cross over in metaphorical exchange. Both are, in any case, media of exchange themselves. There is no more modish topic in contemporary literary theory than the human body. Writing the body, texts as bodies, bodies as sign-systems: in the thick of all this fashionable Foucaulteanism, there has been strikingly little concern with the physical stuff of which bodies are composed, as opposed to an excited interest in their genitalia. The human body is generally agreed to be 'constructed', but what starts off that construction for all of us – milk – has been curiously passed over. There has been much critical interest in the famished body of the Western anorexic, but rather little attention to the malnutrition of the Third World. Perhaps such dwindled bodies are too bluntly material a matter for a so-called 'materialist' criticism. One notable exception to this indifference to the politics of starvation is Maud Ellmann's brilliant study *The Hunger Artists*, which concludes with the following reflections:

> [Food's] disintegration in the stomach, its assimilation in the blood, its diaphoresis in the epidermis, its metempsychosis in the large intestine; its viscosity in okra, gumbo, oysters; its elasticity in jellies; its deliquescence in blancmanges; its tumescence in the throats of serpents, its slow erosion in the bellies of sharks; its odysseys through pastures, orchards, wheat fields, stock-yards, supermarkets, kitchens, pig troughs, rubbish dumps, disposals; the industries of sowing, hunting, cooking, milling, processing, and canning it; the wizardry of its mutations, ballooning in bread, subsiding in soufflés; raw and cooked, solid and melting, vegetable and mineral, fish, flesh, and fowl, encompassing the whole compendium of living substance: food is the symbol of the passage, the totem of sociality, the epitome of all creative and destructive labour.

Ellmann quite properly makes a meal of it. Her paragraph coils like an intestine, the sense slipping from clause to clause like a morsel down the oesophagus. As these lines track the processing of food, so

they in turn process that subject-matter, by the cuisinary transforma-
tions of style, into a delectable feast.

Further reading

Ellmann, Maud, *The Hunger Artists: Starving, Writing and Imprisonment*,
    Virago, London, 1993.
Kinealy, Christine, *This Great Calamity*, Gill and Macmillan, Dublin, 1994.
Murphy, Tom, *Famine*, Gallery Press, Dublin, 1977.
Poirteir, Cathal (ed.), *The Great Irish Famine*, Mercier Press, Dublin, 1995.